What We're Afraid to Ask:

365 Days of Healing for Adult Survivors
of Childhood Abuse

What We're Afraid to Ask:

365 Days of Healing for Adult Survivors
of Childhood Abuse

Sherri L. Board, Jon M. Fleetwood,
Anna M. Jones

Winchester, UK
Washington, USA

WHAT WE'RE AFRAID TO ASK

When children experience abuse it can shatter their souls and their trust in God. Here's a resource that puts words to the questions that broken hearts wrestle with and offers new thoughts and prayers to open the path of healing.

Bill Gaultiere, PhD, author of *Your Best Life in Jesus' Easy Yoke* and cohost of the weekly Podcast: *Soul Talks With Bill & Kristi Gaultiere*

What We're Afraid to Ask: 365 Days of Healing for Adult Survivors of Childhood Abuse utilizes theology and psychology to help survivors recover from abuse and to deepen their spiritual relationship with God.

April B. Butler, *CASA*

I am a psychotherapist and ask tough but necessary Q's everyday in my practice. Pleased to hear of your book.

Shellie Leger, writer at Maine Behavioral Healthcare

As an adult survivor of childhood sexual abuse and trauma that now advocates for other abuse survivors, I found the book, *What We're Afraid to Ask: 365 Days of Healing for Adult Survivors of Childhood Abuse*, a must read for those survivors on their healing journeys and beyond. This book is surely going to touch the hearts of survivors who have struggled with healing and had questions about their abuse, God, and faith. In this book they ask the tough questions that so many survivors have struggled with and may be afraid to ask. With heartfelt questions combined with answers in both a psychological and biblical form, the reader will no doubt find this book to be a great resource and reference to read time and time again. I highly recommend this book to any survivors of childhood sexual abuse, especially those who have struggled with their faith due to trauma and abuse suffered as children.

Elizabeth Sullivan, Founder and Director of EmpowerSurvivors

What We're Afraid to Ask: 365 Days of Healing for Adult Survivors of Childhood Abuse provides a fresh way of looking at what haunts countless souls since childhood. Providing clear examples of how this affliction can be turned around, this book is a gift for all who choose to be empowered by their early life experiences.

David Fishman, author of *The Open Mind: Loving Your Self* and *Into Oneness*

First published by Circle Books, 2016
Circle Books is an imprint of John Hunt Publishing Ltd., Laurel House,
Station Approach, Alresford, Hants, SO24 9JH, UK
office1@jhpbooks.net
www.johnhuntpublishing.com
www.circle-books.com

For distributor details and how to order please visit the 'Ordering' section on
our website.

ISBN: 978 1 78535 123 5
Library of Congress Control Number: 2016935418

A CIP catalogue record for this book is available from the British Library.

Design: Stuart Davies

Printed in the USA by Edwards Brothers Malloy

*What We're Afraid to Ask: 365 Days of Healing for Adult Survivors of Childhood
Abuse* is not a substitute for counseling but a supplement to any therapeutic
counseling process.

We operate a distinctive and ethical publishing philosophy in all areas of our
business, from our global network of authors to production and
worldwide distribution.

CONTENTS

FOR EVERY ADULT SURVIVOR OF CHILDHOOD ABUSE AND
THOSE THAT LOVE THEM

Acknowledgements

For support beyond measure, Sherri L. Board would like to thank the following: God, Dr. Beverly Yahr, Lorelei Logsdon (our editor), Susan L. Jones, Jon M. Fleetwood, and Anna M. Jones.

Jon M. Fleetwood would like to thank his wife, Alexzondra, for her faithfulness, love, and support. He would also like to thank Sherri L. Board and Anna M. Jones for their invaluable contributions to this project.

Anna M. Jones would like to thank God for his grace and unmerited favor. She would also like to thank her parents, Steve and Pamela Jones, for their steadfast love and support, as well as Sherri L. Board, Jon M. Fleetwood and every person who has influenced her faith in Jesus. God is truly good.

Preface

My experiences as a child with sexual, physical, and emotional abuse taught me nothing but lies about God and myself. My psychological foundation was built on shame, terror, and very low self-esteem. Spiritually, I loved Jesus Christ with all my heart. But emotionally, I did not believe that Christ could love someone like me. Furthermore, a fundamental sense of fear followed me out of my childhood and into my adulthood.

In time, I began to trust in God's love for me, which gave me the strength to untangle the false image I held of myself. I did my part in making this happen by committing myself to a therapeutic program which not only sought to heal my soul—my mind, emotions, and will—but also my spirit. This course of therapy and study was, and still is, Christian Counseling.

Indeed, Christian Counseling was in large part the genesis for *What We're Afraid to Ask: 365 Days of Healing for Adult Survivors of Childhood Abuse*. It is my belief that adults abused as children deserve to be enlightened to the healing properties of both psychology and spirituality. Moreover, I trust in the practice in using humanity's psychological therapies as tools and God's Word as the ultimate Healer.

In conclusion, I had asked these 365 questions—whether or not the questions were of a positive or negative vein—with the aforementioned sense of fear. After asking these questions and receiving Jon and Anna's answers to them, however, I no longer possess that fear. Posing these questions simply destroyed what I once perceived to be a threat to my well-being.

The other part of the reason I wanted to see a book like this come to fruition is because there was something I wanted adult survivors of childhood abuse to know—the truth.

Sherri L. Board

Introduction

What We're Afraid to Ask addresses the issues that arise on the front lines of one's abusive past and very present psychological and spiritual battle. 365 questions proposed from a survivor's perspective with the hope that our readers receive truth, validation, and healing. *What We're Afraid to Ask* represents the abused, the broken-spirited, the afraid souls who have deep-rooted questions because of their abusive childhoods and what that means for their faith in God and his Word.

After abuse, fear, shame, mistrust, and rejection can control one's perceptions. The enemy feeds on this deception and uses it to hinder one's true identity in Christ and one's life-sustaining connection to God. 1 John 4:8 states that perfect love casts out fear and we wholeheartedly believe that God flawlessly loves, and his Word and Spirit truly removes one's fear and revives one's soul: one's mind, emotions, and will. We believe, that without the understanding and personal application of the Holy Bible, one's restoration process, one's mental health, and spiritual growth will be hindered. While our devotional's daily journey is about healing from abuse, the healing process is different for everyone. Some suffer from severe depression and need counseling, while others desire to learn about the effects abuse has on one's psyche and behaviors, and most just simply want answers. Nevertheless, it is important to note that if there are questions you do not see yourself in, it is our hope that they will bring about understanding and empathy for others and their suffering.

What We're Afraid to Ask is a beautiful gift that promotes truth, authenticity, vulnerability, and transformation. What one courageously asks and receives will enable personal and spiritual freedom when answers are sought from God's Word, his truth, while understanding one's childhood abuse in correlation to certain psychological concepts and principles. *What We're Afraid to Ask* taps into the unsettled mind and heart, those who feel unloved, ashamed, and afraid, and speaks meaning into one's past, one's present state, and one's glorious future.

Anna M. Jones

And after you have suffered a little while, the God of all grace, who has called you to his eternal glory in Christ, will himself restore, confirm, strengthen, and establish you.
(1 Pet. 5:10)

Question One
January 1st

What is evil?

Jon: "Evil is not a 'thing' in and of itself. Rather, it is the corruption of some good thing. When God created the universe, he made everything good (see Gen. 1:31). A person's body and mind are therefore good. One may, however, use their mind to devise an evil plan and use their body to carry out that plan. It is impossible for evil to occur without the use of something innately good. Evil occurs when something good is used for something that is not good."

Anna: "Evil resists what is good, it is one's abusive antagonist, fleshly vices, and immoral spirits that seek souls. Pain, suffering, and abuse characterize a constant reality that evil pervades and is undoubtedly fatalistic for the unbelieving kind. Its very presence threatens one's belief system, one's rationale, and can profoundly affect one's emotions, behaviors, and relationships when one's identity has been rooted within evil's lies. Relying on oneself to make sense of or cure one's iniquities only exasperates one's issues and causes symptomatic reactions within one's attempts to survive. Because of this inevitability, it is crucial to look at evil from its biblical orientation. Otherwise, confusion, dissatisfaction, self-blame, and disbelief will take over due to one's human experiences and limitations. This will skew one's self-perceptions, one's faith in God's divine plan, and one's unique and sanctified purpose through one's belief in Jesus Christ."

Question Two
January 2nd

If God is such a powerful and loving God, why does he let innocent, defenseless children be born to or be adopted by abusive parents?

Jon: "Man and woman were created in the image and likeness of God (Gen. 1:26) with freedom of the will. Although God didn't want them to eat from the tree of the knowledge of good and evil, he did not restrict their freedom to do so. If God were to force people's actions, their coming to him would not be genuine. We take comfort knowing that God is just: 'For the wrongdoer will be paid back for the wrong he has done' (Col. 3:25)."

Anna: "Human beings are imperfect and through choice have been exposed to both good and evil, which breeds psychological confusion, ambivalence, and dysfunction. When dysfunctional behavioral patterns are entrenched within a family's dynamics, wrongdoing and suffering are inevitable. Unfortunately, children are susceptible to the decisions of adults and are not exempt from experiencing delinquency or abuse. What children are absolved from, due to a limited capacity of awareness and accountability, is eternal wrath and judgment. Ultimately, God will have the final authority on those who have abused others. He does not routinely intervene to establish his recipe for grace, redemption, and to demonstrate the power that genuine faith and belief in his Son provides. God is without a doubt loving and just."

Question Three
January 3rd

What is the human soul?

Jon: "When God created man he 'breathed into his nostrils the breath of life, and the man became a living creature' (Gen. 2:7). We can think of man as composed of two parts: a soul and a body. The soul is the immaterial part of man, while the body is the physical or material part. And while the body will one day die, the soul will continue to live on. Jesus said to the thief crucified beside him, '… today you will be with me in Paradise' (Luke 23:43). The same can be said for the soul of any who place their faith in Jesus Christ."

Anna: "The human soul is immortal, immaterial, yet carried within a vulnerable vessel for a magnificent purpose. It is set apart from but temporarily contained within one's body, is linked to one's psyche, and has the capacity to express one's pain, longings, passions, and childhood traumas. One's soul was created, exists in and passes through this wayward world, and has the God-given power to express itself through one's emotions and physicality. The soul is spirit driven, can be chained to one's past, yet God is ultimately in control and governs one's existence. One's soul is interconnected to one's salvation, and one's destiny will be determined dependent upon what one chooses to believe. When one trusts in Jesus Christ as their Lord and savior, one's soul will have eternal life, reigning in heaven, with the almighty God."

Question Four
January 4th

How would studying the Word of God help us to heal our souls: our minds, emotions, and wills?

Jon: "There is nothing like God's Word; 'For the word of God is living and active, sharper than any two-edged sword, piercing to the division of soul and of spirit, of joints and of marrow, and discerning the thoughts and intentions of the heart' (Heb. 4:12). God's Word is a weapon for spiritual warfare. But it's eternally better than any earthly weapon. Alive and determined to do work, it enters a person's inner being. Perceiving all our thoughts and intentions, it labors with infinite love and infinite power. Open the Bible, and the Bible will open you."

Anna: "God's Word is the unadulterated truth and contains the reasons why one breathes. The Bible holds life's answers and lays the foundations of eternity. Truly understanding biblical principles will transform one's soul, identity, and purpose. Studying Scripture will fortify the believer's mind from self-deception and help one prepare for and combat the attacks of Satan and his demons. The immoralities of humankind have twisted truths into ugly and deceptive lies. The evils of abuse make for an innocent child's mind to grow up and believe that one is unworthy, unloved, and destined for psychological and emotional devastation. God's Word teaches the counter, and this alone, when one's eyes are opened, will change the course of one's conscious mind, one's heart, one's decisions, and one's hope and future."

Question Five
January 5th

What is depression?

Jon: "Scripture refers to depression as a low or contrite spirit (see Isa. 66:2). This state is regarded by most as undesirable. But Jesus said, 'Blessed are the poor in spirit, for theirs is the kingdom of heaven' (Mat. 5:3). Heaven is for those who place their faith in Christ (John 3:16). Accepting this truth requires an awareness of one's need for him. While depression is anything but pleasant, it increases one's awareness of this need. God is not only *there* for the depressed; he is there to give them the kingdom of heaven."

Anna: "Depression is a mood disorder that affects one's mind, emotions, physical being, and behaviors. Attempting to cope with the traumas of abuse only adds to depression's psychologically spirited battle. Bearing a lowly presence is indeed conjointly a spiritual issue that materializes in the physical realm. When a person isolates, self-harms, or has deep self-despair attached to one's existence, godly support and assistance is critical. Depressive symptoms can be exasperated and self-induced by one's beliefs and behaviors. Environmental factors, or a combination of one's circumstances, attitude, and decisions, will profoundly affect one's mental and emotional health. Truthfully examine one's self, because utter hopelessness is not of God's Spirit or influence. Depression is an affliction that can only be healed at its root, through truth, hope, and divine deliverance. Through an authentic relationship with Jesus, the fruits of the Holy Spirit will profoundly and positively affect one's mood and will."

Question Six
January 6th

What is hope?

Jon: "One has hope when they expect something beneficial to happen in the future. 1 Timothy 4:10 says, 'For to this end we toil and strive, because we have our hope set on the living God, who is the Savior of all people, especially of those who believe.' So hope causes something, namely, the ability to strive. In other words, hope is fuel for striving. If our fuel source of hope is in God, and God is eternal, then we have an eternal source of hope. With an eternal source of hope, we can always find reason to push forward."

Anna: "Hope is a belief in something or someone, an expectation of faith's manifestation of the confidence one has in the possibilities. Hope speaks promise into one's existence, desires, passions, and future. Hope can be attached to an aspiration, or a fact that promotes stability, security, and truth. Hope changes one's outlook on everyday and abusively tragic occurrences towards having a legitimate weight and purpose. Healing comes to life through hope's positivity, which nurtures one's body and soul. Intention combined with hope increases one's probability for one's dreams to become reality. Hope allows one to be eternally unrestrained from the psychological, emotional, and spiritual battles of life. Hope manifested through prayer materializes the supernatural due to an inexplicable faith in God and what he is capable of accomplishing, which is absolutely anything."

Question Seven
January 7th

Many survivors of childhood abuse only see the world in black and white, in an extremely simplistic nature. Can purposely looking at other colors, like red, blue, orange, purple, just to name a few, help us to not be so childlike in our thinking?

Jon: "It is very likely that many of us have adopted false impressions of who God is and what he is like. The Book of Revelation provides one of the most vivid and colorful descriptions of God. God is said to have the appearance of jasper and carnelian. An emerald rainbow encompasses his throne while from it extends a crystalline sea. And fiery torches, flashes of lightning, rumblings, and peals of thunder (see Rev. 4:3-5). Anyone who understands God as not some stoic, black-and-white, impersonal robot, but as a robust, active, living, and colorful person, is anything but childlike in their thinking."

Anna: "Color increases one's mental, emotional, and physical vitality through sensation, depth, and creativity. Communication intensifies through hues and their unique properties. Removing the possibilities through polarized thinking manifests in one's splitting process, an inability to see something within balance. When one's perspective is divided into being all good or all bad, delusions are created, emotional walls arise, and dysfunction ensues. Simplicity is essential, but when turned into distortions or denial, then one's perceptions need adjusting. Color activates associations and allows thoughts and imagination to soar. A magnificent world full of color was created by God for one to enjoy."

Question Eight
January 8th

Being betrayed by our parents has left a lot of us distrustful of people and even doubtful of what trust actually means. What is trust?

Jon: "Proverbs 3:5 says, 'Trust in the LORD with all your heart, and do not lean on your own understanding.' We can draw at least two realities about the nature of trust from this verse. The first reality is that trust involves complete surrender of the heart. Trust is not a partial surrender of the heart. The second reality is that trust involves a relinquishing. So we trust when we stop relying or depending on ourselves. Because God never forsakes those who seek him (see Ps. 9:10), we reserve full expression of this kind of trust for him alone."

Anna: "An unmoving belief or certainty in one's purpose displays trust and will change the projection of one's decisions and interactions. Trust is obtainable but more often than not is crushed by selfish, thoughtless, and dysfunctional human behavior. An authentic and trusting soul can be difficult to find, but when discovered is a true blessing in one's life. Just because one is reliable does not mean one will not disappoint or hurt others. Trust does not coincide with perfection or reaching faultless expectations; it boldly sustains one's bond to another and nurtures genuine connection, vulnerability, and growth. Jesus was betrayed by Judas, yet still embodied what was entrusted in faith and certitude, because he fulfilled his purpose and accomplished what God promised he would."

Question Nine
January 9th

A great number of us learned to survive our painful childhoods by numbing out. And now as adults, some of us feel no emotion at all. Can you tell us how we can begin to feel and experience all of our emotions?

Jon: "The Word of God promises, '… if anyone is in Christ, he is a new creation. The old has passed away; behold, the new has come' (2 Cor. 5:17). Notice that this does not mean that the believer in Christ merely *ought* to act as a new creation, but that the believer in Christ *is* in fact a brand new creation. There is no person ineligible to receive a new heart and spirit capable of properly and joyfully experiencing emotion (see Ez. 36:26)."

Anna: "When a child endures abuse, the many emotions associated with that abuse can be so overwhelming and deregulating that one has few options: act out or numb out. As one ages, distressing circumstances rebreathe life into this survival process of self-disunion from deep within. This method to emotionally disconnect is dissociation, and this process occurs at different levels. One can detach from one's current trigger or from one's present reality. To tell one's narrative in a contained environment and calm state is crucial for emotional identification and development, which will prompt self-connection, personal growth, and healing. Emotions are fundamental clues that become appropriately elevated when transformed by God's Spirit, truth, and love."

Question Ten
January 10th

What is faith?

Jon: "Scripture defines faith as 'the assurance of things hoped for, the conviction of things not seen' (Heb. 11:1). Faith grants the mind access to unseen heavenly realities otherwise hidden. It allows God to reveal to us more of himself, his power, his work, and his will. Moreover, faith is necessary for salvation (see Eph. 2:8). When genuinely placed in Christ Jesus, faith becomes the mechanism by which we are immediately forgiven of our sins and granted eternal life (see John 3:36; Rom. 5:2)."

Anna: "Faith is founded upon beliefs greater than one's self yet is directly connected to one's identity and purpose. Faith is freeing, supernaturally oriented, and fundamental for one's gifts in this life and the next. Faith shifts circumstances and shatters perceptions of impossibilities; it saves lives, and releases the shackles of evil upon one's heart, soul, and spirit. One's faith is a series of decisions and profoundly affects one's mental health through overcoming one's childhood abuse and current obstacles. Faith correlates with having a righteous perspective and the knowledge and wisdom to understand that one will not be crushed by the state of the world or by what has happened in the past. Faith is a gift of the promises from God and when fathomed and treasured, one will spiritually soar."

Question Eleven
January 11th

**We anticipate the day our souls—our minds, emotions, and
wills—are healed. Can music help to restore us in these areas?**

Jon: "Steadfastness of heart, pleasure, joy, and gratitude are just
some positive states of being connected with making music unto
God (Ps. 57:7, 135:3, 71:23; Col. 3:16). In Scripture, the goal of
music is not personal gain, but to worship and give praise to the
Lord. Positive personal improvement is merely a byproduct of
God-focused musical endeavors. If we ever feel we have no reason to sing, we can remember we have been eternally saved
through Christ Jesus. We then have an eternal reason to sing and
make joyful noise."

Anna: "When music edifies one's mind and spirit, it has the ability to be deeply uplifting, remedial, and transformative. It trans-
lates through melodies and lyrics a message that stokes, nurtures,
awakens, and brings forth animation to one's emotions and existence. Pleasant sounds and intricate harmonies soothe the soul,
ignite the senses, and tell a story. Music heals on psychological
and physiological levels because it incites congruence within
one's cells and being, and enables personal association and emotional expression. Life can be hard, human behavior is often hurtful, circumstances can be abusive and unfair, and music creates
a grieving highway towards emotional release and healthy escape. Humankind was created to trust, depend upon, and worship God. When praising Jesus through song, one will experience
a marvelous restoration process through honoring, adorating,
and glorifying God."

Question Twelve
January 12th

Since Jesus failed to protect us from evil—letting us down, therefore, and instilling a deep distrust for him in us—how are we to believe that he is dependable?

Jon: "Jesus was triumphant in protecting us from evil. He came to abolish sin and death while bringing life and salvation to those who would believe in him (2 Tim. 1:10). What keeps us from eternity with God is our sin. Though he was sinless, he bore our sins (2 Cor. 5:21; Rom. 5:8). Though we deserve death, he died in our stead (1 John 3:16). Jesus' death on the cross protects us from the worst possible experience: hell."

Anna: "Insecurities, worthlessness, self-hatred, and distrust of others will most likely develop, on some level, within an abused soul. Abuse generates psychological and emotional torment, to an extent, and this promotes one to develop extreme defense mechanisms to protect their being and existence from others. These conscious and unconscious defense strategies ensue due to fear. If one's life on earth has not been safe, then how can one trust the one who created life? An unbiased perspective is key. God is not of the human kind. He is set apart and because of that he is just, righteous, and embodies the emphatic truth. The Bible is dependable and true because it was inspired by God—truth—and he should not be blamed or held accountable for the evil that human beings decide to do."

Question Thirteen
January 13th

Why does God allow us to experience such evil and pain?

Jon: "The Christian has something marvelous that the world will never have: the ability to rejoice in suffering (see Rom. 5:3). How? Because God has made it so that 'suffering produces endurance, and endurance produces character, and character produces hope, and hope does not put us to shame…' (Rom. 5:3-5). Evil and pain are unequivocally wrong. Nevertheless, God's infinite love for us compels him to grow—from the manure of evil—a garden of endurance, character, hope, and respect in our lives."

Anna: "Evil exists, is rampant, and has the tendency to transpire when a chain of disturbing and dehumanizing circumstances unfolds within an individual's environment. Evil moves because the angelic fell and it survives because it can be swift, unseen, and slowly and consistently perpetuated through one's unrighteous living. Abuse was created by the devil yet one carries out his rebellion through one's behaviors. Without evil or free will, would one be able to grasp what is truly precious and good? Without psychological, emotional, or physical pain, would one even slightly comprehend what Jesus went through on the cross for humankind? One's experiences of evil can lead them to the Lord for the distinct fact that God is the epitome of good. One's childhood of abusive experiences can make or break one's soul and the decision must be made. Choose God, choose an abundant life of purpose, and do not let evil prevail."

Question Fourteen
January 14th

Some of us believe that when we were children, we unconsciously took on our parents' unmet needs. Are we obligated as adult children to continue to help our problematic parents?

Jon: "Jesus said the second-greatest commandment is to 'love your neighbor as yourself' (Mat. 22:39). Helping our parents falls under this command. However, Jesus also said, 'if your right hand causes you to sin, cut it off and throw it away' (Mat. 5:30). If helping our problematic parents causes us to sin, that action should be cut off immediately. We are God's workmanship; fearfully and wonderfully made (Eph. 2:10; Ps. 139:14). Helping others never means compromising our own sanctity."

Anna: "One's automatic thought processes, one's intrinsic motivations, one's interpretations, and learned and perceived beliefs have a direct effect on one's identity formation, emotions, and behaviors. Due to the insecure attachment style an abusive parent creates with their child, one will consciously and unconsciously adapt or poorly adjust to fulfill certain roles needed within the family unit. These dynamics create illusions that one's needs are being met. When helping a problematic parent becomes a personal obligation to meet unhealthy motives, one's childhood insecurities, or reach faulty expectations, emotional issues and dissatisfaction will continually fester. Boundaries for protection from self-destructive cycles must be set. Honor one's parents in one's thoughts, intentions, actions, and prayers, yet one's obligation is to their faith's calling."

Question Fifteen
January 15th

What is the Holy Spirit?

Jon: "The Holy Spirit is God. Namely, the third person of the Trinity. Before Jesus ascended into heaven, he bestowed upon his disciples the Holy Spirit to be the dominant presence of God in the world to date (see John 20:22). In other words, everything done by God in this age is accomplished through the Holy Spirit. And he is active in every step of Christian development: from the moment we first believe, to the moment we reach heaven. We mustn't diminish the importance of the Holy Spirit, for everything we receive from God we receive through him."

Anna: "Human nature opposes God's Spirit, the Holy Spirit, and childhood abuse can cause one's soul to be controlled by lies that detrimentally affect one's mind, emotions, and behaviors. One's self-will can fall victim to depravity and be enslaved to the immoralities of emotional neglect when misused and abused. When painful experiences negatively change one's perspective, one's essence, spirit, has been thwarted. Experiencing a corrupted soul can be inundating and eerie when one knows the truth of what is really evolving within one's carnality. When not equipped for the world's vigor, impure psychological, emotional, and behavioral tendencies are created, especially when one's identity has been exposed to continual opposition. The Holy Spirit is God's mighty presence within the Christian, and was sent out to awaken, remind, transform, and lead the believer into the fulfillment of God's will, one's purpose."

Question Sixteen
January 16th

Why don't we feel the power of the Holy Spirit inside of us?

Jon: "A person must 'repent and be baptized… in the name of Jesus Christ for the forgiveness of [their] sins,' before they 'receive the gift of the Holy Spirit' (Acts 2:38). In other words, if a person has not placed their faith in Christ, they cannot feel the power of the Holy Spirit. As for the believer, the Holy Spirit's power in their life may be stifled by sin (see Eph. 4:30; 1 Thes. 5:19). We must inspect ourselves for that which inhibits the Holy Spirit."

Anna: "Inside everyone, a spiritual struggle is occurring. Free will's opportunity can spur illusions of needing to control one's reality, which leads to bondage—for example, anxious and depressive cognitions, abusive behaviors, substance abuse issues, and an array of different vices that silence the truth. Human understanding is limited and self-empowerment cannot sustain without God. Inner and behavioral transformation directly coincides with yielding to God's will, which carries out through his Holy Spirit. God bestows his presence upon and within the believer, which expresses through his righteous qualities. One must choose to let his Spirit lead one's life. Relying upon and surrendering to God's authority allows his essence to manifest through and dominate one's fleshly nature. Through time, one's negative experiences, thoughts, emotions, and behaviors will subdue with spiritual maturity, a conscious righteousness, thoughtfulness, and the Holy Spirit's power."

Question Seventeen
January 17th

We read of the Holy Spirit's divine attributes such as love, truth, and holiness, just to name a few. Many of us were led to believe that we are bad through and through. How can a perfectly good God reside within a bad person?

Jon: "Scripture does say that 'all have sinned and fall short of the glory of God' (Rom. 3:23) and that 'If we say we have no sin, we deceive ourselves, and the truth is not in us' (1 John 1:8). However, to anyone who places their faith in Christ Jesus, God credits righteousness (see Rom. 4:24). We are not righteous or holy, so—through faith—Jesus becomes our 'righteousness and sanctification and redemption' (1 Cor. 1:30). Christ enters us through faith; the Spirit enters through Christ."

Anna: "One's negative self-perceptions are not necessarily truth. After abuse, one's core belief systems become skewed and self-worth can crumble. Survivors tend to lean towards psychological and emotional extremes because of internal conflicts. For example, the idea or belief that one is completely bad and will never be worthy of anything good, which is incorrect. Redemption takes the broken-spirited, mentally afflicted, emotionally downtrodden, and transforms one supernaturally through Christ's holiness. God's love does not discriminate despite one's transgressions, yet one's human nature does disconnect one from God. The Holy Spirit resides in anyone who calls upon Jesus' name. What is purely good cannot be corrupted by evil yet can only inspire evil to become good."

Question Eighteen
January 18th

Childhood abuse has left many of us feeling as though we are floating above our bodies, watching someone else live our lives. Is there a way that we can feel more ever-present inside of our bodies?

Jon: "Scripture reveals one unfailing method for cultivating a mind which feels more ever-present: prayer. Verse after verse we find God's Word directing us to 'pray without ceasing' (1 Thes. 5:17; see also Luke 18:1; Rom. 12:12; Eph. 6:18; Col. 4:2). Prayer causes us to focus on that which we are currently praying about. If we pray often, then our focus will be often on the present. Consistency in prayer brings consistency in feeling more ever-present in the body."

Anna: "Dissociation is a coping strategy utilized to reduce emotional distress. When this response was learned as a perplexed child, this process becomes less than ideal and adapted poorly in most circumstances as an adult. This ingrained yet ineffectual long-term solution, which originally served as an invaluable means for survival, is continually dimming one's security, emotions, and experiences. By increasing one's self-awareness, dissociation can be minimized. Through Christ-like mindfulness, stability can be achieved through a consciousness of one's present truth, while acknowledging and welcoming one's thoughts, emotions, and physical sensations. Being grounded in truth will shift one's perspectives. Experiencing God's love will also strengthen one's ability to open up. Meditating upon his Word and communicating with him daily through prayer will nurture a more sound mind, heart, and existence."

Question Nineteen
January 19th

A great number of us have heard through the years that low self-esteem is the major cause of many spiritual and psychological problems. How can we develop a better opinion of ourselves?

Jon: "King David said if he could only do one thing, he would '… gaze upon the beauty of the LORD' (Ps. 27:4). God is 'the perfection of beauty' (Ps. 50:2), and 'splendor and majesty are before him' (Ps. 96:6). When God made the human race, he said, 'Let us make man in our image, after our likeness' (see Gen. 1:26). We are all therefore of infinite worth as carriers of God's perfect beauty, splendor, and majesty. One life is of more value than all the universe."

Anna: "Self-esteem mirrors one's evaluation of what one believes they are worth. When a person has habitual negative judgments toward their self-image, abilities or purpose, low self-worth proceeds. This deep-rooted issue of self-deficiency will cause psychological and emotional instability, such as depression, anxiety, and dysfunctional behaviors. When one wanders from the truth of who one truly is and solely identifies with one's circumstances, and not the purpose one was created for, and the image one was created after, one's perception has been deceived and distorted. To minimize one's internal unrest, one's soul needs restoration by building from a biblical foundation and truth-centered mentality. One's identity is found in Jesus and his life-giving sacrifice, God's gift of salvation, because one is deeply loved and treasured."

Question Twenty
January 20th

Will you please describe oppression for us as it relates to child abuse?

Jon: "Oppression can take different forms and exist in different contexts. But in Christian circles it is often linked with demonic activity. But this can be dangerous when applied to child abuse. While demonic activity can certainly cause physical, emotional, and psychological abuse (see Eph. 6:12), demons are not always to blame. Sometimes oppression is carried out simply by the free choices of sinful people, which is often the case in child abuse. Why is this important? People don't want to take responsibility for their actions. And when they blame others they make it easier for themselves to carry out sinful actions. With the blame placed squarely on the abuser or potential abuser, their oppressive behavior becomes that much more difficult to carry out."

Anna: "Abuse is oppressive and oppression creates maltreatment. A child does not have the ability to differentiate between the discrepancies within their soul and another's unjust behaviors. Innocence cowers in the presence of cruelty, which is why child abuse is so prevalent. Evil created this advantage. Within oppression there are perceived levels of inferiority and dominance. Children are extremely susceptible to forceful intent because they lack autonomy. This dependence on others leaves them vulnerable to exploitation and attack. God is anti-oppressive because he gives humankind free will and desires for one to choose love, to choose kindness, to choose freedom, to choose Jesus Christ."

Question Twenty-One
January 21st

Some of us are resistant to join a church or therapy group. Can you convince us why we should?

Jon: "The church is the body of believers in Christ throughout all of history. God doesn't inhabit buildings per se; he inhabits people (see Acts 17:24; 1 Cor. 6:19). The moment one places their faith in Jesus, they join the church. People are the church. And the church gathers not only because it is commanded to (see Deu. 4:10; Heb. 10:25), but to worship God collectively (see Col. 3:16). As the body functions properly when all of its parts are present, so too does the church function properly when all believers are present (Rom. 12:3-8; 1 Cor. 12; Eph. 4:1-16)."

Anna: "Building and maintaining a support system is crucial for one's well-being. Conscious experiences of commonality, developing relational trust, nurturing one's vulnerabilities, grieving one's pain, and cultivating personal fulfillment can blossom within group therapy. Opposition to seek help, not utilizing one's resources, or stubbornness against being spiritually fed will hinder psychological and emotional healing, self-awareness, and growth. Sadly, human beings are too often hurtful and abusive. When one has experienced betrayal by a churchgoer, moving forward and taking another leap of faith can be anxiety provoking and even burdensome. When seeking the support one truly needs, one must fully trust in God's promises. Reach out to groups who are in authentic fellowship with Jesus Christ, who consistently delve into God's Word, and who live by his Spirit's power and truth."

Question Twenty-Two
January 22nd

For those of us who did not have an earthly mother, is the Virgin Mary a good role model to follow?

Jon: "Mary was a human being and therefore should not be deified or worshipped (see Ex. 20:3-6). We must 'not go beyond what is written' about Mary in the Scriptures (1 Cor. 4:6). However, when the angel Gabriel told Mary she would bear the Son of God, she responded, 'Behold, I am the servant of the Lord; let it be to me according to your word' (Luke 1:38). We would all do well to adopt this model of obedience to the Lord."

Anna: "Not having a mother to mirror, nurture, or model what a healthy relationship is through the important years of development can lead to a deficit within the scope of having a secure attachment experience. Having a role model or admiring someone should align with one's sought values, character, and beliefs in correlation to a solid foundation of one's obedience in faith. Mary was humble, devout, steadfast, and, most courageously, she firmly believed God and was submissive to his will. Is the Virgin Mary a positive, healthy role model? Yes. Should she be idolized? No, because she is human and not God. She was Jesus' mother, chosen by the Creator himself to carry out one of the most important missions of humankind. Her faith and qualities should be admired and embodied."

Question Twenty-Three
January 23rd

We didn't have caregivers who nurtured our intrinsic gifts. Instead, we had lunatics who turned us into slaves, bridling our spirits. Is God disappointed in us?

Jon: "Far from being disappointed, God promises through his Word a heavenly inheritance for the broken-spirited: 'Blessed are the poor in spirit, for theirs is the kingdom of heaven' (Mat. 5:3). We only grieve God when we rebel against him (see Isa. 63:10). Always remember, 'neither death nor life, nor angels nor rulers, nor things present nor things to come, nor powers, nor height nor depth, nor anything else in all creation, will be able to separate us from the love of God' (Rom. 8:38-39)."

Anna: "One's strengths, weaknesses, and character are shaped and greatly influenced by others. This is what is disappointing: when others do everything in their power to mentally and emotionally extinguish and bury one's worth, passion, abilities, hope, and faith in love. After abuse, it is often difficult to believe in oneself and what one has to offer the world. Despite horrific circumstances, who one was created to be probes one's heart from within. One's temperament tends to not waver in extremes despite negative and positive experiences. God-given gifts never leave and God will use one's abusive past, heartache, and disappointments to mold one into a more effective and powerful vessel to be used for his glorious purposes. God's love cannot waver. Therefore, his love for every single soul is unchangeable."

Question Twenty-Four
January 24th

Our childhoods—the glee, the fun, the joy, the simplicity and innocence—were stolen from us. Is it possible, as adults, to reclaim our childhoods?

Jon: "Joseph's brothers, jealous over his dream, conspired to kill him, threw him into a pit, and sold him into slavery for twenty shekels. The Lord was with Joseph, however, and he would rise to power and provide for his family. When his brothers threw themselves before Joseph in repentance, Joseph said, 'As for you, you meant evil against me, but God meant it for good' (Gen. 50:20). Unequivocally, the God of the universe claims our lives for good."

Anna: "When innocence is stolen from the heart and soul of a child, so are the concepts of security, freedom, and guiltlessness. This is not only tragic but will take some time to reach certain milestones towards truth, self-discovery, and recovery. As a child and adult, it is possible to have corrective experiences within or outside of relationships and feel the simplicity, satisfactions, and joys of life all over again. To find and restore what has been lost is within reach, but one must desire this, choose to believe it through faith, and acknowledge that this is not something that should be done alone, apart from God. There is more good news: Jesus died so humankind could be forgiven, saved, and redeemed. When the Holy Spirit dwells within the believer, fruits like joy from God's beautifully balanced presence are experienced and reclaimed."

Question Twenty-Five
January 25th

What are the spiritual and psychological benefits of taking a walk in nature?

Jon: "The Bible says, 'The heavens declare the glory of God, and the sky above proclaims his handiwork. Day to day pours out speech, and night to night reveals knowledge' (Ps. 19:1-2). When we immerse ourselves in nature we can observe certain characteristics of God. We see that he is infinitely powerful, intelligent, creative, skillful, and excellent. Therefore, taking a contemplative walk in nature inspires us to glorify and worship the Creator of our universe. Understanding that he didn't need to create anything as we behold our existence and the existence of the world around us, we are convinced that God loves us and desires for us to experience his goodness."

Anna: "Walking can decrease stress and help reduce emotional turmoil within one's mind, emotions, and spirit. Witnessing the beauty of nature and strolling amidst the elements can enable wonder and possibility within one's perspective, passions, and purpose. When experiencing the majesty of the ocean or the whimsy of the butterfly, it is difficult not to wonder, become lighthearted, and dream beyond earth's parameters. When overcoming one's painful childhood, nature can enliven one's childlike essence. To be in the present moment and experience what God has created for one to delight in is truly awe-inspiring, powerful, yet calming and rejuvenating for one's psychological, emotional, and spiritual state. Nature is truly divine and was created for one's benefit and pleasure."

Question Twenty-Six
January 26th

What is compassion?

Jon: "Hardship is no discriminator of persons. And it will come. Therefore Galatians 6:2 says, 'Bear one another's burdens, and so fulfill the law of Christ.' Hardship has weight. A spiritual heaviness. So we have compassion when, noticing another's burden, we come alongside them to support that weight. When we do this, we accomplish our purpose as Christians. But it is important to remember that we should not be satisfied by the mere feeling of compassion. True compassion transcends heart to hand. True compassion *does* what compassion inspires."

Anna: "Expressing one's sympathetic heart is a beautiful gift to give. A benevolent nature brings forth kind and generous actions, which when founded in purity and love truly nurture interpersonal connection. When witnessing suffering, one's attempts to help can be deeply humbled and one can feel powerless, when another's burdens do not cease. On the contrary, lacking empathy and being consistently indifferent is emotional and relationship suicide. When one endured childhood abuse, when compassion was nowhere in sight, when one's soul was trampled upon, how does one deter becoming indifferent? Self-awareness toward experienced apathy can shine a light into one's suppressions and disconnected state. Compassion develops from within; it evolves through the power of God's Holy Spirit, and is carried out through one's behaviors. Jesus' selfless death on the cross was the most loving act that ever was and ever will be; a divine act of compassion."

Question Twenty-Seven
January 27th

Why should we worship Jesus for suffering on the cross for us when many of us have suffered as well?

Jon: "Suffering, in and of itself, is never good for people. For this reason heaven will be void of suffering (see Rev. 21:4). Furthermore, God alone should be worshipped (see Ex. 20:2-6). The climax of John's gospel happens in chapter 20 when the risen Jesus appears before Thomas. Seeing Jesus' wounds, and discerning Jesus' power over even death, Thomas exclaims, 'My Lord and my God!' (John 20:28). We do not worship Jesus because he suffered. Rather, we worship Jesus because he is God."

Anna: "The psychological effects of suffering can be devastating and negatively influence many aspects of one's life. When living through trauma, and one is psychologically, emotionally, and spiritually wounded because of the repetitive dysfunctional relational patterns one endured, one's concept of whom they are and what they deserve can be blurred and thrown off course. On the other hand, suffering can increase one's empathy, compassion, selflessness, self-sacrificial desires, and benevolence toward humanity when one's perspective becomes grounded in truth and love. So, even though one suffers, this is why one worships Jesus: he is the Messiah, he overcame suffering, conquered death, and rose from the dead for those who suffer through sin on earth that they might experience redemption, glory, and live eternally with God."

Question Twenty-Eight
January 28th

Many of us who were abused as children have become oversensitive and easily offended. How can we grow thicker skin in this regard?

Jon: "We never want to allow callouses to grow over our life wounds that were not properly healed. However, once we have fully addressed the root problem behind our oversensitivity, we may strategize how to handle future difficulties. Here, Scripture's advice is to shift our perspective: 'Count it all joy... when you meet trials of various kinds... the testing of your faith produces steadfastness. And let steadfastness have its full effect, that you may be perfect and complete, lacking in nothing' (Jas. 1:2-4)."

Anna: "When deeply wounded, abused, and betrayed, one's emotional processes react and defend oneself from uncomfortable experiences. Emotional sensitivity differs from being oversensitive. Understanding why one is sensitive and responds in certain ways, connecting this reactivity with one's hurtful family dynamics, one's inner dialogue and the beliefs they hold about oneself, will help one make sense of why one does what they do. With an accurate measure of one's emotional development, identification and desensitization to specific individuals and situations will increase, one will learn to recognize internalizations and projections, one's skin will grow thicker and self-discovery will ensue. Connecting to and expressing one's heart towards the broken-spirited is doing God's work and will. Having spiritually-thick skin means humbly understanding one's value and purpose, and standing firmly upon God's Word, while graciously loving oneself and others."

Question Twenty-Nine
January 29th

What is forgiveness?

Jon: "Short is the list of words sweeter than this one. For as we excel in needing forgiveness, God excels more so in forgiving. He says, 'I have blotted out your transgressions like a cloud, and your sins like mist; return to me, for I have redeemed you' (Isa. 44:22). Forgiveness is God's light evaporating our clouds of offence. The clouds lifted, we see Christ with arms open. Embracing him, he whispers in love, 'I have redeemed you.' Forgiveness is an eternal embrace of redemption. It is grasping the divine."

Anna: "Possessing goodness and the willingness to overlook something without psychological, emotional, or relational indebting is forgiveness truly established in love. Authentic exoneration does not exploit the weaknesses of others nor does it leverage their guilt or vulnerabilities to misuse for one's advantage. Embodying an enlightened nature is having empathy and mercy toward oneself and others. Survivors of abuse often see the innate value in others, yet find it difficult to love and forgive themselves. When one absolves, they reflect the divine, which exemplifies a beautiful orchestration from above that plants seeds of mercy, salvation, and redemption. Forgiveness can penetrate the receiver's soul and spirit when unearned and expressed with sincerity, compassion, and grace. God's radical vindication of humankind's sins through Jesus Christ's death exemplifies forgiveness flawlessly. God is surely forgiving and good."

Question Thirty
January 30th

Anger. We all feel it from time to time. It is a feeling that can range from a lenient irritation to merciless frustration and rage. As human beings, how does the Lord want us to express our discontent with one another?

Jon: "Sometimes anger is not sinful. Even God becomes angry. However, he is always 'slow to anger and abounding in steadfast love' (Ps. 145:8). Scripture says to humanity, 'Be angry and do not sin; do not let the sun go down on your anger' (Eph. 4:26). While anger is not forbidden, we must be sober, patient, and quick to forgive. A helpful way to know if our anger is acceptable is to ask ourselves, 'Does this anger please God or dishonor him?'"

Anna: "Anger bares pain and is an opportunity for truth to rise amidst what is upsetting and unjust. When the roots of one's frustrations are not exposed, emotional, psychological, and behavioral problems will often manifest. Deciphering the underlying emotions associated to one's past, and addressing one's enraged actions, will help establish a premise moving forward toward awareness, forgiveness, self-expression, and personal growth. Anger can be vindicated, but acting upon it with malicious motives is not just simply absolved or without consequence. God soundly comprehends where one's anger developed and has allowed the emotion to exist for protection, release, moral accountability, and his divine purposes. Expressing one's discontentment within God's boundary system, while maintaining self-control, decency, morality, and not opposing God's Spirit, is righteous expression."

Question Thirty-One
January 31st

At which point is anger sinful?

Jon: "Scripture's response is straightforward: '… whoever knows the right thing to do and fails to do it, for him it is sin' (Jas. 4:17). Notice that sin is not presented as abstract or alien—it is not a force or a substance. Rather, it is a choice. So when we choose to do what we know to be wrong with our anger, we sin. Remember, slowness to anger indicates 'good sense' and 'great understanding' (see Pro. 19:11, 14:29)."

Anna: "Acting upon one's anger, when justified in truth and with cause for a sincere purpose, can be healthy and pivotal in understanding and reshaping interpersonal connections and experiences. One's consciousness of right and wrong is within one's soul and spirit. Behaving angrily with negative intent to hurt, victimize, or emotionally, mentally, and physically destroy another is sinful and will have consequences. Wicked cognitions have detrimental emotions, behaviors, and spiritual effects on one's existence. It is unethical to consciously, to deliberately hurt others in the eyes of God. When anger enables one to do what one understands within that they should not, it is sinful. However, God is a God of mercy, grace, and forgiveness and when one's heart is convicted and one turns away from what is wrong, true transformation transpires."

Question Thirty-Two
February 1st

As young children, some of us learned to internalize our anger. That is, rather than place the blame on our abusers, we placed the charges against ourselves. How can we learn to stop blaming ourselves for the wrongful actions of others?

Jon: "Romans 8:1 is one of the most comforting verses in all of Scripture. It says, 'There is therefore now no condemnation for those who are in Christ Jesus.' If you have placed your faith in Jesus, the God of the universe declares you absolutely free of blame—blame from others, and blame from yourself. We can learn to stop blaming ourselves for the wrongful actions of others by reminding ourselves of Romans 8:1 each time we feel tempted to do so."

Anna: "Children internalize abuse through unconscious introjections, which is adopting the abuse's tainted message as truth. Now, this child's belief system will detrimentally develop through demoralization and self-devaluation. Naturally, anger wrestles within the confused soul and condemnation starts to affect one's identity. The child thinks that if they just behave more appropriately, then the abusive behaviors would stop. When the abuse continues, disappointment, worthlessness, and self-hate evolve. Resolution for this shame requires a cognitive switch and shift in responsibility toward the abuser's behaviors. Healthy expressions of anger are important for survivors of trauma to feel validated and empowered. When one grieves and asks God for healing and wisdom, he will give one understanding and clarity toward one's faulty beliefs; through faith self-blame is released."

Question Thirty-Three
February 2nd

Some of us were raised by very angry fathers. As a result, we believe in every fiber of our beings that God is angry with us as well. Is this true?

Jon: "It is not true that if our earthly fathers are angry with us then necessarily and automatically God is angry with us too. God does not rely on humankind in any way (see Acts 17:24-25). If God is angry with us, it is only because of our sin against him: 'For the wrath of God is revealed from heaven against all ungodliness and unrighteousness of men' (Rom. 1:18). However, if a person is in Christ they will never experience God's wrath (see Rom. 8:1)."

Anna: "When anger, belligerence, and abuses were common occurrences with one's father or caregiver, those psychological, emotional, and physical experiences tend to transfer to and cripple other relationships in ways. One's concept and image of God connects to one's earthly father experience especially when one has not felt or does not understand the depth of God's love and grace. God's anger is blamelessly just and focused toward one's sinful thoughts, intentions, and behaviors, not one's being and worth. Those who have been beat down by another's anger, especially children, this sincerely displeases God and there is natural, relational, and spiritual consequences for one's words and actions. God's wrath exists because evil exists; it is not toward those whom evil has charged. God created humankind from his abundant wisdom and love."

Question Thirty-Four
February 3rd

Is it right to be angry with God?

Jon: "If you are angry, Scripture says, 'Cast your burden on the LORD' (Ps. 55:22). While it is right to share our anger with God, we must be careful not to blaspheme him. In other words, if our anger causes us to disrespect or speak evil against him or his character, we have sinned. It is a privilege to communicate with the Creator of the universe. It is a greater privilege to communicate our adverse feelings with him."

Anna: "To have anger toward evil and the horrendous abuse one endured is not wrong. However, to blame and be angry with God for what a flawed individual has done is widely common, yet not just. Anger can be tricky because if it prompts one to action, to protect, to sacrifice, to resolve an issue or mend a relationship, it can be a powerful catalyst for change. Yet if anger causes one to act immorally, build resentments, creates passive aggression, rumination, or causes one to be self-righteous and blinded by pride and selfishness, anger has turned into what is now considered wrong and unpleasing. Anger is an indicator that one is not at peace and in emotional and spiritual unrest. God can handle all things, especially one's anger, but remember he is the ultimate source of power, love, restoration, and peace. When one offers up their indignation to him, one becomes more accessible for psychological and emotional healing."

Question Thirty-Five
February 4th

Generally speaking, what does peace feel like?

Jon: "In the Bible, peace is presented as something which is constantly worked for. Peace is sought after and strived for (see Ps. 34:14; Heb. 12:14). It is what we make and live in (see Jas. 3:18; 2 Cor. 13:11). Scripture says, 'For to set the mind on the flesh is death, but to set the mind on the Spirit is life and peace' (Rom. 8:6). Peace then is a daily discipline of moving one's thoughts and desires into harmony with God's."

Anna: "When at peace, one is in a psychological, emotional, and physical mode of contentment and spiritual accordance. Inner peace is connected to an understanding of pure freedom, divine power, identity, self-worth, and purpose. This awareness minimizes intense, negatively skewed emotions, such as anxiety, and fear, as well as stress. When one is peaceful, how one approaches and grasps challenging situations changes. Having peace of mind does not mean one will not feel and experience difficult emotions and the complexities of being. Quite the contrary: with personal peace, one will enjoy life more presently and fully. Peace intertwines with one's thoughts and belief systems because genuine serenity achieved through biblical truths and promises transforms one's perceptions. To truly live peacefully, a spiritual transformation must take place through God's Holy Spirit, which will reside within and exude from one's being. God's peace, supernatural peace, feels amazing."

Question Thirty-Six
February 5th

What is shame, and why do we feel it so deeply in the core of our beings?

Jon: "God is all-good and all-knowing. He has perfect understanding of what is and is not good. Made in his image, we obtain a finite understanding of what is and is not good. We feel shame because we recognize that we have done wrong. We sense that our actions have not met God's standard of goodness. Shame is powerful because through it we perceive that we have offended a holy and righteous God. But there is still hope in shame. 'For godly grief produces a repentance that leads to salvation...' (2 Cor. 7:10)."

Anna: "When abused, from one's very first moments and memories, recollected experiences carry a message of blame, that one is bad, dirty, unacceptable, or deemed a toy to be played with and disposed of. This shatters one's feelings of significance and negates one's internal being. This leaves a child feeling humiliated, crushed, and dejected by those who were created to love and look after them. The believed shame in that alone is perceived as unbearable. Shame exploits one's inability to be perfect, and cruelly exemplifies the reality and brokenness of one's humanness. The concept of disgrace has proliferated from dysfunction and humankind's disobedient nature, which sadly enforces the enemies' evil plan. With unadulterated faith in Jesus, one will be brought into God's glory and spiritually mended from their self-condemning lies of shame."

Question Thirty-Seven
February 6th

What are the spiritual and mental health benefits of writing?

Jon: "While there are no passages in Scripture that directly comment on the benefits of writing, there is powerful indirect evidence throughout the Psalms of the benefits of expressing oneself verbally. For example, at the beginning of Psalm 4, King David shares his feelings of distress and shame with the Lord. By the end of the psalm he is able to say, 'In peace I will both lie down and sleep; for you alone, O LORD, make me dwell in safety' (Ps. 4:8). Like King David, expressing ourselves verbally during times of distress can often bring peace."

Anna: "Writing for creativity and pleasure or writing to cope with life's circumstances has tremendous cathartic and therapeutic benefits. Revealing one's thoughts, emotions, ideas, dreams, personal history, etcetera, enables healing from experiences, self-validation, and allows for desires and deep-rooted feelings to be released and explored. Expressing oneself through journaling enables one's subconscious and emotional self to surface. One's well-being is correlated with one's ability to engage in and have the willingness for authentic self-expression. Writing plays a primary role in life's experiences and is crucial for documenting truth, understanding history, and validating the life and testimony of Jesus Christ. The Holy Bible was written through God's Spirit so humankind could come to know truth by those who believed in and were inspired by humankind's true God."

Question Thirty-Eight
February 7th

Can analyzing our dreams bring us to a greater understanding of ourselves?

Jon: "God often spoke through the dreams of both Old and New Testament figures. Daniel, for example, interpreted King Nebuchadnezzar's dreams as prophecy concerning future kingdoms (see Dan. 2, 4). Joseph, Jesus' adoptive father, was told by an angel in a dream to stay with Mary when he doubted her fidelity (see Mat. 1:18-25). While it is possible for God to use dreams to increase self-understanding, be cautioned: a dream may simply be the result of an active mind (see Eccl. 5:3)."

Anna: "The psychoanalytic interpretations of dreams can be fascinating when understanding the unconscious messages and signals of one's emotional processes. Dream symbolism and translation is complex, individualistic, and difficult to measure. At times, dreams can bring to light one's innermost passions, traumas, repressed feelings, and latent content, which can aid one in gaining a more comprehensive self-perspective. However, dreams are not the be-all of perception and should be interpreted therapeutically within the broader context of one's unique story, cognitive development, and personal exploration. Dreams are only a small facet in better understanding reality, and interpretation is not free from error. One's soul has been gifted the ability to dream, for release, enjoyment, and warning. God knows you better than anyone; his Word and Spirit should be the primary sources where one births self-conception and self-purpose."

Question Thirty-Nine
February 8th

Because of childhood abuse, most of our lives have been manipulated by faulty compasses. For us, even when we know that the correct direction to go is north, something inside takes us south. Is there a way that we can fix our broken, internal compasses?

Jon: "Jesus said that the Holy Spirit 'will convict the world concerning sin and righteousness and judgment' (John 16:8). We can therefore rely on the Spirit of God to be our compass through life. Moreover, the Lord has given us his divine Word with the Bible as a literary guide. We have his Spirit, we have his Word, and we have hope knowing he has promised everything (compasses included) will one day be made new, 'for these words are trustworthy and true' (Rev. 21:5)."

Anna: "After abuse, of any kind, one can be psychologically and emotionally confused. These offenses stir up mistrust in others, core beliefs of being worthless and damaged, trouble regulating one's emotions, and possible feelings of intolerance and chaos within one's relationships. This is not a healthy or fulfilling way to exist. An abused person cannot fix or heal this internal disorientation and pain alone. Every human being was created to be dependent upon God. When one has faith in Christ and the Holy Spirit is leading and directing one's life, then one's decisions, one's understanding of who one is and which direction one needs to go in profoundly and supernaturally deepen, yet become more clear."

Question Forty
February 9th

What is the proof that the Holy Spirit is inside of us?

Jon: "Speaking to the great multitude Jesus said, 'each tree is known by its own fruit' (Luke 6:44) and 'every healthy tree bears good fruit' (Mat. 7:17). Therefore, we know the Holy Spirit is inside of us when we bear the fruit of the Spirit: 'love, joy, peace, patience, kindness, goodness, faithfulness, gentleness, self-control' (Gal. 5:22-23). Ultimately, however, to confess, 'Jesus Christ has come in the flesh,' proves both that 'you know the Spirit of God' and are 'from God' (1 John 4:2)."

Anna: "When abused one has felt dead inside, lost, rejected, and hopelessly powerless. Living without faith is like searching for truth yet not believing it when found, pointless. The Holy Spirit transforms the believer from the inside out, through one's belief systems, thought processes, self-worth, identity, and passions. The eyes and hearts of those who follow Jesus are opened and they yield fruits that stand out from the characteristics of the world. For example, becoming more patient and disciplined will manifest within and exude from one's spirit, words, and behaviors. Proof is in one's testimony, proof is in one's internal and external transformation, and proof is in how God uses one's life to plant seeds of forgiveness, salvation, and love. Prove the Holy Spirit exists by encouraging others in Jesus' name and by living out God's will for one's life."

Question Forty-One
February 10th

If Jesus was without sin, how could he possibly understand what we're going through?

Jon: "Scripture says that Jesus was tempted in every way we are (Heb. 4:15). Notice it is not that Jesus was tempted with the same *things*, but in the same *way*. He faced the same moral dilemmas we face—anger, pride, theft—not in our modern context, but in his ancient context. Moreover, if Jesus had sinned as we do, salvation would be impossible. It is his sinlessness that becomes our sinlessness and allows our entrance into heaven. And Jesus understands sin better than we ever could. He alone bore the full penalty of the sins of the whole world."

Anna: "As free-willed beings personal pain causing disunity between one's innate purpose and self-concept is often created. Jesus was completely man while perfectly God. He walked the earth to seal dysfunction's fate and experience firsthand what those he died for encounter. He did not deserve what he endured, just like one's abusive childhood. He survived betrayal, as well as emotional, verbal, and physical abuse, and was despised by the very same people he became a man to save. Jesus lived a sinless life, yet he was tempted, mentally tried, and experienced intense emotional states. He withstood psychological and spiritual torment and was ruthlessly tortured. His life was profoundly affected by the behaviors of others, yet he persevered and carried the weight of the world on his shoulders when crucified for humankind's sins."

Question Forty-Two
February 11th

Trust does not come easily for us, because we were let down by the very people who were supposed to instill trust. How, then, can we trust that the Bible will not let us down?

Jon: "People are fallible and sometimes speak untruthfully or erroneously. God the Father is not human—rather, he is the most perfect being (see Ps. 18:30; Mat. 5:48). When he speaks, he 'never lies' (Ti. 1:2). If the Bible is 'breathed out by God' (2 Tim. 3:16), it is therefore truthful and will not lead into error. God's Word is our 'sword of the Spirit' (Eph. 6:17) and 'was written for our instruction, that… we might have hope' (Rom. 15:4)."

Anna: "Because people are imperfect, trusting others involves risk, high and low, depending upon one's belief systems and behavioral patterns in correlation to their mental and emotional state. Distrust can be a powerful indicator as to when to protect oneself and deter from negative situations. However, when suspicion causes improper inhibitions in one's thought processes, biased thinking, paranoia, fear, or a complete loss of faith in humanity may evolve. From a flawed, human perspective, being able to trust can be built, maintained, established, broken, and shattered. From the divine perspective, God secured his trustworthiness from the beginning through his prophetic Word. The Bible has not changed nor will it ever change, it has withstood time's test. God's truth, integrity, and love will never waver or fail."

Question Forty-Three
February 12th

What is a blessing?

Jon: "One is blessed when they receive favor from another. We usually think of blessings as from God, but we can bless others and others can bless us. We may even bless God (see Ps. 103:1-2). James 1:17 says, 'Every good gift and every perfect gift is from above, coming down from the Father of lights with whom there is no variation or shadow due to change.' We are exceedingly thankful as we consider every good thing—from all that is between the stars of the night sky and the dust of the field, to our salvation through Christ Jesus—a blessing from God."

Anna: "A blessing may have distinctive meanings, for different people, tied to different affiliations and outcomes. Gratitude and sound perspective are directly connected to one's belief system, attribution style, and mental health. Thankfulness blesses one's attitude, mood, and character, yet one's outlook and behaviors are not what predicts one's worthiness of grace or protection. Blessing others through caring actions, especially after surviving psychological, emotional, or physical traumas, releases oneself from enslavement through humility, selflessness, and love. Recognizing truth's blessing is a choice because one's decisions profoundly affect one's state of mind and emotions. One's blessings come from God. One must choose to appreciate, honor, and worship God for who he is and what he has done: giving one life, the gift of salvation, sanctification, and eternal glorification through Jesus Christ, one's greatest blessing."

Question Forty-Four
February 13th

Are adults who abuse children possessed by Satan?

Jon: "Satan is a created being—an angel who was cast out of heaven long ago (see Rev. 12:9). He, like all other created things, is finite in power and influence. It is therefore impossible for him to be in more than one place at one time. He cannot influence more than one person at any moment. Though it is possible for Satan to strongly influence a person (see Luke 13:16, 22:3, 31; Acts 5:3), it is more likely that abusers act voluntarily."

Anna: "Acting upon one's desires or being possessed by Satan or his demons are not one and the same. There are confused souls who serve Satan and choose to engage in satanic acts of worship, which may include sexual deviances, torture, and human sacrifice. Adults who abuse children choose to behave immorally and what they do, even though it may be of demonic influence, is not Satan acting himself. Those who abuse have malignant forces to conquer and frequently have a tragic history of abuse themselves. Most often, those who desecrate have serious psychological, emotional, and spiritual issues, yet are not necessarily under demonic possession. Satan is an expert of deception, and when one follows him, is into the occult, or has conjured spirits to possess one's body, immoral anarchy is profoundly compelled. God does not tempt. Therefore, any enticement is of one's human nature or succumbing to temptations of external or spiritual influence."

Question Forty-Five
February 14th

If Satan is only able to be in one location at a time, does he have an army of demons that he sends out to negatively influence others?

Jon: "Not only does Scripture affirm the existence of Satan, but also of dark rulers, authorities, powers, and forces of evil in the world (see Eph. 6:12). Even Jesus had multiple encounters with demons (see Mat. 12:22; Mark 9:25; Luke 8:27, 13:11). While we are not immune to these forces, we must remember that if we have the Spirit of God within us through faith in Christ, we need not fear them, 'for he who is in you is greater than he who is in the world' (1 John 4:4)."

Anna: "Satan is often underestimated and not taken seriously as seen by the way most people operate within his secular guise. He is to blame for the fallen world, for abuse, yet one must choose their side. Satan is not omniscient or omnipresent and he has already lost because Jesus died on the cross and rose again, which conquered evil. Satan knows this and desires to take anyone he can down with him. He has been disgraced and has a legion of fallen angels, demons, who submit to his authority in this universal war against God and his creation. Yes, demons are vengefully sent out to torture human souls and weaken righteousness in the world. However, do not succumb to lies. Satan is not greater than God. God triumphantly prevails."

Question Forty-Six
February 15th

Can we express and heal from our angst by dancing, by moving and amplifying our bodies?

Jon: "Genesis shows us that God created humankind to fill, rule over, work in, and care for the earth. We were not made to be sedentary creatures, but creatures who actively pursue their purpose. Too much inactivity then places us outside of God's will, and therefore into sin, which will ultimately produce negative effects in our lives. Our body is no exception to this principle. Being active in our body in a way that is honoring God not only expresses our fundamental purpose as human beings, but it may also keep us from or even lift us out of a negative state of being."

Anna: "Having the freedom and ability to express oneself is a privilege. One's body is beautifully designed, a vessel that can do incredible things, which adds value and meaning to one's life. A healthy body is an extension of self-esteem, self-worth, and one's earthly and divine purpose. When one takes care of oneself, this correlates with self-respect, honor, wisdom, and an appreciation for the body one has been given. Anxiety, stress, sadness, and shame can be minimized, explored, and coped with by dancing and openly expressing oneself. When one is uninhibited to be vulnerable and authentic, fear subsides and confidence wins. God desires for one to worship him and feel safe enough to righteously release one's emotions and gratitude in mind, body, and spirit."

Question Forty-Seven
February 16th

Many of us are perfectionists: people who set their personal standards so high that they are constantly striving for bigger and better. This sort of persistence only causes stress and misery. And the irony is—nothing is ever good enough. Thus, it feels as though it's not so good to be a perfectionist. Is it not so beneficial?

Jon: "Jesus says in Matthew 5:48 that: 'You therefore must be perfect, as your heavenly Father is perfect.' This is not in relation to any worldly aspirations, however. In fact, he is instructing his followers to do the opposite. The world says to love one's neighbor and hate one's enemy. To Jesus, being perfect means loving one's enemy and praying for one's persecutors. Perfection then is not striving after personal standards but striving after God's standards. There is no better way for a person to live life than in sincere imitation of God."

Anna: "Aiming high, self-belief, pushes one to excel, which at times is necessary to exceed one's internal restrictions. However, when one's thoughts lead to the dismissal of what is natural and then is equated to unworthiness, this becomes a faultfinding approach for a self-demeaning and self-disproving model. When perfectionism leads to dehumanizing one's existence just like the abuse did, one's perspective has been bound by dysfunction's deceptive grip. Human beings are flawed yet created by an exquisite God, to be made righteous through Jesus, and to display his magnificent glory through one's relatable story."

Question Forty-Eight
February 17th

Scores of us parent ourselves just as our parents parented us. For example, if we were beaten, yelled at, abandoned, then that is how we treat ourselves. We are cruel to our inner kids. How can we stop being abusive to ourselves?

Jon: "Scripture responds: 'Do you not know that you are God's temple and that God's Spirit dwells in you? If anyone destroys God's temple, God will destroy him. For God's temple is holy, and you are that temple' (1 Cor. 3:16-17). God takes very seriously any cruelty we endure—including self-inflicted cruelty. In the times we feel we deserve abuse, we can remember that the God of the universe has chosen to make us the dwelling place of his Holy Spirit."

Anna: "For survivors of trauma, the dilemma of accepting responsibility versus deflecting blame can be a painful and confusing process. Abusers tend to hone the projection and delivery of shame and excessive guilt onto others. Self-accusation, unworthiness, demoralization, and self-harm can blossom from this disorganized attachment to one's abuser. This convoluted relational dynamic causes deception, emotional chaos, and psychological cruelty within a person. In attempts to stop this abusive internalization, one needs to acknowledge, process, and release responsibility for their abuser's spiritual state, emotional issues, and immoral behaviors. God Almighty forgives graciously, so why does one have such trouble forgiving oneself? Learning to love oneself through truth's eyes and the heartfelt Spirit of God is what will minimize self-abuse and personal disfavor."

Question Forty-Nine
February 18th

As children, when some of us expressed our true selves to our parents and/or caregivers, we were beaten. This caused us to hide our authenticity. As adults now, how can we finally let our guards down and show others who we really are?

Jon: "Scripture uses the metaphor of a body to depict the total collective of Christians (1 Cor. 12:12-31). In a body, each part fulfills a different function. If even one part is not fulfilling its function, the body cannot work at its full potential. Likewise, if one believer is not fulfilling his or her function, the church body cannot work at its full potential. When you let your guard down and share with others your unique gifts, the church functions properly and thrives."

Anna: "With time, the hope is that one will learn to shed the weight of negative experiences. With encouraging realizations and a faithful outlook, one's intended self will blossom. When one feels accepted and secure, one starts to feel it, believe it, and be it. Genuine healing does not occur without emotional validation and one's eternal comprehension. After abuse, one is psychologically, emotionally, and relationally stifled. Who the abused have become, on some levels, are not the people they were created to be on other levels. Yet, one can use their childhood heartache to mold and propel one into one's future. When the authenticity of one's divine identity has been laid, God's will beautifully transpires from deep within one's soul."

Question Fifty
February 19th

A lot of us feel bad about ourselves. Can you convince us that we are deserving of good?

Jon: "The last six of the Ten Commandments forbid evil actions and thoughts between people. Scripture not only prohibits evil, it instructs us to go further. For example, Jesus said the second-greatest commandment is to 'love your neighbor as yourself' (Mat. 22:39). God's Word commands that others bring you not evil, but goodness and love, because you are deserving of goodness and love. If your faith is in Christ, then you are guaranteed an eternity with the greatest good: God."

Anna: "Negative thoughts and emotions expose one's belief systems and affect the way one perceives the world and how one behaves. Having the support and encouragement of others is important to help shape and build self-esteem yet believing that oneself is worthy and lovable is a personal decision. Oftentimes, having the feeling or experience of being deserving of 'something' is directly correlated with how one has been treated by others, especially as a child. When abusive conduct is how one bases the measurement and extent of their value, the perceived odds have been stacked against them. God valued humankind so much that he sent his Son to die on a cross to cover humanity's sins. The Creator of the Universe made it blatantly clear that through Jesus Christ, one is sacrificially loved and deserving of what is exceptionally good."

Question Fifty-One
February 20th

Some of us hate our perpetrators so much; we want to see them suffer as much as we did. What do we do with this kind of red-hot hatred?

Jon: "Our hatred of evil demonstrates that we have been made in the likeness of God, for God 'hates the wicked' (Ps. 11:5). Just as God's hatred of evil never becomes sin, neither should ours. If it does, we have not only allowed ourselves to sin against God, but we have allowed our offenders to cause more destruction in our lives. Lay down sin-causing hatred, 'since indeed God considers it just to repay with affliction those who afflict you' (2 Thes. 1:6). We don't have to repay because God will."

Anna: "Hatred is an indicator of severe disgust and one's malice toward demeaning experiences. Abuse is attached to such deep painful emotions and personal suffering that one's frustration often cannot be explained. Contempt not only expresses the un-settling feelings one holds within, it can erode one's sense of compassion and empathy. Hatred for the evil acts of abuse coincides with justice, but when one's revulsion for the abuse turns toward the abuser and his or her soul, mercy and forgiveness have vanished. Time can heal but not faithfully when apart from God's Spirit and power. Pray and ask God to continue to transform one's heart and mind, so his love, forgiveness, and grace will subdue, minimize, and extinguish one's deep hatred toward others that lies within."

Question Fifty-Two
February 21st

Is there a positive way to express hatred?

Jon: "The word *hate* is used nowhere in the Bible more frequently than in Psalms. The psalmist, often vexed by hate, would pray: 'Out of my distress I called on the LORD; the LORD answered me and set me free' (Ps. 118:5). When we express our hatred honestly to God, we are set free from offending others and set free from bottling up our feelings. Genuinely pray *for* the object of your hate, and be set free of that hate entirely."

Anna: "When anger is not addressed, it can elude and sabotage one's rational, reasoning, and conflict resolution problem-solving skills. When rage is suppressed, it can be projected, like a volcano, in the most destructive ways. Constructive expressions of what have been deemed as negative emotions when they are not are necessary for mental, emotional, and relational balance. Hatred can reside deep within a person and, when expressed healthily, can help one grieve. This process enables emotional release and validation. For personal stability, recognize and identify one's anger at its root, express it through verbal, emotional, and creative outlets, safely and constructively. When one's intent is to feel and forgive, confessing one's uncomfortable emotions and severe dislike to God and counselor will help one heal from one's intense pain and move forward."

Question Fifty-Three
February 22nd

Love. For those of us who were emotionally, physically, and/or sexually abused by the very people who were supposed to protect us, there is no such thing. Do you disagree? Convince us, then, that love does exist.

Jon: "Scripture characterizes love as patient, kind, not envious, not boastful, not arrogant, not rude, not insisting, not irritable, not resentful, not joyful at wrongdoing, joyful over truth, forbearing, trusting, hopeful, and enduring (see 1 Cor. 13:4-9). If you have seen, given, or received any of these qualities, then you have witnessed the existence of biblical love. Moreover, Colossians 1:17 says, '… in him [Christ] all things hold together.' Your continuing existence—every breath and heartbeat—is constant proof that God's love for you exists."

Anna: "Love exists, yet from one's human heart, it develops impurely. Human love and God's love can be compared but are worlds apart coexisting through truth and faith. Love prevails regardless if one chooses to abuse it and disregards its divine message and purpose. Biblical love differs from secular love, as one has experienced through abuse. Think about your deep-seated needs and desires. Most desire to be accepted and valued for who they innately are, which is love. Genuine selflessness and concern for others promotes a healthy, secure attachment, and nurtures loving relationships. God created and manifests love therefore he loves excellently. The most whole and fulfilling love one can ever receive or experience is from him."

Question Fifty-Four
February 23rd

What is a positive expression of self-love?

Jon: "A positive expression of self-love is one that does not bring glory to the self, but brings glory to God. We must be careful not to merely seek the gratification of the flesh. 'For,' Scripture says, 'if you live according to the flesh you will die' (Rom. 8:13). The greatest positive expression of self-love is to place oneself in the correct relationship with God. Living according to God's direction gives us the freedom to act in favor of oneself without acting selfishly."

Anna: "To humbly love oneself through truth is the goal, and is fundamental for psychological, emotional, and spiritual survival. False humility or seeking the approval of others can dilute love's intention and purpose. Love can mean many things depending upon the perspective, beliefs, and values one holds. Positive expressions of self-love are self-acceptance through healthy thoughts and behaviors, which promote a positive well-being. Being self-assertive, believing in one's gifts and talents, and acting upon one's worth, is self-adoration. A consistent, grounded, realistic self-evaluation with the intent to be Christ-like and accountable for one's priorities and decisions is self-love in motion. Upholding one's faith, acting upon self-care, valuing one's mind, body, and spirit is embodying love for oneself. Loving others through self as God loves, despite one's flaws and weaknesses, is love truly understood."

Question Fifty-Five
February 24th

Some of us would rather please other people than please ourselves. It is as if we desire to continue to abuse ourselves, as our parents did before us. (Comforting ourselves feels odd.) How do we begin to love ourselves first?

Jon: "Reflecting on his future death, Jesus affirmed, 'Greater love has no one than this, that someone lay down his life for his friends' (John 15:13). It is Christ-like to give oneself for others as long as it does not result in sin. The only reason we love is because God 'first loved us' (1 John 4:19). Since he is morally perfect (Ps. 92:15), everything God does is right. If God loves us, then it is right for us to love ourselves."

Anna: "The desire to be liked, appreciated, needed, and valued is deep within the heart of those who have been abused. It is as if the 'people pleasers' behave toward others how they desire to be treated: with effort, acceptance, and sacrifice. When one's motive to help is validation, and one's self-worth and happiness is dependent upon uncontrollable factors, this may end poorly because others can be unappreciative, unreliable, and misguided. Self-love is nurtured by truly grasping the importance of one's existence and purpose. Bestowing consistent love upon oneself will undoubtedly transform one's attitude and behaviors. Genuine self-love is believing why Jesus sacrificed himself for humankind: one is chosen, blessed, and undeniably loved and worth dying for."

Question Fifty-Six
February 25th

A lot of us think about everything except what we are doing in the present moment. How can we teach ourselves to remain in the present?

Jon: "Remaining in the present is a natural product of inner peace. God's Word advises we train our minds to contemplate, moment by moment, what is true, honorable, just, pure, lovely, commendable, excellent, and worthy of praise (Phil. 4:8). If you make a practice of setting your mind on these things, 'the God of peace will be with you' (Phil. 4:9). We can rejoice and be glad in the present by remembering, 'This is the day that the LORD has made' (Ps. 118:24)."

Anna: "Mindfully grounding oneself within one's present moments, an authentic awareness, and taking the time to enjoy life and its beauty are vital for one's emotional stability and mental health. Anxiety in correlation with the past only muddles the present and instills fear and doubt when thinking about or preparing for the future. Valuing the moment can go against what one was taught, pushed into, or was modeled within their family system and environment. When one comes from an anxious or fear-based family structure, one's current circumstances and present state can feel highly uncomfortable and unsafe. By appreciating and focusing on the gift of life, one can be taught to remain present and thankful. When one knows who they are and their purpose, daily tasks become more meaningful and one's mission can be established with every step."

Question Fifty-Seven
February 26th

Many of us understand insanity to mean: "The definition of insanity is doing the same thing over and over and expecting different results." An example of this is to continue to expect empathy from someone we clearly know does not possess the capacity to express compassion. How can we stop seeking that which is surely unavailable to us?

Jon: "God's Word casts pursuing that which we know will produce harmful results in an unpleasant light: 'Like a dog that returns to his vomit, is a fool who repeats his folly' (Pro. 26:11). However, it is not that we should stop seeking entirely. Rather, Christ encourages us to reevaluate the primary focus of our seeking when he said, 'seek first the kingdom of God and his righteousness' (Mat. 6:33). For God is both infinitely available and worth our infinite seeking."

Anna: "People are fundamentally similar, yet often relate so differently. When one's personality is understood, one's natural characteristics deciphered, unique perceptions of how one will self-express will arise and settle. It is worthwhile and adaptive to deduce what people truly want. To pursue something from someone that they are incapable of giving can be hurtful, exhausting, and detrimental to one's psyche, emotions, and self-esteem. When one chases others to meet their unmet desires, one will never truly be satisfied. God genuinely fulfills one's needs, yet when one is given opportunity to be loved from another in this life, it is a beautiful God-given gift."

Question Fifty-Eight
February 27th

A lot of survivors of childhood abuse have a propensity to make assumptions; to draw conclusions without proof. For example, perhaps someone forgot to pick us up from work. Instead of calling the person in question, we tell ourselves that this person doesn't like us and thus didn't pick us up. We absolutely believe this to be true. We find a way to work and learn that the person was in the hospital. How can we stop this cycle of falsehood?

Jon: "The psalmist experienced a similar cycle. He humbled himself before God, saying, 'Deliver me, O LORD, from lying lips, from a deceitful tongue' (Ps. 120:2). Genuine confession and repentance unto God are the first steps toward breaking the cycle of falsehood—daily asking for deliverance and strength from his Spirit. Every urge of distress we feel is a signal to pray for deliverance. How glorious that from our deceitfulness and distress, the Lord brings us into closer communication and into a closer relationship with him."

Anna: "Any cycle of misconception festers within a person's mind and spirit. Assuming the worst when internalizing another's actions comes from feelings of inadequacy, unworthiness, and fearing rejection or abandonment. Low self-esteem often presumes that miscommunications have negative connotations. To lessen this fallible process, minimize speculations and emotional reactivity and attempt to not evoke the issues created within one's thought processes, which could self-fulfill one's sabotage. Surrender the madness, and allow God to transform one's beliefs through his Word and Spirit."

Question Fifty-Nine
February 28th

Does the Bible say anything about expressing emotions as opposed to knowledge?

Jon: "We want to have such control that we can freely express knowledge *and* emotion without hurting others or ourselves. But our tongues are troublesome. Scripture describes the tongue as a fire, a world of unrighteousness, a restless evil, and full of deadly poison (see Jas. 3:5-8). Without God's assistance, 'no human being can tame the tongue' (Jas. 3:8). To avoid the many cataclysms caused by the tongue, we must strive to consider whether our words are honoring God before we speak."

Anna: "The well intentioned soul is still imperfect and acting strictly upon emotion can be foolish, misleading, and established upon faulty premises. Emotions can be astute and affect the way one rationalizes and behaves. Emotions, like one's mind and body, are greatly influenced by humankind's fall into sin. Therefore, they can be polluted by one's sinful nature, experiences, passions, and desires. However, emotions do have the ability to gauge what is real and what is not. Please remember, chaotic emotions are of this world, and not of what is pure and righteous. God's knowledge surpasses human emotion, but just as knowledge can be misleading when it is grounded in secularism, emotions are powerful and meaningful when brought on by God's Word, his truth's convictions, and his mighty Spirit."

Question Sixty
March 1st

A lot of us make our lives more difficult than they need to be. For example, life would be simpler if we could just ask others for help. Thoughts?

Jon: "Scripture does not deny that life is often difficult. Jesus said, 'Come to me, all who labor and are heavy laden, and I will give you rest' (Mat. 11:28). Because Jesus is God, he is omnipresent, or present everywhere at every time. Because Jesus is everywhere at every time, we may come to him wherever and whenever we need help. In Christ, then, we have someone who affirms our struggles, who is eternally available, and who has the desire and infinite power to assist us in our time of need. How simple it is that this is attainable at the turning of one's heart to God in prayer."

Anna: "Humanity is made up of billions of souls, so to continually hurt and struggle in solitary is downright detrimental and heartrending. Accepting and experiencing support from others when distressed and in need not only encourages unification but also enables genuine connection and substantiates one's significance. However, potential problems arise when asking for help drags along expectations that bring disappointments. Usually, fearing mistrust due to past abuse hinders one from living out one's true desires within relationships. Seeking counsel and engaging in communion is biblical. One was not created to always be alone; one was created to humbly and wholeheartedly depend upon God while in authentic fellowship with Christ's followers."

Question Sixty-One
March 2nd

What is wisdom?

Jon: "Job 12:12 says, 'Wisdom is with the aged, and understanding in length of days.' If knowledge is acquired information, wisdom is the proper utilization of knowledge. Knowledge can be gained in an instant. Wisdom can take a lifetime to gain. In other words, the wise don't simply possess knowledge. They know when and when not to use it. Oftentimes, therefore, wisdom will be heard loudest not in the words spoken, but in the words left unspoken. The skilled musician does not play all her notes at once. She knows the importance of the space between them. In the same way, the wise know the importance of the space between their words."

Anna: "Insight complemented by a patient, mature, and informed disposition shows wisdom. When one has discretion and intentionally deciphers when to act or not, a wise perspective is revealed. Upholding personal and spiritual boundaries, flexibility in love while not wavering upon truth or following the world's ways for fleeting gain is wise. Refrain when tempted to retaliate and appease one's childhood traumas, because wisdom is having self-control at one's most crucial hour. Learning from one's mistakes while nurturing one's core beliefs rooted in love is astute, yet not long lasting when relying solely upon one's strength. Wisdom recognizes concealed truths, heeds instruction, walks the honorable path, and righteously leads. All wisdom, pure and true, comes from God, the Creator of the Universe, whose ways are brilliant."

Question Sixty-Two
March 3rd

Some of us have heard that listening to the sound of running water can aid in quieting the mind. Is this true?

Jon: "The Bible recommends obtaining a quiet mind. Doing so will yield many positive influences. For example, Proverbs 14:30 says that tranquility of mind 'gives life to the flesh.' While there is much value in contemplating God's creation, could there be anything more effective at quieting the mind than running water? Psalm 93:4 says, 'Mightier than the thunders of many waters, mightier than the waves of the sea, the LORD on high is mighty!' There can be no better remedy in calming the mind than setting it upon the One who created the seas and calms them by his Word."

Anna: "The natural sound of water, whether it be a breathtaking waterfall or the majestic ocean's activity, can undoubtedly soothe one's abused soul. When senses are fostered by the rhythm of the waves, relaxation occurs due to the slowing of one's energy and thought patterns. Water stills the mind through allowing one to simply be, relax, and narrow in on that specific frequency to soothe one's cells, worries, and distractions. This meditative process can alleviate anxiety's stress, one's bodily tension, and one's racing thoughts while calmly rejuvenating one mentally, physically, and spiritually. God created water sources for humankind's needs, pleasure, leisure, and purification, so allow oneself to reap all its benefits while one's presence and mind quietly reap from God's wonderful creation and plan."

Question Sixty-Three
March 4th

How can we show more empathy toward others?

Jon: "Empathy begins with understanding that every person is of great worth. This worth comes from being created in the image of God, who is of infinite worth. Understanding that people are of such value motivates us to empathize with those who are in need of emotional personal interaction. Scripture says the next step is to 'Rejoice with those who rejoice, weep with those who weep' (Rom. 12:15). Sometimes emotions are too heavy to be carried alone. We can lift some of that weight for another if we simply share in their emotional state alongside them."

Anna: "Expressing empathy transpires from experiencing and understanding one's human condition and worldly struggles. The ability to identify with why others are the way that they are, and why they do what they do so one can truly have an emotional connection is empathy. Simply thinking of others' needs and meeting them enables empathic intentions to unfold in such beautiful ways. Empathy's ability should be valued and respected, because every soul needs love, compassion, and selfless acceptance. Naturally being empathetic is a God-given gift that truly blossoms through one's relationship with Christ, and the power of the Holy Spirit. When one desires to show more empathy, one must have a genuine concern for what others are going through while selflessly listening and validating their experiences. Ask God in Jesus' name to open one's heart and mind to others' needs and pain."

Question Sixty-Four
March 5th

What is a soothing definition of grace?

Jon: "Grace is freely receiving something good unconditionally and undeservedly. Grace is a gift. Being perfect and holy, God owes us nothing. Yet he gives us eternal life by grace through faith in Christ (see Eph. 2:8). Being finite and sinful, we owe God everything. Having no means with which to pay God the price for our sins, he became the means himself by offering himself as a sacrifice in our stead. God needed nothing, yet he created the world, humanity, and humanity's way unto salvation."

Anna: "Grace is unearned and it has been perfectly destined from the beginning of time. Selfless rewards or bestowing mercy upon another can be one of the most powerful gifts in building rapport, displaying love, and affecting one's life. Grace not only has the potential to heal a relationship and completely redeem a situation, but to profoundly influence one's state of mind, demeanor, and behaviors. Grace is powerful and pivotal for humankind's purpose. Without God's grace, humankind would be hopeless and unfulfilled in this life and the next. Grace is a divine blessing and it establishes one's future through faith in Jesus. Grace soothes one's psyche, emotions, and spirit because of its very nature and mission: to lead the believer into eternal glory through love's forgiveness, salvation, and redemption."

Question Sixty-Five
March 6th

A lot of us spent our lives trying to earn the love of our victimizers, treating these abusive monsters as if they were loving gods. We ignored the one true God. Will God punish us for not having put him first?

Jon: "In the first commandment God states that we are to have no other gods beside him (see Ex. 20:3). The second commandment states that we are not to idolize any created thing (see Ex. 20:4-6). To break these commandments is sin. Since God is perfectly just, the consequence of sin is punishment and ultimately death (see Rom. 2:5-6, 6:23). However, God has made it so that these consequences do not apply to those who believe in Jesus Christ (see Rom. 8:1)."

Anna: "The difference between humankind and God is that God loves justly and always will, because he cannot waver. His love is not earned, and that will never change. Human beings are flawed, can be self-serving, self-righteous, often have the audacity to make others prove their worth, and thrive on conditional love. A full awareness of God holds one to a standard of accountability, and innocence, naiveté, and ignorance are often redeemed. Blindness and confusion in suffering differs from blatant defiance or the conscious rejection of righteousness. There are consequences in life yet God, who sees all, has the ultimate authority over one's life. He is a merciful God and will take all things into consideration when judging his creation."

Question Sixty-Six
March 7th

Childhood abuse is so rampant throughout the world. Why doesn't the Bible speak more against it?

Jon: "Morality doesn't come from the self. If it did, anyone could create their own morality. For example, the child abuser could create for himself or herself the morality that child abuse is right. But child abuse is wrong regardless of anyone's opinion. So morality doesn't come from the self, but from an outside source: God. For God alone is perfectly holy and righteous as well as able to uphold moral reality. He is the standard of what is right and what is wrong. And if the Bible alone is God's Word, then the Bible is the loudest voice in the world speaking against moral evils such as child abuse."

Anna: "Child abuse is a heartbreaking epidemic and cultural failure. Sexual, physical, and psychological deviances are disgraceful due to the evil repercussions had on one's identity, soul, and spirit. In relational systems, the family unit is complexly connected to one another and within these dynamics; each individual affects the whole. Within theological principles, this is paralleled with how the church body affects one another. A biblical standard is set on how believers should behave toward believers, non-believers, and children, behaviorally, relationally, and spiritually. The wording 'child abuse' is not mentioned verbatim but is undoubtedly unacceptable by God. The disapproval of anyone being abused is overtly implied, commanded and written about within God's Word, and shown through Scripture's teachings."

Question Sixty-Seven
March 8th

Some of us literally hold our breath, not realizing that we are suppressing our very life force. Can you offer us a way to remind ourselves to breathe?

Jon: "Scripture says it is God 'who created the heavens and stretched them out, who spread out the earth and what comes from it, who gives breath to the people on it, and spirit to those who walk in it' (Isa. 42:5). Breathing is automatic. Our body will continue to breathe whether we are conscious of it or not. If only it were the case that we just as regularly considered who gives us that breath. We can take advantage of those times we catch ourselves breathing and remember that our breath is a gift. It is not us who holds our breath, but God."

Anna: "To breathe, to be amidst the atmosphere, can truly be breathtaking. When one's oxygen has stopped reaching one's lungs, asphyxiation will cause one to gasp and will literally suppress one's very life force. To thrive and not just exist or merely breathe, is psychologically, emotionally, and spiritually freeing. To be present and appreciative takes awareness and action. Grounding one's beliefs and thoughts anchors one's soul to one's present state and one's ultimate purpose. Focused breathing aids one's ability for self-control, mind and body, and as circulation increases, one's physical being is revitalized. God created the air and wind for life. Inhale, exhale, and take it all in one breath at a time because you are loved."

Question Sixty-Eight
March 9th

For many of us growing up, we had to take on many adult responsibilities such as raising our younger siblings, protecting our siblings (the best we knew how) from violence, and laboring when we should have been playing. As a result, we became adults who feel as though we have to be liable for far too much. That said, what are our responsibilities in this life?

Jon: "An expert in Old Testament law once asked Jesus, 'Teacher, which is the great commandment in the Law?' (Mat. 22:36). He responded, 'You shall love the Lord your God with all your heart and with all your soul and with all your mind.' This is the greatest and first commandment. And a second is like it: 'You shall love your neighbor as yourself.' On these two commandments depend all the Law and the Prophets' (Mat. 22:37-40). All our responsibilities stem from loving God and our neighbor."

Anna: "An abusive system's rules and roles sets tremendous weights upon those within the dysfunction. Deciphering between what is an appropriate or even reasonable interaction can be challenging due to the disorganized and disrupted attachment styles formed. Feelings of inadequacy, confusion, frustration, and resentment build due to a projected and perceived inability to reach unrealistic standards and pressures. From a developmental perspective, once one is consciously aware and has the ability for autonomy, one's obligations increase. Yet, without God and his Holy Spirit, one will not adequately meet their true and divine responsibilities in this life."

Question Sixty-Nine
March 10th

Can anything compensate for never hearing our offenders say, "I'm sorry"?

Jon: "It is possible that our offenders will never take responsibility for their actions. It is possible that for our entire lives we will never hear the words, 'I'm sorry.' We will not, however, allow our offenders to still so negatively influence our lives. Instead, when we feel the need for an apology, we can replace it with feeling thankful for all we have been forgiven by God. We can use it as a cue for confession and say, 'I'm sorry' to God, knowing that 'he is faithful and just to forgive us our sins and to cleanse us from all unrighteousness' (1 John 1:9)."

Anna: "Realization and confirmation is important within one's grieving and healing process. Whether one receives an apology or not from their offender, family member, or witness, acknowledging and processing the invalidation is a pivotal juncture in the development of one's personal progression and spiritual conversion. What can compensate for not receiving acknowledgement or closure from others? God's grace, compassion, favor, wisdom, and his healing powers truly can. God's might and Word restores, forgives, and speaks truth into the hearts of humankind and penetrates the believer's soul. The Holy Spirit is one's supernatural comforter and God's love when sought, will deeply compensate for the unmet needs and suffering one endured."

Question Seventy
March 11th

There is an old cliché that states, "Sometimes we hurt the ones we love," the ones most precious to us. As human beings, we realize that it is an impossibility never to get mad at those closest to us. That said, many of us wish to make amends to our loved ones, who we have hurt with our unkind words and/or bodily injury to them. Can the Lord offer us some helpful actions that we can take toward them?

Jon: "First, we acknowledge and take responsibility of our sin before ourselves and before God. There must be genuine repentance: a sincere desire to change. The next step is to candidly admit fault and humbly ask for forgiveness. Scripture puts it this way: 'confess your sins to one another and pray for one another, that you may be healed. The prayer of a righteous person has great power as it is working' (Jas. 5:16). Don't underestimate the power of prayer in seeking reconciliation."

Anna: "When a relationship is ruptured, to repair it is truly a liberating notion. Humility, honesty, and sincerity play integral roles in mending communication. Within behavior, motives and emotion truly set the tone. Both parties must desire reconciliation to strengthen restoration and even with the best intentions, one must prepare to handle another's truth. Have faith through prayer and your dedication to God's will. Ask God to perform a miracle within their soul, and to show them the truth of your heart and how deeply they are loved."

Question Seventy-One
March 12th

What is mercy?

Jon: "Mercy is not receiving a deserved punishment. For example, the defendant who is convicted of a crime but is given a lighter sentence than he or she deserves has received mercy. Or, the debtor whose debtee cancels the debt owed has received mercy. God most greatly expresses mercy toward us in that while our sin places us in condemnation before him, he removes that condemnation immediately upon our faith in Jesus Christ. If God is great in his mercies toward us, great should be our mercies toward others (see Mat 5:7)."

Anna: "To show one mercy, to be legitimately compassionate toward another, can be demonstrating clemency at a life-changing crossroad. Mercy is unique because it does not usually just happen naturally. To be gracious toward another when they certainly do not deserve it, shines a light upon the wisdom and foresight one has in regards to human purpose, connection, and love. Mercy reaches out and diminishes powerful emotions and belief systems that breed disdain, shame, guilt, indignity, and unworthiness. This can happen within the psychological and emotional framework of the wrongdoer and forgiver alike. If one were justly punished for their behaviors, Jesus would not have died on the cross to cover humankind's sins. God's grace is life giving, and represents the theme for humankind's biography and unfolding future. His mercy is abundant and selflessly anew."

Question Seventy-Two
March 13th

Because of our childhood neglect—limited food, shelter, and medical care—many of us are prone to depression. How can we turn this sadness into happiness?

Jon: "Scripture says, '… rejoice insofar as you share Christ's sufferings, that you may also rejoice and be glad when his glory is revealed' (1 Pet. 4:13). Jesus was born into and lived in poverty, was forsaken by his friends and family, brutally tortured, and murdered. His sorrows and sufferings are glorious, however, in that they atone for the punishment we deserve for our sins. If, as 1 Peter 4:12 affirms, when we sorrow and suffer we share in Christ's sorrow and suffering, then sharing in Christ's sorrow and suffering means sharing in his glory. If we share in God's glory, we have great cause to rejoice and be glad."

Anna: "Self-despondency creates a woeful mind, a profound sadness, and a lack of hope in one's purpose. When one has been neglected, it is common to introject this minimization of one's existence by devaluing one's soul and significance. In order to turn things around, validate your pain in correlation to past and current experiences, believe in yourself, and take action toward your hopes and your future. To consistently be sad is an excruciating reality and causes intense desperation within the mind and heart of the sufferer. Ask God in faith to break one's spiritual bondage because he removes the darkness and cures the afflicted by his grace, power, and love."

Question Seventy-Three
March 14th

How do we turn the shame we feel about ourselves, damaged and opposed, into pride, blessed and chosen?

Jon: "Scripture says that we are blessed by God, 'even as he chose us in him before the foundation of the world, that we should be holy and blameless before him' (Eph. 1:4). This means that those faithful in Jesus Christ have been set apart by God since before the universe came into existence. For almost fourteen billion years, then, God has been waiting to bring you into existence on earth for a purpose that no one else but you can carry out. Your next action, therefore, is the culmination of a God-made fourteen-billion-year-old plan."

Anna: "Shame is a lie. To turn this deception into a catalyst for change, one must genuinely believe that they are worthy despite the past. A self-acceptance of one's abusive upbringing shows honesty, humility, and growth. The ability to separate one's immoral experiences from their chosen mission takes absolute truth and wisdom. The world's truth differs from divine perspective. The world succeeds on an individualistic, independent notion that one exists to live, thrive, and die in one's own strength. Spiritual truth embodies one being dependent upon and forgiven by God's grace that one has been chosen for a purpose greater than oneself. One needs the Holy Spirit to truly understand this heavenly gift: One is blameless, forgiven, and undoubtedly blessed through one's belief in Jesus Christ."

Question Seventy-Four
March 15th

What is dignity?

Jon: "God is innately worthy of infinite honor and respect. He has infinite dignity. Made in his image, human beings inherit a finite portion of God's infinite dignity. Human beings are therefore worthy of honor and respect. We have dignity. Galatians 3:28 says, 'There is neither Jew nor Greek, there is neither slave nor free, there is no male and female, for you are all one in Christ Jesus.' There are no ranks among humanity. There is no better or worse. All are of equal value. All are of equal dignity. We are brothers and sisters. We are all sons and daughters of God."

Anna: "When respect and esteem are the core principles behind human interaction, trust and connection have the ability to thrive. The abused heart understands admiration's longing, yet one's past encounters may abolish this reality through one's traumatic experiences. When one is treated with indecency, prejudice, unworthiness, or brutality it tampers with one's intrinsic value and sense of security. Abusive behavior, of any kind, is dishonorable and the deteriorating effects it has on its entangled souls are truly heartbreaking. When an individual believes that they have the authority to deem another as unimportant, they not only need a reality check, but a truth-immersed heart-examination. Encountering honorable treatment can influence one's self-perspective, self-confidence, and motivation. Every being was created by God from his infinite love to be reestablished by one's faith in Jesus, humankind's savior, who through love dignified humanity."

Question Seventy-Five
March 16th

Does the Lord hold us accountable for the condition of our subconscious minds?

Jon: "Scripture affirms the 'natural limitations' of humanity (Rom. 6:19). We are limited in our ability to control our subconscious. Since God is just (see Isa. 30:18), he does not hold us accountable for the limited control we have over our subconscious. He does not forsake us here: '… the peace of God, which surpasses all understanding, will guard your hearts and your minds in Christ Jesus' (Phil. 4:7)."

Anna: "Accountability coincides with knowledge, understanding, wisdom, and the realization of one's motives behind one's thoughts, words, and behaviors. How can one be legitimately held accountable, eternally speaking, for what one is not aware of intellectually, experientially, spiritually, or even subconsciously? Even more so, if common decency or dignity for oneself and others were not valued, established or modeled by a primary caregiver, how can one be measured and judged the same as another where that standard was set, met, or rejected? In the end, it simply would not be just to do so. When abused, naturally one's subconscious and spirit have been affected. The Lord will hold each person accountable for what one knows, confesses, comprehends, was taught, and what one consciously and intrinsically is aware of to be righteous and true. Surrender to God's will, study his Word, and ask him to reveal and heal what lies deep within you."

Question Seventy-Six
March 17th

By what means can we turn our disrespect for our offenders into prudence?

Jon: "Proverbs, the book of wisdom, says, 'The prudent sees danger and hides himself, but the simple go on and suffer for it' (Pro. 27:12). Here is an example of a positive lesson one may learn from a dominantly negative situation. Solomon intimates that past offenses give us the wisdom to avoid similar future ones. He makes his point stronger by rebuking those who do not heed his advice. With Solomon's advice in mind, we may foresee evil coming not only in our own lives, but also in the lives of those around us, so that we may assist in delivering them from evil."

Anna: "When psychologically, emotionally, or physically offended through abuse to the point where one's dignity has been completely violated, understanding, forgiveness, and discretion are needed in attempt to move forward and to obtain personal peace. To be discerning does not mean one's emotions and pain are invalid. It simply means that despite one's deep-rooted suffering and intense experiences, one can progress and minimize relational turmoil and emotional reactivity. The believer in Jesus is not called to respect evil by any measure. One has been called to persevere despite it, to believe in and acknowledge truth, and to lift up one's abuser in prayer. Prudence comes from God, and it is by his wisdom and grace that one can truly see others clearly."

Question Seventy-Seven
March 18th

Many of us have been beaten down so badly that we are constantly fearful. How can we learn to be courageous in this life?

Jon: "When two people fall in love, they often become so infatuated with each other that they lose awareness of the world around them. Unaware of the world, nothing in the world could cause them to fear. The Bible has always affirmed this principle: 'There is no fear in love, but perfect love casts out fear' (1 John 4:18). Passionately expressing and cultivating an infatuating love for God—who already loves us perfectly—will render the world utterly incapable of causing us fear."

Anna: "When abused and faced with threats, fear can pervade. For self-protection, one will either override their fears to oppose evil or retreat. Either way, boldly acting does not mean one is completely fearless. Oftentimes, overcoming apprehensions is a process for abolishing one's prior belief systems and understanding one's limitations. When alarmed, one's anxiety increases, and may cause intense panic or an extreme emotional response. When one comes to awareness and determines that fear can be overridden by something more meaningful, courage is born. To have been beaten down throughout childhood and have the desire and ability to continue on and persevere, one is brave. To choose to do what is right without the intention of acknowledgment will be consequentially rewarded by God in this life or the next."

Question Seventy-Eight
March 19th

What does the Holy Spirit have to do with the credibility of Scripture?

Jon: "Jesus said to his disciples, '… the Helper, the Holy Spirit, whom the Father will send in my name, he will teach you all things and bring to your remembrance all that I have said to you' (John 14:26). So the Holy Spirit makes Scripture credible in two ways: 1) He confirms internally to the believer that the Bible is true; and 2) He taught the authors of the Bible and brought to their remembrance all that God desired to be written within it."

Anna: "What is perceived as truth is connected to one's reality, one's senses, and one's substantial experiences. The Holy Spirit brings Scripture to life and is the manifestation of God's biblical truths within the believer. The Holy Spirit is a gift that allows one to experience and exude God's character on a supernatural and palpable level. For starters, God promised his Spirit to the believer, and through one's experience of the Holy Spirit, he has fulfilled his Word. Within mental and emotional healing, actions tend to trump words, which is experiential proof. Following through and keeping one's word is crucial for nurturing healthy attachment and in building trust. The Holy Bible is believable because God is credible and he has proven this through Jesus' death and resurrection, one's testimony, and the attributes of his Spirit transforming all who believe."

Question Seventy-Nine
March 20th

We grew up having to stuff our feelings, never allowed to express the broad range of our primal human emotions. Are emotions sinful?

Jon: "The book of Ecclesiastes says, 'For everything there is a season… a time to weep, and a time to laugh; a time to mourn…' (Eccl. 3:1-4). Not only does God permit us emotions, he desires we share in the emotions of others: 'Rejoice with those who rejoice, weep with those who weep' (Rom. 12:15). However, when emotions manifest within us 'sexual immorality, impurity… idolatry… enmity… jealousy, fits of anger' (Gal. 5:19-20), they have crossed the line into sin."

Anna: "Emotions play an integral role in human development and the quality of one's life. One's initial or pattern of emotional responses may vary dependent upon one's temperament, upbringing, personality, and subjective experiences. Emotions are vital for the concepts of attachment, free will, and faith. Emotions can be positive, negative, short-lived or long lasting. Emotions can weigh one down like one is drowning in life's misery, and they can set one free and give pure authenticity to one's experiences and personal journey. When emotions lead to impure thoughts, motives, and behaviors, then sin comes into play. Being selfishly entrenched in one's emotions and blindly or impulsively acting upon them can lead to sinful states and consequences. God has called one to rely on his Word and to be vulnerable to his Spirit, and to not be misled by simply how one feels."

Question Eighty
March 21st

Some of us prefer to remain in a state of drunkenness rather than face the issues brought on by childhood abuse. If we're not hurting anyone, what's the harm in this?

Jon: "The Bible repeatedly forbids drunkenness both in the Old and New Testaments (see Pro. 23:20; Gal. 5:21). It is a sin. Therefore, when we become drunk we harm not others, but ourselves. Notice what it says in Ephesians 5:18: 'And do not get drunk with wine, for that is debauchery, but be filled with the Spirit...' So be drunk, but not with alcohol. Rather, cultivate a life in which you often become intoxicated by the Holy Spirit of God, by Scripture, by prayer, and by communion with Jesus Christ."

Anna: "When one chooses to escape through alcohol they are not only hurting themselves, but also affecting those who love them. God understands why one chooses to drink instead of facing one's pain. Nevertheless, it is not a healthy or fulfilling way to cope with life's problems. The devil waits to attack, especially those who are inebriated to escape their broken and abusive past. When one's mind is not clear, one will be led away from God's Spirit and truth. Resist the allure of psychological and emotional escape and be alert. Focus on God's Word, his will, and one's immoral addictions will fade. The temptation for worldly things can be strong, yet the spiritual appeal of what is required for eternity is stronger."

Question Eighty-One
March 22nd

Many of us have heard that if we get more sleep, we will be less sensitive to negative emotions, such as fear. Is this true?

Jon: "Proverbs 3:24 says, 'If you lie down, you will not be afraid; when you lie down, your sleep will be sweet.' Is it that easy? We go back three verses for the answer. Verse 21 says to 'keep sound wisdom and discretion.' Verses 23 and 24 are consequences of obeying verse 21. So if you want to sleep sweetly and unafraid, then you must keep wisdom. How do we become wise? 'The fear of the LORD is the beginning of wisdom' (Pro. 9:10). Better sleep is a consequence of properly revering God."

Anna: "The benefits and implications of sleep are staggering. When one has peace within, one will fall asleep more effortlessly. A lack of sleep can affect one's cognitive abilities such as difficulty concentrating, problem solving, and simply processing one's ideas like one usually does. When one does not receive physical rejuvenation, one's psychological and emotional well-being is affected. When fearful, anxious, and internally deregulated, one's circadian rhythm changes due to unrest, because it coincides with one's psyche, environment, and sleep patterns. Fear is not faith. When one is in direct communion with God, fear subsides and faith's security overrides one's worries. When content, one will be less emotionally reactive upon outside forces and negativity. Resting in God's Spirit will rejuvenate one's mind, body, and soul."

Question Eighty-Two
March 23rd

A lot of our parents deny that we were ever abused. And from time to time, we find ourselves questioning the truth as well. Would it be better for us to join our parents in their disbelief?

Jon: "That we avoid spreading falsehood is so important to God that he made it the central principle underlying the ninth commandment (see Ex. 20:16). The suppression of the truth indicates unrighteousness and brings about wrath and fury (see Rom. 2:8). However, dispensing truth brings freedom, sanctification, growth, and unity (see John 8:32, 17:19; Eph. 4:15, 4:25). Promoting truth is not merely good in itself, but as God promises, it will bring about a multitude of subsequent blessings in our lives. Therefore, it is always better to join oneself with truth than falsehood."

Anna: "Acknowledging and living out the truth is essential for one's healing and a transformative life. Being shackled and weighed down by one's reality is the opposite of freedom and faith. Denial and disbelief are harmful to the healing process and limit one's existence. Not being able to grasp or comprehend why certain things happen is a painful part of life but when one is getting in their own way due to distressing aspects of their past, doubt needs to shift toward honesty of one's abusive history. Denial continues the cycle of abuse in its unique and rare form. Disbelief is not honoring those who abused you; it's dishonoring oneself and your testimony for God."

Question Eighty-Three
March 24th

When confronted with bad news, some of us regress, more often than we'd like, by crying and/or staying in bed. How can we begin to change this sort of unhelpful behavior?

Jon: "If we respond in an unhealthy way when confronted with something negative, we are not prepared for it. We are surprised. We are caught off guard. We have no choice but to respond instinctively, whether that instinct is healthy or not. Scripture offers us the remedy for this problem. 1 Peter 4:12 says, 'Beloved, do not be surprised at the fiery trial when it comes upon you to test you, as though something strange were happening to you.' If we live in daily awareness that trials are inevitable, we will be mentally and emotionally prepared when we encounter them. Not surprised, we will be able to respond in a healthy manner."

Anna: "Processing the abuse and pain that trigger this unhelpful process is crucial for change. When one's needs and emotions are invalidated and unmet, life's events become difficult to handle due to one feeling inept, overwhelmed, and alone. When one's conflicts persistently receive no resolution, faith in self and others dwindles. This takes one back to feeling as they did when younger, with no power or control. Complete honesty about one's dysfunctional patterns and a sincere will and plan to change is a humble place to begin. God knows why one regresses; ask him to reveal and heal one's inner kid."

Question Eighty-Four
March 25th

What does it mean to be spiritually alive?

Jon: "We are made spiritually alive when God causes us to be 'born again to a living hope through the resurrection of Jesus Christ from the dead' (1 Pet. 1:3-4). While this is not something we observe directly, we can observe it indirectly. Some outward evidences of regeneration are a lessening of sinful behavior (1 John 3:9), an increase of righteous behavior (1 John 2:29), and bearing the fruit of the Spirit such as love, joy, and peace (Gal. 5:22-23)."

Anna: "Separation from God, the rejection of God, and a contin-ual state of disobedience toward God equates to existing in a sort of a psychological, emotional, and personal purgatory. Follow-ing this route or succumbing to this lifestyle will lead to or end in one's spiritual death, an eternity cut off from God's majesty. Regeneration, through the Holy Spirit, is what will liven one from a spiritual death. So, to be spiritually alive would mean to accept Jesus as your Lord and savior so that the Holy Spirit will be alive in you. The revival of one's soul and spirit through Jesus Christ will follow when one commits their life to serving the Lord. To be awakened in Christ and freed from sin's strong hold is an amazing gift that enables one to be fulfilled and eternally alive."

Question Eighty-Five
March 26th

Are not we all born into this world inherently good?

Jon: "There is much debate as to whether or not the Bible affirms people are born sinful. However, there is no debate as to whether or not the Bible affirms that people *are* sinful. 'For,' says Scripture, 'there is no one who does not sin' (1 Ki. 8:46). Even if we came into this world inherently good, we will inevitably sin. A dependence on Christ then becomes imperative. Though we are sinful, our belief in him makes his righteousness our own before God."

Anna: "Humankind has been born into transgression, unfair or not, or whether one wants to believe it or not, every person behaves immorally. People's definition of what is acceptable and good often varies. For some, being a good person is purely following the land's laws or just being decent to others from day to day. In psychology, being 'good' aligns with being true to oneself, being true to one's emotions, experiences, and one's personal understanding of one's morality and spirituality. Goodness from a worldly perspective cannot measure to God's standard, his excellence in truth. Inherently, humankind is sinful, but through one's belief in Jesus, one is identified as good purely for choosing faith. Remember, God is always good and naturally humankind is not, yet one is redeemed through Jesus, which is salvation's saving grace."

Question Eighty-Six
March 27th

Many of us act out: punch holes in walls, throw things, even harm our own bodies. We do these things because we are unable to express ourselves in any other fashion. Help?

Jon: "According to the Bible, the admission to God that one's actions are wrong or sinful, and that one is unable to keep him or herself from committing those actions, is halfway to redemption and recovery. The next step is placing one's faith and hope in Jesus Christ, who, though he was tempted, did not sin. He is in this respect not only able to sympathize with our weaknesses, but, being the only person who triumphed over every encounter with sin, he is literally the best possible figure to seek advice and help from. 'Let us then with confidence draw near to the throne of grace, that we may receive mercy and find grace to help in time of need' (Heb. 4:15-16)."

Anna: "Verbalizing one's pain, utilizing creative emotional outlets, and engaging in activities of interest like dancing or martial arts are beautiful avenues to self-expression. When revealing one's innermost feelings leads to self-destruction, worthlessness pervades as shame becomes aggravated and deeply entrenched. When desperately depressed, one may act out to cry out, because one is in great need of acceptance, support, and love. Feeling insignificant is a lie straight from the enemy's tongue. Believers are called to value one's body, one's temporary vessel, that has been given to be used for God's glory."

Question Eighty-Seven
March 28th

An initial search on the Internet tells us that the specific types of child abuse are: sexual, neglect, physical, emotional, and family violence. What we don't see listed is child spiritual abuse. Isn't there such a thing?

Jon: "Sin is not a physical but a spiritual problem. Notice how Jesus speaks of child abuse in this context: '... whoever causes one of these little ones who believe in me to sin, it would be better for him to have a great millstone fastened around his neck and to be drowned in the depth of the sea' (Mat. 18:6). In other words, whoever causes a child to sin is spiritually abusing that child. There is such a thing as childhood spiritual abuse, and Jesus reserves his harshest language for those who would commit such an action."

Anna: "When one is abused, one's soul, identity, and spirit are tormented and oppressed. Spiritual abuse, which is connected to all abuse, leads one astray from their divine worth and purpose. Living life on planet earth causes one's being and flesh to be tried and tested. Anything that is not of God or functions apart from a belief in God's Son is unrighteous. When being subjected to the world's corruption, immorality's messages test and victimize one's mind, will, and decisions. Children are most susceptible to spiritual abuse because of their naiveté, limited capacities, and dependency upon flawed human beings. Sadly, evil and humankind are the carriers of abuse, yet love will win."

Question Eighty-Eight
March 29th

Most of us have heard that helping others helps us to feel better about ourselves. Is this true?

Jon: "There is one commandment that when obeyed guarantees fullness of joy from God (see John 15:11). Jesus said, 'This is my commandment, that you love one another as I have loved you' (John 15:12). In this context, the goal in helping others is not self-betterment, but to obey God's command to do so. So self-betterment is a byproduct of helping others. Helping others for the sake of self-betterment may give us momentary happiness. But helping others for the sake of obeying God's commands will give us fullness of joy."

Anna: "Helping others with selfless compassion will move what is truly important into perspective and beautifully connect one another. Altruism, at its best, is a divine blessing; but at its worst, yet still impactful in ways, it can be evasive. If one is constantly caring for others to escape or so as to not address one's problems, or one is not feeding their soul, obstacles toward healing and one's spiritual growth arise. When one through charitableness is unconsciously nurturing defective thought processes that one is unworthy of care or last on the list, then negative reinforcement is in motion. Helping can alleviate self-dejection and increase positive emotions, but in order to be at one's brightest and most moving, one must learn to truly love one's self through God."

Question Eighty-Nine
March 30th

Is it healthy to fear God?

Jon: "When the Bible talks about fearing God, it uses the word *fear* in a special way. To fear God is to keep his commandments, obey his voice, and serve and hold fast to him (see Deu. 13:4). Scripture says, 'let us cleanse ourselves from every defilement of body and spirit, bringing holiness to completion in the fear of God' (2 Cor. 7:1). A complete fear of God does cause us to cower before him, but brings a healthy holiness to our lives."

Anna: "When fear deludes reality or gets in the way of one's functioning, emotional and psychological concerns have transpired. Fear can magnify anxiety, which can birth panic attacks and serious and debilitating phobias. Fear has the ability to manipulate, create, and taint one's existence and quality of life. Fear can be intrinsic, instinctual, learned, imitated, and generated. Realistic expectations and experiences correlated with fear used as a protective measure and adaptation is evolutionary and crucial for survival. When distressed, acting upon one's fears can create more problems and manifest the very things one was afraid of. When righteous fear is grounded within and built upon God's Word, prophecies, and laws, it serves one's eternal purpose. Fearing God is healthy and wise when it reminds, ignites, and guides one's love and commitment to Jesus Christ."

Question Ninety
March 31st

If an adult abuses a child to the point of taking that child's life, should the murderer receive the death penalty?

Jon: "God is wholly sacred. He created humanity in his image and after his likeness. All human life is therefore sacred. No human being has the right to take the life dubbed sacred by God of another human being—especially an innocent child. However, Romans 13:4 says of government, 'But if you do wrong, be afraid, for he does not bear the sword in vain. For he is the servant of God, an avenger who carries out God's wrath on the wrongdoer.' Wrongdoing deserves punishment. And sometimes God allows government to wield the sword that carries out that punishment."

Anna: "When an abuser receives the death penalty for causing a child to die, for ultimately committing murder, many would call this poetic justice or sweet revenge. The murder of a child is not only evil; it is unfathomable for most. An abuser has a story, too, meaning: an abuser has a higher probability for having been abused themselves. Now, this does not excuse the abusive behaviors, but sheds light on the abusive cycle and dysfunction's snare. Just like one usually desires to be forgiven for one's mistakes, abusers are often no different. Whether a murderer has genuine remorse or not, the death penalty may or may not be appropriate, spiritually speaking. God will rightfully judge every choice everyone has made. Consequences are biblical and inevitable."

Question Ninety-One
April 1st

Some of us project our difficult feelings onto others. For example, an unfaithful spouse might accuse his or her innocent partner of having an affair. How do we stop projecting our troublesome emotions onto others?

Jon: "The adulterer feels uneasy because he or she has committed adultery. Projection is more often than not a byproduct of sin. If you kill sin, you kill projection. Romans 8:13 says, 'For if you live according to the flesh you will die, but if by the Spirit you put to death the deeds of the body, you will live.' We need no help living in sin. We need help killing it. And help is provided by the Holy Spirit of God, attained only through faith in Jesus Christ. Whereas projection is a byproduct of sin, the death of sin is a byproduct of the Spirit's dwelling within you."

Anna: "Projection is charged by denial, guilt, shame, anger, and a defensive reactivity when unable to sit with uncomfortable resolve. The aftereffects of assigning unsettled issues onto another can severely affect that person's sense of security, confidence, and trust within the relationship. The projector tends to negatively alter their self-perspective because they are left to pick up the pieces of their pride after they have hurt, offended, or blindsided another without warning or premise. To stop this, one must take accountability for one's behaviors, confess to God, and not blame and judge others for the very things that one does."

Question Ninety-Two
April 2nd

Do we inherit the sins of our ancestors?

Jon: "All persons sin (see Rom. 3:23). We are condemned in ourselves then before anyone else's sins may be ascribed to us. However, Scripture says, 'The son shall not suffer for the iniquity of the father, nor the father suffer for the iniquity of the son' (Ez. 18:20). While it is true that some children inherit propensities toward certain sins such as substance abuse or anger, no generation inherits the sins of another. Since 'God is just' (2 Thes. 1:6), and it would be unjust to punish one person for the sins committed by another, he will never do so."

Anna: "Sin is inescapable for every human being, so yes, from one perspective we have inherited sinfulness from Adam and Eve, one's ancestors, and parents. Ancestral sins trickle down through generations due to the deep and inevitable consequences that immorality has within families, and coexisting with flawed individuals. From another perspective, just because someone's parent or relative has an issue with addiction, for example, does not necessarily mean that person will, due to one's beliefs, decisions, and strength of will. Therefore, sin is inevitable, but the measure and extent of sin in one's life need not equate to another. Every day one makes choices and due to the morals, ethics, and spirit one has, these will accompany the sinful actions in one's life. Having the Holy Spirit indwelling and truly leading one's life will help decrease one's immoralities."

Question Ninety-Three
April 3rd

As hard as this may be to comprehend, many of us who were abused would rather be nice to our offenders than express our hurt feelings to them. Is this a skillful way to protect ourselves?

Jon: "Jesus taught his followers to love their neighbors and turn the other cheek when struck. Because of this some people believe they are to avoid all confrontation. But if we look at Matthew 18:15-17, we get a much different picture. In this passage Jesus teaches a four-step plan for confronting someone who sins against us. The very first step is to express oneself to their offender. So the skill is found not in avoiding expression of hurt feelings, but in following the steps of biblical confrontation without forsaking love and humility."

Anna: "In this scenario, using the defense mechanism reaction formation for self-preservation is doing what conflicts with what one truly desires to do. Learning to not be or create a problem naturally unfolds out of abusive dynamics and reiterates the message that the survivor and their feelings are unimportant. Sadly, when one continuously devalues and underestimates their intrinsic need for acknowledgment and self-empowerment, what will become of one's true self and self-worth? Contradictory processes and behaviors can alleviate one's anxiety temporarily but the lasting effects can be psychologically, emotionally, and relationally crippling. God must desire for one's mind, heart, and behaviors to be congruent and authentic while having patience in love for oneself and others."

Question Ninety-Four
April 4th

Apathy, an air of indifference, the absence of emotion and regard for another's well-being. Most of our parents displayed apathy toward us. Does this mean that we will be the same: heartless?

Jon: "2 Timothy 3:2-5 affirms humanity's tendency toward selfish behavior. We are likely then to become apathetic and heartless inasmuch as we rely on our own ability to care for and love others. The Christian, however, depends not on his or her own power to sympathize with others, but on God's. If the Holy Spirit naturally produces the fruit of love and kindness (see Gal. 5:22), and he resides within those who believe in Christ (see Eph. 1:13), then God himself will ensure that love and kindness toward others are natural parts of our lives."

Anna: "To be unkind is a conscious decision. The effects had on the abused do not claim permanency over mirroring the behaviors from one's caregiver. Concern and sensitivity toward others is attached to one's beliefs, values, empathy, awareness, understanding, intentions, and experiences. Insensitivity and detachment stem from creating defenses to protect oneself from re-experiencing pain. Caring for others is intrinsic, modeled, and learned but is not limited to replication. Choosing to love shows that one's mindset and desires are moving in truth's direction, and though this does not mean that one will love perfectly and without fault—only God does that—one was not created to be heartless. When willing, God's Holy Spirit will teach one how to passionately care."

Question Ninety-Five
April 5th

It is hard to feel gratitude when so much has been taken away from us. What do we have to be thankful for?

Jon: "How thankful would we be if God told us his will for our lives? 1 Thessalonians 5:18 says, 'give thanks in all circumstances; for this is the will of God in Christ Jesus for you.' God's will for us is that we give thanks in all circumstances. Notice it is not *for* all circumstances we give thanks, but *in* all circumstances. In other words, we're not necessarily to be thankful for a bad circumstance. But we can be thankful that we know God's will for our lives through any circumstance—good or bad."

Anna: "When the most precious parts of one's core being have been stolen, and one is holding onto dignity with all their might, thankfulness is not always effortless. Appreciation's hope is to arise from tragedy, but this will take time depending upon one's past, their present mindset and spiritual state. Gratitude is an outlook, and when established in humility and purpose, its impact is unstoppable. Being broken, whether caused by others or self-inflicted, is hopelessness when not understood in connection to Jesus' death and resurrection. A grateful demeanor transforms one's mind, emotions, and will and is obtainable no matter what one has been through. Reach for and embody thankfulness because Jesus withstood so much so that humankind could be spiritually alive and free."

Question Ninety-Six
April 6th

A lot of us want to come together and form prayer groups and pray for those adults who were abused as children and also for today's children who may be experiencing abuse. Do you believe in the power of group prayer?

Jon: "After being filled with the Holy Spirit, Peter delivered a sermon in Jerusalem on the day of Pentecost that brought about three thousand people to believe in Jesus Christ. Acts 2:42 says, 'And they devoted themselves to the apostles' teaching and the fellowship, to the breaking of bread and the prayers.' The following verses indicate that unification of these believers in activities such as prayer brought many powerful manifestations of God. From group prayer we can expect to experience awe, signs, unity, communion, joy, and worship. Prayer is one of the most powerful things we can do for the abused children of our time."

Anna: "Prayer is one of the most powerful abilities one has, and when one's heartfelt intent righteously coincides with others, miracles happen. Prayer not only enriches one's faith, it brings people together beautifully. Whether one prays for healing, the unification of one's family, or for comfort and strength within one's soul, intercessory prayer is crucial to enable change. The hope in possibilities plants seeds toward the growth of one's unmoving beliefs. Undivided confidence and authentic communication with God is one's supernatural weapon. Group prayer is biblical and when believers come together in Jesus' name, heaven's will flourishes."

Question Ninety-Seven
April 7th

What is the most basic birthright of every child?

Jon: "One could say that we have the right to be loved. But it's not that we are entitled to be loved by others as much as it is that others are commanded to love us. It's not about what we deserve, but about how others ought to treat us. Remember, we are commanded by God to love one another (Lev. 19:18; Mark 12:31). So any newborn, or any person, ought to be loved by every other person. The problem is that people do not always do as they ought to. But this doesn't mean that we shouldn't be loved, or that we shouldn't continue to love others."

Anna: "A newborn has no say when coming into the world and one's rights will either be valued or abused. What is deemed rightful in one's life comes down to one's belief system and values. It is simple; without a solid awareness of what is truly important, one's perspective can be completely swayed and will have discrepancies. One's worldly heritage may be manipulated, convoluted, given or taken away through unfortunate, unfair, or cruel circumstances. However, every human being has purpose, was created with significance, and is deeply loved. When one's earthly legacy coincides with God's will, one's inheritance will bring eternal rewards. One's birthright to inherit God's kingdom is through Jesus, but one must choose this honor so that one can spend an eternity in heaven."

Question Ninety-Eight
April 8th

Why should we care about the condition of our souls?

Jon: "If the soul is the part of a person that continues to live on after the body dies, the question is, 'Where does the soul go?' Jesus said that the unrighteous '… will go away into eternal punishment, but the righteous into eternal life' (Mat. 25:46). In other words, there are two potential destinations for the soul: heaven or hell. Therefore we should care about the condition of our souls because, according to Scripture, they will reside for an eternity in either heaven of hell."

Anna: "The condition of one's soul has serious spiritual implications that determine one's future. Experiencing cognitive dissonances within life's journey, and feeling that one is not valuable, not worthy, or not gifted, is hard to accept when one has intrinsic needs to be cared for and loved. Having clashing or opposing thoughts, beliefs, and experiences that affect one's sense of spiritual balance is confusing and painful especially when one lives and acts upon intrusive or obtrusive lies. The essence of one's soul—whether one believes it is limited or limitless matters, and it is attached to one's spirit and inspirations. Even though one's soul is distinct in that it gives purpose to one's body, the driving force is attached to all other aspects of one's spiritual existence. One's soul is a precursor to one's eternal destiny and should not be taken lightly. Your soul is special and it yearns for God's righteousness."

Question Ninety-Nine
April 9th

Is there a difference between the soul and the spirit?

Jon: "There are two dominant theological positions here. *Trichotomy* is the view that man is composed of three parts: a body, a soul, and a spirit. *Dichotomy* is the view that man is composed of only two parts: a body, and a soul. Dichotomy is the more widely accepted view because Scripture, while it affirms the existence of an immaterial part of man, does not divide that immaterial part into more parts than two. It may be helpful to consider the terms 'soul' and 'spirit' to both denote our inmost being."

Anna: "The spirit breathes life into one's physical body. One's spirit is distinguished through characteristics and this affects one's temperament, thoughts, and actions. Every being has a soul, but not every being has the same spirit. The abused know this concept deeper than most and have experienced firsthand how one's spirit can be deceptive and mistrustfully wavers when not rooted in what is pure and good. The spirit can be oppressed, suppressed, and manifest itself through depression, anxiety, fear, bitterness, or hopelessness. One's soul will exist whether one's spirit is good or evil, but one's spirit will decipher one's legacy and if one is truly fulfilled in this life and the next. Just because one has breath does not mean one is truly full of life. Believers in Jesus are legitimately alive because their spirits are truly connected to God."

Question One Hundred
April 10th

If unbelieving child molesters assault children their whole lives but suddenly on their deathbeds accept Christ as their savior, are their sins forgiven?

Jon: "Technically speaking, faith in Jesus Christ is sufficient for salvation (see Eph. 2:8). And this offer is available to everyone (see John 3:16,18, 36; 6:40). Jesus Christ is God. Therefore, his death on the cross is of infinite worth. There is no sin that Christ's infinitely powerful sacrifice cannot atone for. So as long as one's confession of faith is genuine, they are saved (see Rom. 10:9). This reality causes us joy because its truth guarantees us eternal life. Let our focus not be on the ones who are saved, but on the one who saves."

Anna: "Sexual attraction differs from the act of molestation and it is false to assume that all pedophiles are abusers. Many pedophiles have been abused themselves and are sadly stuck in re-creating and controlling the sexual experiences that were imposed upon them when defenseless. Now, this is no excuse or justification for pedophilic behaviors, but should shed some light on the viciousness of this deeply rooted spiritual issue. One can be forgiven for all one has done but that does not mean one will not face responsibility or penalty for the choices one has made. Even though certain crimes are heinous and cause serious harm, repentance, forgiveness, and salvation through Jesus are attainable for every person who chooses to believe."

Question One Hundred And One
April 11th

What are defense mechanisms?

Jon: "There are good and bad defense mechanisms. A bad defense mechanism is an unhealthy and even sinful emotional or psychological barrier we set up around ourselves when confronted with difficult situations. A good defense mechanism is one which God has dispensed to us for our good. For example, Scripture speaks of righteousness as a breastplate, faith as a shield, and salvation as a helmet (Eph. 6:14-17). Using all of these, we are 'able to stand against the schemes of the devil' (Eph. 6:11). If a defense mechanism attempts to bring glory to the self, it ought to be cast off. If the defense mechanism attempts to bring glory to God, it ought to stay."

Anna: "They are involuntarily created within one's mind to shift or discredit the truth. Defenses shield one from awkward interactions and attempt to minimize negative thoughts, emotions, and behaviors. When traumatized or abused, the psyche will do anything required to survive within the moment and then attempt to endure the wreckage left behind. Physical, emotional, or psychological fortitude is not automatic or inevitable. Many unconscious and conscious systems work together to help one withstand their fears and the most painful aspects of life. However, one must choose courage. Wholeheartedly ask God to reveal these unconscious facets of one's essence for awareness, healing, and wisdom to be more equipped for his purpose."

Question One Hundred And Two
April 12th

Have you heard of the catchphrase, "Fake it 'til you make it?" If so, do you think that if some of us fake feeling confident that eventually we will get to the point where we don't have to pretend self-assurance anymore?

Jon: "If my confidence is in myself, my confidence will be finite. If my confidence is in God, however, my confidence will be infinite. For when I am weak, 'I can do all things through him who strengthens me' (Phil. 4:13). And when I cannot accomplish something on my own, 'The Lord is my helper' (Heb. 13:6). So God is not only by our side, but he empowers us to accomplish his will for our lives. Let's make God's confidence our confidence."

Anna: "In order for one's heart and mind to truly trust, build, and coincide to promote one's ambitions, one must believe. To live out one's dreams requires acting upon one's convictions. Self-assurance, at its best, is rooted in a definitive identity and divine purpose. Superficial attitudes or fakeness exude insecurities and permeate doubt within one's belief systems. If one truly trusts in one's calling and worth, one's thoughts and actions will follow. Unwavering tenacity, vivaciousness, and hope in an absolute aim greater than oneself is rare but dazzling to witness. Authentic faith in God and self is not an act, and therefore prompts one's passions, confidence, and behaviors to supersede the norm and be extraordinary."

Question One Hundred And Three
April 13th

What does it mean to be accountable for our own actions?

Jon: "First, it means that we are responsible for *what* we say and do. Our words and actions are the result of our own free will. Second, it means that we are responsible for the *consequences* of what we say and do. We deserve the appropriate praise or punishment our words and actions fairly bring. Spiritually speaking, although there is punishment for sin, Christ bore the punishment for the sum of the sins of humanity on the cross. Through faith in him, our sins are accounted to Christ while his righteousness is accounted to us."

Anna: "Life's responsibilities typically increase with awareness, understanding, and developmental maturity, but in many cases this does not happen consecutively, for varying reasons. Adult children of abusers were not taught healthy moral commitments through the consistent modeling of a functional standard. When a parent hinders and devalues their child's efficacy and well-being, how does that child then grow up to deeply value and empower oneself with a negatively skewed self-perception? One's concept of personal duty and self-worth comes from one's environment but also flourishes from within. Accountability, whether acknowledging one's hurtful words or simply facing the repercussions of one's behaviors, begins in one's heart, mind, and manifests in one's character and actions. Fortunately, the Holy Spirit convicts the believer when one's attitude and behaviors deviate from God's will so one becomes accountable through Christ."

Question One Hundred And Four
April 14th

Do you think that one can choose to be happy?

Jon: "We cannot choose to be happy. But we can choose to do things that bring about happiness. Jesus says in Matthew 6:33, 'But seek first the kingdom of God and his righteousness, and all these things will be added to you.' So if we want to be happy, we do not pursue happiness itself. We pursue righteousness. In other words, happiness is a byproduct of righteous living. Only to the extent that one chooses to live righteously does one choose to be happy."

Anna: "A baseline of where one is cognitively, emotionally, intellectually, and spiritually will affect one's state of mind and contentment as a whole. Desiring to be happy or having an overall positive attitude is divergent from and not equated to experiencing a natural, emotional, human response to a painful situation. An optimistic individual can experience all the other so-called negative emotions at any given moment due to the circumstance at hand. When one is despondent, oftentimes one's fundamental choice and will is muddled and stifled by psychological, emotional, and physiological symptoms. Choosing to be unhappy seems to be more common in present times but should not be misconstrued with a clinical diagnosis, spiritual warfare, or demonic oppression. Within the secular perception, evil forces are not overtly acknowledged, but are connected to the deception toward one's state of mind and the perceived inability to not experience God's peace and happiness."

Question One Hundred And Five
April 15th

If God doesn't get his purposes fulfilled by certain people, does he find others to implement them?

Jon: "Remember how Jonah fled to Tarshish after being called by the Lord to prophesy in Nineveh? Aboard the ship, Jonah introduced the mariners to the God of heaven and 'the men feared the LORD exceedingly, and they offered a sacrifice to the LORD and made vows' (Jon. 1:16). Although Jonah was disobedient, it was God's purpose to bring those mariners into a relationship with him. Even if we flee from him, 'I will accomplish all my purpose,' says the Lord (Isa. 46:10)."

Anna: "Personal responsibility, purpose, and destiny are at the core of psychotherapy. Duty goes hand in hand with commitment, accountability, and repercussion. There are consequences for all one does, negative and positive, unseen and seen. Think about the times you have made a mistake, ruptured a relationship, a situation, or just simply missed an opportunity. Most importantly, think about the aftermath, the possible openings you had to make it right or not, or to make the decision to utilize what has happened for the common good of self and others. There is always the option to implement what has been missed or discovered to benefit someone. God's goodness is merciful, he operates fully with purpose, and has ultimate sovereignty; he will utilize one's missed opportunities favorably to help any soul that is willing and able."

Question One Hundred And Six
April 16th

Our minds have been trained to focus on the negative. Can replacing these negative thoughts with positive ones help us to heal our minds?

Jon: "The Bible uses war imagery to describe what we are to do with negative thoughts. 2 Corinthians 10:5 says to 'take every thought captive to obey Christ.' Notice the two steps here. The first step is to acknowledge the negative thought. We detain it at the forefront of our consciousness, not letting it cause us harm. The second step is to bring the thought before God, allowing him to work. So we do replace negative thoughts with positive ones—thoughts of our God and Savior."

Anna: "One's thoughts and core beliefs are connected, yet different, and can yield a very distinct weight and outcome depending upon one's psychological development and impressionability. Thoughts can and will change abruptly, but one's belief systems may take time to impact and evolve. The way one thinks surely can change the way one feels. Corrective experiences attached to positive emotions can be influential and empower cognitive restructuring when one is aware and open for change. When one's thoughts are futile and rejecting of one's very nature, it is not surprising that emptiness and self-loathing surface. Human beings are in a spiritual battle and the enemies' tactics are to attack, cloud, and deceive one's mind, will, and spirit. For unmatched psychological healing, allow God's Holy Spirit and Word to transform one's soul."

Question One Hundred And Seven
April 17th

Some of us choose to heal... spiritually, psychologically... and to establish stable homes and healthy interpersonal relationships. Some of our siblings, on the other hand, choose to maintain the opposite, remaining depressed and destitute. We have tried to be good examples for our siblings. Are we our siblings' saviors?

Jon: "We want to help our siblings in every way possible, but we are not their savior. Jesus Christ is: 'And there is salvation in no one else, for there is no other name under heaven given among men by which we must be saved' (Acts 4:12). In this regard, the greatest help we can be to our siblings is to point away from ourselves and toward Christ. Doing so will not only lighten our burden, but also leave our siblings in the infinitely capable hands of God."

Anna: "Sibling relationships can be convoluted, tumultuous, and meaningful, yet the pressures to rescue or save someone one is genuinely connected to can be overwhelming. When a parental relationship is unresolved, a sibling may have the conscious or subconscious pull to step in the emotionally absent parent's shoes and become the caretaker, guardian angel, or hero. Now, to aspire to protect family or assist those one loves is admirable, but to expect oneself to deliver another from mental illness and spiritual warfare is too big of a burden to carry. To help and be used by God is one's divine purpose, but there is only one true savior of humankind, Jesus Christ."

Question One Hundred And Eight
April 18th

Can adults who were abused as children suffer from PTSD, Post Traumatic Stress Disorder?

Jon: "In 2 Samuel 12 we read that David and Bathsheba had borne a son who became very ill. On behalf of God Nathan informed David that David's son would soon die. David became so distraught that he slept on the ground and refused to eat. Verse 18 says that on the seventh day of his illness the boy passed away. Upon hearing the news, 'David arose from the earth and washed and anointed himself and changed his clothes. And he went into the house of the LORD and worshiped' (2 Sam. 12:20). For David, it was worship, obedience to the Lord, and the knowledge that heaven awaited him (vv. 22-23) that aided him after his traumatic experience."

Anna: "Adults and children can be diagnosed with and suffer from PTSD. Without the proper knowledge, support, and care, one can feel completely trapped within their past abuse's reproach. Suppressed anxieties can manifest persistent, intrusive thoughts, which will pervade one's functioning when belittled or ignored. Dysphoria is miserable and affects one's psyche, behaviors, relationships, and when ongoing takes a tremendous toll on one's emotional well-being. When one does not face and give their childhood trauma to God with the intent to truly process and grieve, one's deep-seated fears attack vigorously to destroy, and can become post-traumatic stresses. Ask God's Holy Spirit to heal one's pain, one's soul, so one's past does not drastically surface."

Question One Hundred And Nine
April 19th

Why do some of us who were traumatized in childhood have a hard time making decisions?

Jon: "Many would call difficulty in decision-making a weakness. And it may be, but this is to our advantage. For God says, 'My grace is sufficient for you, for my power is made perfect in weakness' (2 Cor. 12:9). If we can do something on our own, we are less likely to ask God for help. But if we cannot do something on our own, like make a decision, we are more likely to ask for and therefore receive help from God. We can boast in our weaknesses because they grant us access to the power of God."

Anna: "Challenges arise when one did not receive consistently healthy stimulation. When exposed to repetitious threats, whether physical, psychological, or emotional, one's cognitive drive is often stifled. When abused, one's innate gifts, willpower, and decisiveness are overthrown with every vicious word and behavior. Avoidance of conflict and pain become natural defenses for protection. Making simple or difficult decisions can escalate one's stress and minimize one's perceived emotional strength. When one has low self-efficacy due to the internalization of an abuser's projections that one is defective or incompetent, one's insecurities arise and override instinctive conclusions and problem-solving skills. Experiences of intense uncertainty would cause most to feel unsure at times, so have faith: seek God for conviction and clarity, for he is never unsure."

Question One Hundred And Ten
April 20th

A lot of us get irritated with people who keep telling us to just let   the pain of our pasts go. Isn't the healing process different for everyone?

Jon: "The prophet Jeremiah prayed for deliverance from pain and despair. He cried out, 'Heal me, O LORD, and I shall be healed; save me, and I shall be saved, for you are my praise' (Jer. 17:14). What was Jeremiah's process? He turned to the Lord and affirmed that his healing would come as surely as his salvation. It is likely that the healing process is different for everyone. But for Jeremiah, there simply wasn't enough room for considering the pain of his past while in the midst of his faith and praise."

Anna: "The grieving process is personal and needs compassion and authentic exploration. Acknowledging one's afflictions but not allowing them to consume one's thoughts, negatively affect one's behaviors, or skew one's identity and future hopes within the moment can be humanly challenging. To attempt to thrive where one has no peace or little support is frustrating, discouraging, and downright lonely. One's hardships may cause psychological torment and prop the open door for demonic forces to abide when not properly discerned and addressed. Abuse's aftermath manipulates one's mind, can leave one's emotional state in shambles, and must be taken seriously, so that self-medicating escape is not sought. God alone fully understands what one has withstood, seek him for he is one's ultimate comforter."

Question One Hundred And Eleven
April 21st

To cope in this life, some of us have developed multiple personalities. Is this sinful?

Jon: "If we willingly assume a personality we know is not our own, we lie to others and to ourselves. Verses rebuking falsehood and lying abound in God's Word. For example, Colossians 3:9 says, 'Do not lie to one another, seeing that you have put off the old self with its practices.' When we place our faith in Christ we are created anew. The old self who depended on coping mechanisms is replaced with the new self who depends solely on God for refuge and strength and deliverance. One personality devoted to the Lord is worth infinitely more than a million personalities devoted to anything else."

Anna: "During and after severe trauma, to cope, one creates tactics to survive in attempts to escape suffering and gain control of one's reality. Within Dissociative Identity Disorder, one's being is completely fragmented, which manifests a deficiency to combine distinctly complex facets of one's self functionally. This differs from having a conscious alter ego or persona. When enduring repeated, horrific events, perplexing personality characteristics arise to weather hell, which is uniquely complicated but not sinful in and of itself. As human beings, when faced with opposition or evil, there are formidable truths to overcome that affect one's sensibility and behaviors interdependent upon one's consciousness, perceptions, and memories. When aspects of one's personality causes immorality or deliberate autonomy from God, sin then emerges."

Question One Hundred And Twelve
April 22nd

Is it good and cleansing for our souls, for our minds, emotions, and wills, to shed tears?

Jon: "Lazarus, the brother of Mary and Martha, had died. Distraught, the sisters sent for Jesus. Upon his arrival, he found friends and family consoling the sisters. All were weeping. Deeply moved in his spirit and greatly troubled, Jesus wept with them (John 11:33-35). Now, Jesus—being God in his divine nature—only did what man ought to do. In other words, he only did what is morally right or good. Therefore, if Jesus shed tears, it is good that we shed tears at the appropriate time."

Anna: "Shedding one's tears manifest a purging process that allows for the release of one's deepest emotions that cleanses and validates the soul of one's experiences. Tear ducts were masterfully created to protect one's sight and to aid the expression of one's innermost being. Not only are tears essential for one's health, but are truly fascinating in regards to their intricacy. When one cries, a distinct message is conveyed. It is a powerful form of communication that yearns for deep understanding and reciprocation. The Bible graciously shares that Jesus shed tears: God in human form, who knew what was to come, intensely broke down when he walked the earth. Knowing this, then how much more might we release tears and weep to grieve and survive this life?"

Question One Hundred And Thirteen
April 23rd

For many of us, if someone does something kind for us, we feel like we owe them the world, that we must give all of ourselves away to them. How do we find balance here?

Jon: "1 John 3:16 says, 'By this we know love, that he laid down his life for us, and we ought to lay down our lives for the brothers.' So we do give everything we can for others. But what is the reason we give? It's not because others did something for us first, but because Jesus has already done everything for us. We give our lives for others *because* Jesus gave his life for ours. Balance in giving comes when God is the focus of giving."

Anna: "Thankfulness and behavioral reciprocation to show generosity or mutual respect, when genuine, solidifies one's experience and appreciation toward an exchange. When not given the safety and security one needs to feel validated, valuable, or special, it is common for one to latch on to what is perceived as out of the ordinary when indeed it is *not* extraordinary. Blindly clinging to anyone's and everyone's positive behaviors is codependence at work. Humankind was created with a burning need for love, and deciphering between sound desire and deceptive desperation will bring more self-awareness and balance to one's thoughts, emotions, and behaviors. One's devotion belongs to Jesus and personal and relational equality is obtained through manifesting God's love, his attributes, and stabilizing Spirit."

Question One Hundred And Fourteen
April 24th

Why are a lot of adults who were abused as children addicted to toxic people?

Jon: "Many times Jesus says that while Christians are *in* the world, they are not to be *of* the world (see John 15:19, 17:14). Jesus wouldn't repeat this reality if it weren't a great threat to believers. In other words, it is incredibly easy for someone to become influenced by worldly toxins. Our frail and finite condition as humans only compounds the problem. In Christ, however, we have an appropriate person to whom we may devote ourselves. Christ will never toxify our lives; he will only purify them."

Anna: "Abuse stirs into psychological disarray the concept of what healthy relationships are. When toxicity surrounds families, it is difficult to differentiate between what one receives and what one truly deserves. The cycles birthed are not only addictive but can be so fixed into one's psyche and beliefs that its remnants will be replicated and played out in many aspects of one's life. When toxic relationship patterns are modeled from a young age, there is an innate pull to desire the familiar correlated to a twisted internal dialogue and worldly perspective. Toxic spirits are like wolves hunting for the bruised and broken to prey upon, until nothing is left to devour. Toxicity taints and exudes an evil stench that gravely needs holy fragrance. It is damaging, and only God's goodness can truly vanquish it."

Question One Hundred And Fifteen
April 25th

What is resilience?

Jon: "Resilience is enduring hardship without succumbing to it. 2 Corinthians 4:8-9 puts it this way: 'We are afflicted in every way, but not crushed; perplexed, but not driven to despair; persecuted, but not forsaken; struck down, but not destroyed…' And this is not the result of our own strength, but the result of God's strength working through us. It is the power of Christ's resurrection that resurrects us time after time from the hardships we experience. It is Christ's resilience to sin, destruction, and death that energizes our resilience to the very same."

Anna: "Having the will to redeem one's momentum after affliction or adversity is an admirable and inspiring strength to have. The courage to surmount one's obstacles, no matter the emotional and psychological beating, takes a fighting and tenacious soul. The world's nature will undoubtedly attempt to destroy one's innermost self, attitude, dreams, and hope. A fundamental understanding of permanence, the distinction between what is temporary and long lasting, is key to resiliency. To not give up and to keep contending under trying and abusive circumstances demonstrates one's determination and application of self-belief and purpose. Rediscovering and standing firm in one's true identity and striving for something greater is a gift from God whose existence and love is overflowing and eternal."

Question One Hundred And Sixteen
April 26th

Is it true that if we smile even when we don't feel like it, smiling nonetheless will lift our spirits?

Jon: "The Bible says that if we make a practice of thinking about whatever is true, honorable, just, pure, lovely, commendable, excellent, and worthy of praise, 'the God of peace will be with you' (Phil. 4:9). While doing so may provoke a smile, there is a deeper truth here, namely, that contentment must be cultivated. It's not easy to constantly be aware of our thoughts while directing them toward virtuous realities. But a content spirit is only wrought in this way—slowly and deliberately."

Anna: "Incongruence with one's thoughts, emotional state, and behaviors is inauthentic and masks what is truly happening. Depending upon the problem's severity and weight of one's emotions, smiling may or may not help. Have you been sad, and then someone cracks a joke, and suddenly things are not so hopeless? This is a beautiful reminder that faith exists within sorrow. When one's depression perceives no way out, attempting to smile would appear almost pointless, possibly offensive, and could harmfully minimize one's pain. Wearing an emotional façade is lonely, deceptive, and inhibits others to truly connect with and support the one in emotional disguise. Smiling can uplift one's soul, but continual concealment of one's true self will hinder God-given relationships and psychological, emotional, and spiritual development."

Question One Hundred And Seventeen
April 27th

Some believe that the God of the Old Testament possesses the same characteristics that our abusers did: wrathfulness, vengefulness, and murderousness. Isn't God a god of love?

Jon: "The Old and New Testaments separate the Bible into sections, not God into gods. Scripture says God is 'the same yesterday and today and forever' (Heb. 13:8) and in him, 'there is no variation or shadow due to change' (Jas. 1:17). People change. God doesn't. Neither does his perfect upholding of justice, which compels him to enact punishment on the wicked—including those who abuse the innocent. But God is simultaneously compelled by his love to provide opportunity for salvation: 'As I live, declares the Lord GOD, I have no pleasure in the death of the wicked, but that the wicked turn from his way and live; turn back, turn back from your evil ways, for why will you die…?' (Ez. 33:11)."

Anna: "A definite track record of complete holiness distinguishes God from any human being. An abuser is not justified for vindictiveness yet their denial persists. God is not spiteful; he hates immorality, but he does not hate the one who is immoral. His character is never changing and his existence is never-ending. He is fair and consistently implements his wrath against evil, dysfunctional mentalities and hypocrisy, and yet he is still a God of mercy, grace, and forgiveness. God is a loving God and he cannot be anything other than who he perfectly is: love."

Question One Hundred And Eighteen
April 28th

What is *unconditional* love?

Jon: "Perfect love is personified in God. The Bible says, 'God is love' (1 John 4:16). It is not that *love* is God, but that *God* is love. In other words, it is his nature to express perfect love at all times. This love has existed within the Trinity since before the foundation of the world (see John 17:24), and it will exist for all eternity. This is cause for great joy. For, although we have witnessed this love in Jesus' sacrifice of his life for ours, in heaven we will be unhindered by worldly obstacles to experience God's infinite love for all eternity."

Anna: "To embody and deliver unconditional love is truly a conscious decision that permeates through one's heart. Love's manifestations attach to different senses, emotions, and experiences. Proven love requires self-sacrifice, compassion, empathy, patience, esteeming others, and utilizes and exemplifies many other qualities and traits that are spirit-driven. Absolute love does not sway depending upon the moment, person, or behaviors. When love is irrefutable, this does not mean one is to allow others to trample upon, use, chew up or spit out what one has undeniably given or offered up. Love defends because it deeply values. When adoration and devotion coexist within one's experience, security and loyalty strengthen. Unconditional love materializes and epitomizes God's divine purpose for humankind to coexist with him for eternity."

Question One Hundred And Nineteen
April 29th

Some of us who were sexually molested when we were children grew up preferring same-sex relationships. Are we going to hell?

Jon: "Absolutely not. Scripture says, 'Whoever believes in the Son has eternal life; whoever does not obey the Son shall not see life, but the wrath of God remains on him' (John 3:36). In other words, only those who do not place their faith in Jesus Christ do not inherit eternal life. While it is true that sin of any kind is *condemnable* before an infinitely holy and just God (Rom 6:23), it is also true that sin of any kind is *pardonable* through and only through faith in Jesus Christ."

Anna: "What molesters generate within the souls of their targets is deep, controversial, and immersed with abysmal consequences. Molestation has difficult-to-understand psychological and spiritual effects that reach beyond human comprehensions. The acts of homosexuality bring forth such disputation unlike any other biblical issue because it attacks one's perceived sense of soul-identity, which the devil has used for his malicious advantage. No matter the lifestyle one has indulged in, those who truly believe in Jesus will be preserved. Being a Christian does not mean one is excused from the ramifications of free will, yet forgiveness and salvation are truly found in Christ. When repentance through God's love is experienced, righteous intention through one's actions, not perfection, will follow."

Question One Hundred And Twenty
April 30th

Do we have the right to expect others to make us feel good about ourselves?

Jon: "Jesus said that the second-greatest commandment is to love your neighbor as yourself (see Mat. 22:39). In this sense, insofar as others ought to follow the teachings of Jesus, they ought to love us. Ideally, we love others as much as we desire to be loved by others—as they do the same. But we understand that people are finite and prone to miss the mark (see Rom. 3:23). Knowing this, we are prepared for those times when others do not love us as they should."

Anna: "Verbalizing one's needs instead of placing unreachable expectations upon others is a vital part of establishing healthy communication. Assuming others can mind-read is unfair, and it forces the relationship dynamics to bear a heavy disadvantage. Setting boundaries early on so that both parties are aware of what is expected is critical to building trust and imperative toward the development of communication. It is fair and appropriate to desire considerate treatment, but it will not always occur. One's thoughts and emotions depend highly upon one's belief system. Attempting to control another's behaviors is simply disrespectful. Own the authority one has over what one thinks about and how one treats others. When loved ones let you down or hurt you, remember: God has proven himself through his Son's sacrifice to legitimize his love, your worth, and your eternal place in his heavenly kingdom."

Question One Hundred And Twenty-One
May 1st

For many of us growing up, there were people around us who simply turned a blind eye to the abuse: the bruises, the broken bones, the bloodied lips. The screams. How do we behave toward these people if they are still a part of our lives?

Jon: "God implores human beings to '... do good; seek justice, correct oppression; bring justice to the fatherless...' (Isa. 1:17). We have a responsibility to minister to the well-being of those around us. However, humankind is sinful (Rom. 3:23) and therefore susceptible to cowardice and the inability to discern the right course of action. Remember, when Jesus was marred 'beyond human semblance' (Isa. 52:14), slandered, tortured, and crucified, he said, 'Father, forgive them, for they know not what they do' (Luke 23:34)."

Anna: "One's values, convictions, and motives set the framework as to why one takes action or not. A blind eye toward injustice often comes from selfishness. What is black or white to one may be gray to another. One's behavioral system is directly connected to one's mindset. Others' choices can be manipulated, but ultimately one opts to act. When others' actions or lack thereof do not align with one's morals and have profoundly influenced one's life, what does one do? Relying on God's Spirit, grieve, possibly confront, rebuild, and heal the best one can. Forgiveness, acceptance, and hope promote healing, decrease burdensome emotions, and send a powerful message to one's abuser: with God one will persevere and overcome."

Question One Hundred And Twenty-Two
May 2nd

Some of us, even when we are told that we are wonderful and caring people, just do not see these attributes in ourselves. Indeed, we could have spent our whole lives caring for the poor but never have felt a sense of doing enough. How can we learn to accept and witness the goodness in ourselves?

Jon: "James 1:17 says, 'Every good gift and every perfect gift is from above, coming down from the Father of lights...' So it is not that *we* produce good, but that God produces good *through* us. We truly are wonderful then, not because of anything we do, but because the God of the universe chooses to use us as instruments of goodness. We are literally divine conduits of God's love and generosity. Simply being that conduit is the greatest gift we can give."

Anna: "One's core belief system is deeply connected to one's experiences with their primary caregivers. Once one is conscious of held self-misconceptions and why, what one needs is to rediscover their beliefs, identity, worth, and shift one's perspectives. Until one understands that the ability to identify, acknowledge, challenge, and change one's destructive cognitions comes from within, one will not have increased self-awareness or purpose. Goodness and human nature coexist through love, faith, and salvation. The Holy Spirit indwells the believer, and because of God's righteousness that exudes from his perfection and power, from him is where one's virtue extends."

Question One Hundred And Twenty-Three
May 3rd

This world could certainly use more laughter. Do you think that God has a sense of humor?

Jon: "Since we have been made in his image, and have the ability to perceive and express humor, it would seem that God has the same ability. Indeed, Scripture says God literally laughs at the wicked (Ps. 37:13, 59:8) and those who would try to injure him (Job 41:29). However, Ephesians 5:4 insists that we refrain from 'crude joking' that might offend or injure. The sorrowful take heart in Jesus' promise, 'Blessed are you who weep now, for you shall laugh'(Luke 6:21)."

Anna: "Not only do humor, laughter, and joy positively affect one's mental, emotional, and physical state, they help one unwind, rejuvenate, and break down walls one has built for self-protection. Laughter is a blessing to the spirit and soul. Laughter can help heal one's psyche and create an escape from what is burdensome in life. Humor can be key in changing the course of a tragic day and laughter can make a bitter moment sweet. Laughing releases natural chemicals in the brain to promote stimulation, pleasure, and peace. Therefore, on all levels, mind, body, and spirit, laughing is essential for one's health. God so graciously allows humankind to experience and understand playfulness, its influence, and purpose; so, with deductive reasoning, the conclusion would appear to be that God's sense of humor would profoundly trump humankind's limits, expectations, and imagination."

Question One Hundred And Twenty-Four
May 4th

Will not forgiving others prevent the Holy Spirit's power from healing our souls?

Jon: "Sin keeps us from God (see Isa. 59:2). And we sin. The greatest healing we need from God therefore is his forgiveness of our sins. Jesus said, 'but if you do not forgive others their trespasses, neither will your Father forgive your trespasses' (Mat. 6:15). Notice that we cannot separate our forgiveness toward others and God's forgiveness toward us. So we can think of forgiving others not as a loss, but a gain. That is, when we forgive others we make the way clear for God to forgive us. To forgive is to gain."

Anna: "When one has an unforgiving nature, it undoubtedly affects their entire being. An attitude and demeanor of anger, bitterness, self-righteousness or hate only corrupts one's mind and sends a negative message to the transgressor. When one does not forgive, psychological and emotional limits are not only placed on that person and relationship, but restraints are set on one's personal growth and spiritual formation. Relational progress can mirror interpersonal healing from within. The Holy Spirit will move in the midst of an unforgiving person because when one is feeble, God's power still soars. One's broken spirit or hard-hearted character can and will be used to teach oneself and others to love and glorify God, yet there are natural repercussions to being merciless and unforgiving."

Question One Hundred And Twenty-Five
May 5th

Some of us get upset when people don't notice us or want to hide when they do. Can you help us in this regard?

Jon: "1 Thessalonians 2:4 says we should seek 'not to please man, but to please God who tests our hearts.' Now, this does not mean that we consider others irrelevant. In fact, God commands us to love others (see Mat. 22:38-39). So what does it mean? It means that if our concern is focused on how God sees us, we will be less concerned with how others see us. In other words, *fully* focusing on God will help us *appropriately* focus on others."

Anna: "Ambivalence within relationships grows when one's needs are not securely met. Poor modeling pushes a child to develop distorted tactics due to stress, anxiety, and uncertainty as to how their emotions will be handled. This child will often grow up creating hypersensitivities toward other people's moods and behaviors. As an adult, this can turn into reliance upon others, unrealistic expectations, emotional resistances, anger, or self-blame for relationship complications and failures. Insecurities continue to be cultivated when one's emotional pattern is to irrationally make what is small catastrophic through a subconscious or conscious means of receiving love and attention. God's healing through his Word will increase one's self-worth, personal freedom, and emotional stability when self-awareness through his truths are sincerely sought."

Question One Hundred And Twenty-Six
May 6th

Is it true that there are certain types of people who can uplift other people's spirits?

Jon: "Tychicus was sent by the apostle Paul to 'encourage' the hearts of the Ephesian and Colossian churches (see Eph. 6:22; Col. 4:8). In Acts 4, the apostles give one disciple a nickname which means 'son of encouragement' (Acts 4:36). Romans 12:8 even suggests that *encouragement* may be a spiritual gift the Holy Spirit grants to some. While there are some individuals who seem to excel in encouraging others, Scripture affirms that we may all encourage one another by reminding each other of the hope we have in Jesus Christ (see 1 Thes. 4:13-18)."

Anna: "Uplifting others is truly a God-breathed gift and an ability that lies deep within one's heart, soul, and is ignited by one's spirit. One can reassure anyone through one's attitude, demeanor, words, and behaviors. Through honor, encouragement, exhortation, and psychological, emotional, and spirit-driven inspiration, one's life can truly strengthen and transform. Encouragement waters one's intrinsic needs and one's spiritual seeds can become revitalized. God's Holy Spirit elevates the believer to aspire to be great but not as the world would see it. To be impactful in God's eyes is to uplift the broken-spirited, to deliver his good news, and to willfully brighten one's light for the glorification of his present and future kingdom."

Question One Hundred And Twenty-Seven
May 7th

Do you both believe that the truth does hurt?

Jon: "Truth is what accurately corresponds with reality. Sometimes information about reality can be off-putting or painful to hear. However, Jesus said, 'and you will know the truth, and the truth will set you free' (John 8:32). Regardless of how it affects us, all truth is liberating. It frees us from the bondage of ignorance. For many, the knowledge that we are sinners in need of salvation through faith in Jesus is off-putting. Nevertheless, that truth gives us the opportunity to be liberated not only from ignorance, but also from that which keeps us from God."

Anna: "The truth does not always cause pain, but it most definitely can, depending upon the messenger's intent and the recipient's understanding and openness. At times, the truth or differing perspectives can be shocking, difficult, and unpleasant to swallow. Nevertheless, the truth can also be freeing and heartwarming, and can bring sustenance to one's soul when truly put into sound perspective. In order to thrive, one must be established in authenticity in regards to where one has been, where one currently stands, and where one desires to be. Reliant upon one's approach, the truth can be delivered with an awareness of one's motives to lessen the blow, because words can be extremely effective. God's truth, though eye-opening, weighted, and vast, ultimately brings healing, contentment, and peace to the believer."

Question One Hundred And Twenty-Eight
May 8th

Why do some of us achieve a greater sense of our identity from Satan rather than from Christ?

Jon: "1 John 3:10 says, 'By this it is evident who are the children of God, and who are the children of the devil: whoever does not practice righteousness is not of God, nor is the one who does not love his brother.' Hatred and evil works are the trademarks of one who identifies with Satan. So long as we continue in these, we will remain in him. The good news of Romans 11 is that even though we may now belong to the root of Satan, God has the power to cut us off from it and graft us into his own. Belief in Christ assures us his love, his righteousness, and his identity."

Anna: "Certain people cling to Satan's darkness because they identify with being bad, tainted, forgotten, and have been pushed too far; thus, a psychological connection to something delusively different transpires. This notion makes one feel unique, powerful, and can feed one's delusional god-like persona. When a child is treated sadistically, naturally an adverse reaction occurs because a premature soul cannot handle the torment. Liberation, when disassociated with truth, is often sought through destructive beliefs and behavioral patterns. The irony is that Satan is abusive; his very nature opposes one's identity because true deliverance is God-breathed. It is not manmade, nor concocted from an opposition to what is good."

Question One Hundred And Twenty-Nine
May 9th

Will you please explain what it means to feel a healthy guilt?

Jon: "1 John 1:9 says, 'If we confess our sins, he is faithful and just to forgive us our sins and to cleanse us from all unright-eousness.' We see at least four steps here for handling guilt. First, we make a genuine admission of wrongdoing. Second, we direct that admission toward God. Here is where it gets interesting: The third step is to affirm within that God *has* forgiven us of that wrongdoing. And the final step is to affirm that God *has* cleansed and restored us."

Anna: "Comprehending the weight of one's thoughts, words, beliefs, and actions and having an upright conviction can catapult one into lasting transformation. A genuine sense of remorse, a realistic expectation of one's capacities, being humble yet graciously regarding one's flawed nature, is imperative for self-efficacy and authentic growth. Minimal self-awareness with a lack of conscience enables psychological confusion, emotional anguish, and spiritual devastation. Remorse linked to one's destructive behaviors may be helpful, whereas shame can be deceptively planted within one's soul. Guilt derives from rebellion and a divine boundary system and is an indicator either that one is not abiding within God's will or deeply believing the enemies' lies: that one is unworthy and deserved the abuse. Jesus died for humankind's sins, so let go of your shame, address your convictions, repent of your immoralities, and embrace God's grace, forgiveness, and love."

Question One Hundred And Thirty
May 10th

Why do people make such a big deal about self-care: clothes, makeup, and white teeth? A lot of us were not taught these things, and they are not for us.

Jon: "Scripture says that we are to honor God with our bodies because they are where his Holy Spirit resides (see 1 Cor. 6:19-20). We treat our bodies not as our own, but as God's. In other words, we are stewards of the bodies God has given us. This means that we must avoid negatively affecting our bodies as we pursue positively affecting them. Although self-care is important, we don't want to cross over into sinful indulgence or hedonism. Careful inspection of one's priorities, Scripture reading, and prayer are necessary to find where this line is."

Anna: "Vanity, self-obsession, and self-absorption are catalysts for varying degrees of identity distortion. When one's outer appearance is the sole qualifier to one's worth, deep reflection and confrontation of one's core beliefs need to be addressed. On the other hand, when one's body and mind are valued, appreciated, and taken care of, it can be evidence of one's inmost convictions to show one's utmost respect for one's body, one's temple. Self-care is extremely important and is an outer representation of one's soul, but overcompensation and pressure to meet unreachable worldly standards can lead to false insecurities, perceived inadequacies, and continual self-demoralization. God's love is not superficial; he loves perfectly, and values one's heart."

Question One Hundred And Thirty-One
May 11th

It is impossible to avoid negative people. How can we feel less disturbed by them?

Jon: "Matthew 12:34-35 says, 'For out of the abundance of the heart the mouth speaks. The good person out of his good treasure brings forth good, and the evil person out of his evil treasure brings forth evil.' A perpetually negative attitude is a good indicator that Christ is not fully occupying one's heart. For, a heart full of Christ will overflow out of the mouth. We ought to feel grieved and burdened for those who do not know Christ's fullness. They are in great need of our prayer and patient witnessing of the gospel."

Anna: "When grounded in one's true identity, clarity and hope equips one to elude or endure negativity. Nevertheless, perpetual skepticism can suck the life out of anyone if given the authority to do so. Doubt and frustration can spread like a virus and infect others. It takes wisdom and strength to not become ensnared by displeasure's allure. Negativity manifests from painful experiences and uncomfortable emotions and it can dilute one's state of mind, which prompts one's words and actions. To have a pessimistic outlook and to adversely affect others, one's soul is truly unsettled. Good and evil forces exist, and one or the other influences everyone's behaviors. Being disturbed or angry at evil is just, but the mismanagement of one's resentment can breed animosity and unrighteous behaviors, which is not of God."

Question One Hundred And Thirty-Two
May 12th

When some of us were very young, child molesters did unconscionable things to our bodies. As a result, bodily experiences that would normally be pleasurable are painful. Please, does a response even exist for this?

Jon: "Jesus says to our abusers, 'Truly, I say to you, as you did it to one of the least of these my brothers, you did it to me' (Mat. 25:40). Great honor is given to the greatly afflicted here. As intimate as our afflictions are to us, they are so intimate to Jesus. In the moment we were afflicted, he was simultaneously afflicted. Our loss of pleasure is Jesus' loss of pleasure. Our pain is Jesus' pain. And now, Jesus' resurrection to new life is our resurrection to new life. His restoration is our restoration."

Anna: "Sexual acts were intended to be enjoyable, within marriage, between two consenting adults. When traumatic experiences rob and violate one's safety, one's mind and body will react. A strong correlation between trauma, the psyche, and physiological responses coincide to validate, project, and re-create one's hurtful experiences. To minimize reliving horrific memories, grieving and spiritual cleansing must transpire. Sexual pleasure may seem distant but can be reached when one believes they are loved, worthy, safe, accepted, and unrestrained to be their authentic self. When one is ready to allow God to restore one's negative perceptions of sex and intimacy within his will, his power, grace, and comfort can counter one's painful experiences."

Question One Hundred And Thirty-Three
May 13th

Oh so many of us love to play the victim, experiencing crises and blaming them on everyone else except ourselves. How can we stop playing the victim?

Jon: "1 Peter 2:24 says of Jesus, 'He himself bore our sins in his body on the tree, that we might die to sin and live to righteousness. By his wounds you have been healed.' Jesus literally endured the punishment we deserved for our sins. Not only for our sins, however, 'but also for the sins of the whole world' (1 John 2:2). Whatever punishment for sin has been deserved by all people throughout history, Jesus bore. The depth of his suffering is unfathomable. It becomes difficult to feign victimization when confronted by Jesus' undeserved, deadly real, and unfathomably painful victimization."

Anna: "An abused child is a defenseless victim exposed to evil's disorder, and reliving this crises or dramatizing reality is not uncommon. Needing to make sense of or displace fault onto another for the cause of chaos within one's soul helps one to defend against the dysfunction. Pleading naiveté for one's current actions, because of the past, is not justification for absolving one of consequences. As awareness increases, so does one's accountability. Acknowledge the past, accept what is, do what one truly can, and choose to live within one's divine identity. Jesus was a blameless victim who humbly and steadfastly carried humankind's sins; use what was evil to victoriously help oneself and others."

Question One Hundred And Thirty-Four
May 14th

What is grief?

Jon: "Grief is an emotion of deep sorrow common to all people, including God the Father (see Gen. 6:6), the Son (see John 11:33, 35), and the Holy Spirit (see Eph. 4:30). The psalmist expresses his grief: 'Be gracious to me, O LORD, for I am in distress; my eye is wasted from grief; my soul and my body also' (Ps. 31:9). Notice that grief penetrates one's whole being. It affects not only the soul, but the body and the senses as well. But to all those in Christ the promise is given, 'You will be sorrowful, but your sorrow will turn into joy' (John 16:20)."

Anna: "When grieving, one's soul and spirit aches for what has been lost. Mourning personal anguish can make it difficult to function. Sorrow burdens one's will and tests one's beliefs, mentality, and endurance. Many different kinds of loss that vary in individual importance affect one's grief. When disappointment and unexpected tragedy lead to the perceived ruin of one's life, different emotional responses ensue dependent upon one's psychological, emotional, and spiritual state. A sudden loss will affect one distinctively than when loss is foreseen and prepared for. Bereavement is sad no matter how it comes about, but different factors affect one's grieving process and outcome. God knows all and consummately comprehends one's afflictions. Wholeheartedly elect to depend on him first to bear the calamities of life."

Question One Hundred And Thirty-Five
May 15th

How do we express our grief in a healthy way?

Jon: "Grief will come to all of us. And sometimes, it comes relentlessly. In other words, grief can be impossible to manage directly. But Scripture shows us how to manage our grief indirectly. The apostle Paul said that when he was sorrowful he would simultaneously rejoice. He was 'sorrowful, yet always rejoicing' (2 Cor. 6:10). We don't work to stop grieving; we work to start rejoicing. One of the deepest comforts we can experience as human beings can only come by rejoicing in God through our suffering."

Anna: "The grieving process can be highly personal, deeply complicated, and considerably circumstantial. Articulating one's sufferings to a caring and safe presence will help one mourn. In times of darkness, one can feel hopeless and completely alone, so it is critical to seek support. Isolating oneself or suppressing one's true thoughts and feelings can cause an illusory existence that will enable more personal and relational troubles. Healthy expressions of grief can look and be experienced quite differently. Encouragingly, this process can be individualized to help one reveal deep pains and frustrations to bring forth relief and personal reinforcement. One desperately needing counseling to treat depression and self-confinement differs from one who simply requires some solitude to weep. Meditating upon God's Word and his promises are critical for one's soul and spirit. Remember, you were created to fellowship with believers for comfort, encouragement, and support."

Question One Hundred And Thirty-Six
May 16th

A lot of us are told that we should be more tolerant of others. What is tolerance?

Jon: "Ephesians 4:2-3 says we are to treat one another 'with all humility and gentleness, with patience, bearing with one another in love, eager to maintain the unity of the Spirit in the bond of peace.' This does not mean we have to give up our opinion. This does not mean we have to adopt someone else's opinion. Tolerance means we don't hate those who disagree with us. It means we treat others with the dignity and respect one created in the image of God deserves."

Anna: "Having the capacity and intention to treat others with dignity despite their personal convictions or behaviors, in essence, is the basis for tolerance. Yet, respecting someone does not mean one is continually exposed to destructive or abusive behaviors. To carelessly empower what is wrong, or yield consciously to the inappropriateness or projections of another's false beliefs, to comply because it is the norm or what the majority believes despite one's convictions, is not tolerance—it is conformity rooted in fickleness. Accommodation to not disrupt perceived harmony or minimize another's dysfunction is not admirable, it is enabling. One can be tolerant in love while disagreeing with and not condoning another's harmful decisions. As a Christian, a believer in Jesus Christ, one's allegiance is to God; stand firmly upon his Word, with confidence, while spiritually driven in love."

Question One Hundred And Thirty-Seven
May 17th

Is it true that if we know ourselves better then we will understand others more?

Jon: "Paul tells young Timothy, 'Keep a close watch on yourself and on the teaching. Persist in this, for by so doing you will save both yourself and your hearers' (1 Tim. 4:16). There are two practices that yield the best results for ourselves and for others: holiness and love for God's Word. If we persist in these, we will not only preserve our relationship with God, but others' as well. In other words, the more God's light shines in our lives, the more it will shine into the lives of those around us."

Anna: "It takes a conscious effort to put oneself in another's shoes, to genuinely attempt to understand their position, feelings, and state of mind. When one dives into emotional depths to explore one's innermost parts, clarity can emerge out of the murkiness of any situation. Taking the time to connect the whys of one's discontentment, one's family dynamics, the childhood traumas or lack thereof will help in comprehending why one has evolved into who they are. If more people transferred this process of conceptualization toward others, empathy and tolerance would blossom more effortlessly and the world would be a much safer and loving place. Through one's relationship with Jesus, compassion and wisdom will flow from God's Holy Spirit, and manifest within oneself onto others through one's supernaturally influenced qualities and behaviors."

Question One Hundred And Thirty-Eight
May 18th

Some of us curse the name of the Lord for what he has permitted to happen to us! Why shouldn't we?

Jon: "We should be honest with God. Proverbs 3:6 says, 'In all your ways acknowledge him, and he will make straight your paths.' When we turn to the Lord, whether in anger or love, he hears us (see Ps. 34:4). And he wants to hear us because he loves us (see 1 John 4:19). Knowing he loves us, we are inspired to obey his command to not curse him (see Ex. 20:7). No matter how much they curse his name, God will never cease to love and forgive his children (see Ps. 57:10; 1 John 1:9)."

Anna: "Anger for having one's human rights abused and violated is fitting and justified. To heal, one needs to acknowledge the pain and grieve one's heinous experiences. Hatred directed toward the evil one has faced and the hold it has had on one's mind and will is not wrong. Having the discernment to distinguish between the roots of others' actions in correlation to one's purpose is maturity and divine wisdom. Worldly immorality is consistent with biblical prophecies. To curse God is to surely bane oneself. Denouncing the Lord's name sanctions spiritual disconnection but also brings psychological, emotional, and supernatural torment upon oneself. God's faithfulness to heal one's animosity and the past's bondage for one's sake is bottomless; God's love exists eternally. God is not the enemy, Satan is."

Question One Hundred And Thirty-Nine
May 19th

Childhood trauma has left many of us bitter and not wanting to set a day aside to worship God. What's the point?

Jon: "No one worships nothing. We all worship something. And whatever we worship becomes our god. So the point is to worship the right thing. Money, self, power, and material objects are not worthy of worship. Only God is. 'For,' says the psalmist, 'great is the LORD, and greatly to be praised; he is to be feared above all gods' (Ps. 96:4). Because God has created us and sustains us and our world in being, he deserves not only one day per week of worship, but a lifetime (see Col. 3:17; Ex. 20:8-11)."

Anna: "One's childhood trauma, though unfair and wrong, was due to an abuser's destructive behaviors, not because God did not care. One's bitterness and pain needs healing from the Creator himself for one to find peace. True worship is sacrificial, a spiritual cleansing, and a deep acknowledgment of what has been done for humankind. Abuse affects one's perceptions and when psychological and emotional turmoil becomes bondage, this can turn into distaste for God and will affect one's spirit. Worshiping God acknowledges him and his love for you, and allows one to experience his essence through a supernatural connection. Acting in faith despite one's past and pain reflects a humble heart and a deep understanding of one's worth."

Question One Hundred And Forty
May 20th

Yes. For some of us, the rage we feel inside has caused us to kill another. We most certainly can blame it on our childhood abuse. Can't we?

Jon: "Serious brain trauma may cause our cognitive faculties to not function properly. Some behaviors therefore may be the result of such trauma. However, 1 Corinthians 10:13 says, 'No temptation has overtaken you that is not common to man. God is faithful, and he will not let you be tempted beyond your ability, but with the temptation he will also provide the way of escape, that you may be able to endure it.' Unless our cognitive faculties have been adequately damaged, we are to blame for our sins (see Ex. 20:13). Yet forgiveness is always available through Christ (see 1 John 1:9)."

Anna: "The execution of a human life brings forth repercussions of its own no matter the reason or justification. To snap and displace one's pain and vengeance onto another so severely that they no longer have breath is abusive, and taking life into one's own hands. One can attribute their beliefs and mindset to the abuse one endured, but this does not mean one will be free from ramifications. Remember, awareness upholds accountability, and seeks out justice. Something to ponder: when one kills when in deep psychological and emotional distress, spiritual turmoil, where does the blame fully lie? God is just and he is one's final judge. Repent, because one is shamelessly loved."

Question One Hundred And Forty-One
May 21st

Some of us watched our parents commit adultery, and we followed in their footsteps. We feel as if we were (are) just doing what we were taught. We follow by example, right?

Jon: "1 John 4:1 says, 'Beloved, do not believe every spirit, but test the spirits to see whether they are from God…' Because there is so much falsehood in the world, we have to evaluate the sources from which we derive moral direction. We don't want to follow the direction of anything that leads us in the wrong moral direction. Fortunately, God's Word always leads us in the right moral direction (see Ps. 119:105). Always following God's will, Jesus Christ is the perfect example of whose footsteps we ought to follow."

Anna: "Immoral actions enable one's innate drives and kindle instant gratification without weighing one's conscience within the moment. One's rationale and cognitions distinguish between what one desires and needs. One's beliefs and internal code are attached to one's worldly examples of conduct whether appropriate or not. It takes less discipline within the moment to be morally unsuccessful, but the aftermath is definitely not easier or free from emotional, psychological, or physical pain. One's human experience is definitely vulnerable and highly susceptible to temptation. Without God's Holy Spirit, his divine direction, and conscious self-discipline and accountability, one will not truly have the upper hand on one's inherent desires and generational impositions."

Question One Hundred And Forty-Two
May 22nd

Many of us steal today, as we did when we were young, because we have no food or clothing. How else are we to survive?

Jon: "We sense that it is wrong to steal. This sense corresponds to God's command not to steal (see Ex. 20:15). How are we to survive without breaking this command? 2 Timothy 2:15 says, 'Do your best to present yourself to God as one approved, a worker who has no need to be ashamed, rightly handling the word of truth.' The Lord approves of the worker. In fact, this passage implies that working is one of the *best* ways we can obtain his approval. Work bestows not only honor, but a means to survive."

Anna: "Understanding one's mindset and motivation as to why one stole is crucial for one's moral awareness, self-forgiveness, and present and future hope. When one is hasty and cannot control oneself, then one may have a serious issue. However, when one is desperate to purely survive and is truly in need, then the psychological and behavioral implications genuinely change. Human beings were born with internal compasses that give life and conviction to one's experiences. When one steals, there are unique emotional and heartfelt consequences that can affect one's self-esteem and self-worth. One is to survive on their hardworking efforts, and upon others when truly dependent or in need. Depend upon God because he will supernaturally comfort when one does not have what one desires and needs."

Question One Hundred And Forty-Three
May 23rd

Most of us could use a miracle. Do you believe in miracles?

Jon: "Since God is all-powerful, he has the ability to manifest miracles in this world or to empower us to do so. In fact, there are over one hundred such miracles recorded in the Bible. Of these, Jesus performed about three dozen. And he said in John 14:12, '… whoever believes in me will also do the works that I do; and greater works than these will he do…' If you have been saved by grace through faith in Christ, you have experienced and been the benefactor of the greatest miracle possible: the redemption of a soul."

Anna: "Defying worldly limitations are inspired through a source. Miracles happen daily, and not always in the way one expects. They can take place anywhere, but are truly significant when experienced within one's mind, emotions, and willpower. One's essence can be miraculously transformed, and through one's dominating spirit, one can overcome the past and accomplish amazing things. A divine commissioner or phenomenon can be perceived to appear by chance, coincidentally, or be logically explained away, when in truth it was an ordained celestial being sent down to carry out goodness. This type of occurrence bewilders those who do not have faith. Disciples of Jesus experience God-breathed revelations, exude an emblematic light from within, and testify that the unexplainable can be elucidated by God, through his supernaturally written Word and miraculous Holy Spirit."

Question One Hundred And Forty-Four
May 24th

People tell a lot of us to listen to our intuitions. Is this sound advice?

Jon: "There may be instances where our intuition is guiding us [so to speak] away from a dangerous situation. 1 John 4:1 says, 'Beloved, do not believe every spirit, but test the spirits to see whether they are from God, for many false prophets have gone out into the world.' This probably applies to our more subtle intuitions than feeling in danger. But the point is that any of the feelings that influence the important decisions we make ought to be brought before God and his Word. If our intuitions concord with God's commands and aren't leading us into sin, we are justified in following them."

Anna: "Human intuition can be powerful, sharp or inaccurate, and can bring forth false assumptions about others. However, the motives, intentions, or ethics of an individual are important to weigh when based on factual occurrences. Being overly analytical to where misconceptions have been created in one's mind causes internal and external troubles. Partial and impaired insight will lead to having poor and erroneous judgment. Yes, one needs to be aware of and pay attention to their instincts, but do not just impulsively act upon them. When the Holy Spirit lies within, wisdom divinely unfolds, and deep truths are revealed through the mind and heart of the believer."

Question One Hundred And Forty-Five
May 25th

Some of us have shared our stories of abuse with people who we thought were our friends. Once we told them, we no longer heard from them. What did we do wrong?

Jon: "Some people can't handle truth. Jesus spoke many truths that turned away even the religious leaders of his day. And they would eventually kill him over those truths. Ephesians 4:25 says, 'Therefore, having put away falsehood, let each one of you speak the truth with his neighbor, for we are members one of another.' Notice it doesn't say to only speak *easy* truths. It says speak *the* truth. And this ought not separate us, but unite us as neighbors and members of the same body. Others' resistance to adhere to God's Word is no wrong of ours."

Anna: "Many are not equipped to constructively adjust to the complexities of reality. An empathetic being will not just abandon another because of one's childhood abuse. Now, if one's trauma causes chaos within one's current friendship, then a sincere confrontation of the unhealthy dynamics needs to be addressed, and boundaries established. Broken and misused trust replay inside the mind of the abused, and the rejection one feels for simply being who one is is abandonment. Sharing one's past and vulnerabilities is intimidating yet rewarding when non-judgment and understanding are conveyed. God knows everything one has been through and he loves completely despite it all; true awareness is remarkable because one will realize that with God, one is truly never alone."

Question One Hundred And Forty-Six
May 26th

Some of us who were abused as children feel the only way out of our pain is to abuse our own children. Can you help us to break this vicious cycle?

Jon: "If we believe that the abuse we suffered was wrong, then we believe that abusing others is wrong. And it is (Mat. 22:34-40). Knowing how terrible it feels to be abused motivates us to never abuse another. If we do abuse others, we affirm with our actions that it is okay for one person to abuse another. In other words, we show that our abusers did no wrong when they abused us. Even if we never had the opportunity to personally confront them, we can stand up to our abusers every time we refuse to abuse another."

Anna: "The projection of one's painful childhood is not one's way out. Admittance of one's abusive nature and the desire and will to stop one's misconduct must be authentic for change to occur. Seeking assistance to express the emotions one feels may alleviate one's psychological burdens and secrets, but this alone is not enough. Abuse is tragic and should be intolerable. Children are helpless, dependent, unsuspecting, and as one knows, will be seriously affected by abusive processes, words, and actions. One's abusive behaviors derive from one's deep-rooted pain, insecurities, desperately wanting control, and a perceived impulsiveness towards minimizing one's powerlessness. God's Spirit will transform one's willing soul, yet one must take accountability and action."

Question One Hundred And Forty-Seven
May 27th

The authority figures we experienced throughout our c hildhoods hurt us. Why should we respect authority now?

Jon: "We don't respect bad authority. We respect good authority. And God is infinitely good (see Ps. 25:8, 145:9). Therefore God deserves our infinite respect. Moreover, if God is perfectly good, then his Word is good (see 2 Sam. 22:31). So Scripture is authoritative as well. It deserves our respect. While we may respect other good sources of authority, God and his Word deserve our highest respect. This means that when other authorities don't comply with God and his Word, we don't comply with them (see Rom. 13:1-7)."

Anna: "Those privileged to have authority over another are not all bad. Yet, many do take advantage of their position, which is unfortunate in that what could be used as a platform for change is corrupted and perpetuates misery. When one has a lack of morality, self-respect, self-worth, and self-love, one stands on the precipice of self-war. Authentic respect toward others aligns with one's awareness, one's understanding of decency, and one's manifestations of a conscientious integrity and conviction of what is right. Respect for others, even when not deserved, is a reflection of one's heart, and a shining example of what wisdom and love truly are. When one esteems God's laws and others, one is demonstrating a devout reverence, is truly walking in humility, and is a beautiful reflection of Christ himself."

Question One Hundred And Forty-Eight
May 28th

Prayer is very foreign to some of us. How do we pray?

Jon: "We can think of prayer as sincere conversation with and only with God. Jesus suggests proper content for this conversation in Matthew 6:5-15. First, prayer acknowledges the supreme holiness of God. Second, prayer places God's will above our own. Third, in prayer we ask God to supply our daily needs. Fourth, in prayer we ask God to forgive our sins as we forgive those who have sinned against us. Finally, in prayer we ask for the strength to reject sin. When prayer is difficult, we have hope knowing that the Holy Spirit of God will intercede on our behalf (see Rom. 8:26)."

Anna: "Prayer is a reflection of one's faith, one's heart's desires, and without question is one of the most powerful gifts given to humanity. It personifies one's beliefs regarding miracles within the supernatural, and brings forth change that is extremely influential and beyond one's capabilities. When confessing one's past and present abuses, through one's faithful prayers one can receive mental, emotional, and physical healing. Victory succeeds through prayer and one's well-being is connected to faith's hope. To communicate with and petition God because one believes that he can do anything, that he wants to fulfill one's needs, is a phenomenal belief system to abide in. To seek God's will in Jesus' name, with a humble, sincere, and patient heart, is most definitely a beautiful place to start."

Question One Hundred And Forty-Nine
May 29th

Our five senses... seeing, tasting, hearing, smelling, and touching... all have remnants of our molesters coursing throughout them. How can we purify our fives senses of them?

Jon: "It may be that our senses are not fully purified until we reach heaven. But Jesus said, 'The thief comes only to steal and kill and destroy. I came that they may have life and have it abundantly' (John 10:10). Our abusers came to take away from us. Jesus came to give us more than we have. Even if our senses are tainted, God will always give us more. Through faith in Jesus Christ, we receive something greater even than our senses can perceive: eternal life and an intimate relationship with God the Father."

Anna: "Senses are vital toward one's functioning and quality of life, and inspire action and enticement into one's experiences. When one's innocence and physical body have been corrupted and exploited through sexual deviances, it is challenging to not let one be controlled or limited by these devastating traumas. When one's sexuality has been affixed to an abuser's inflictions through serious violations, deceptive beliefs become instilled deep within one's subconscious. An emotional, psychological, and spiritual purification, through a conscious effort with one's dependence upon a supernatural process, is pivotal for restoration. Through one's faith in Jesus is how one will truly transcend their negative earthly experiences; ask God for purification through his powerful Holy Spirit."

Question One Hundred And Fifty
May 30th

Do you believe that people need to suffer to become better people?

Jon: "1 Peter 2:21 says, 'For to this you have been called, because Christ also suffered for you, leaving you an example, so that you might follow in his steps.' Suffering is inevitable in this life. The difference for the believer — the *called* — is that their suffering causes them to be more like Jesus. In the way God brought the greatest good upon humanity through and only through what Jesus suffered, God will bring great good upon our lives through and only through what we suffer. If suffering is inevitable, more so is the good that God will bring through it."

Anna: "Adversity challenges one's resilience, persistence, and perseverance. Physical, emotional, or psychological torment can be used to build one's character and push one to live the life one was truly intended to lead. At times, it can be difficult to accept why God would allow abuse and oppression to exist. However, when suffering is due to one's poor decisions, the emotional realities of this can create inner complexities that are humbling to admit and overcome. When condemnation is awakened within one's psyche, shame and guilt override the fact that one is loved and was created for a profound purpose. Suffering shapes impactful souls but it also breaks the spirit of many. What truly makes one 'better' is to submissively allow God's Spirit to transform one's will to align with his."

Question One Hundred And Fifty-One
May 31st

What is codependency?

Jon: "The Bible largely presents our relationship to sin as codependent. We give ourselves to sin, and sin gives us destruction. In spite of this, we return to it over and over again. In fact, Scripture says we are slaves to sin (see John 8:34; Rom. 6:20; 2 Pet. 2:19). This is one reason why the gospel is called 'good news.' The good news is that Christ offers us freedom from the bondage of sin. The Son sets us free (John 8:36). So we are not codependent with, but dependent on Christ. We give ourselves to him, and he gives us eternal life."

Anna: "Codependents thrive in unhealthy relational systems. When a disproportionate need for emotional or psychological endorsement is quenched to establish one's worth, identity, or direction, one's perspective and intentions are misaligned, unhealthy, and misused. Enmeshment, which enables obscure boundaries, often unknowingly devalues personal growth and authentic connection. Codependent behaviors, which can be addictive, create a delusional world in which one perceives oneself to be all right, when underneath it all one is overwhelmingly insecure and internally malnourished. Within any relationship, codependent behaviors can cause division, confusion, and strife because discord develops out of manipulations, unfair motives, and enabling dysfunctional behavioral patterns. A blind dependency or extreme devotion to anyone or anything other than God is idolatry. Entrust oneself fully to God so that he can fulfill one's needs, because he is the only one who loves flawlessly."

Question One Hundred And Fifty-Two
June 1st

What does it mean to set spiritual and psychological boundaries?

Jon: "Before the elders, heads, judges, and officers of Israel Joshua stood. He was their leader, the successor of Moses. And he was about to die. In his parting speech he reminded Israel of the countless times God graciously and miraculously delivered them from oppression and exile. He said, '… choose this day whom you will serve… But as for me and my house, we will serve the LORD' (Josh. 24:15). Rejecting false gods, we set up spiritual boundaries when we choose to serve exclusively the One and Only God who has and is able to deliver us."

Anna: "Setting emotional boundaries, which is connected to one's spirituality, can be difficult to accomplish when one's childhood boundary system was nonexistent, blurred, or consistently infringed upon. One's worth and role within any relationship is crucial to recognize and cultivate, so as to maintain one's personal standard of care. When individual experiences and emotional expressions vary, consistency with relational expectations is needed, so the boundary line does not become internalized and then emotionally projected by the other. Without boundaries, violations will occur which perpetuate abusive tendencies, emotional manipulations, enmeshment, codependency, and the suppression of a flourishing self. Setting one's boundaries is to maintain personal protection, authentic connection, and reach relationship goals. Being faithfully yoked within God's spiritual boundary system will ignite optimal relationship preservation and blessing with others who do the same."

Question One Hundred And Fifty-Three
June 2nd

What is judgment?

Jon: "2 Corinthians 5:10 says, 'For we must all appear before the judgment seat of Christ, so that each one may receive what is due for what he has done in the body, whether good or evil.' Judgment is receiving whatever we deserve for our good or evil actions. It is from God. And it is inevitable. Not only for the Christian, but for the unbeliever as well. Although both will stand before Christ after death and be judged, there is a difference for the believer. Namely, that we will be judged righteous because we've obtained Christ's righteousness through faith."

Anna: "An objective framework is critical for common sense to flourish. Determining the intent of one's behaviors as opposed to condemning the individual takes compassion and prudence. After abuse, perceived self-judgments can turn into harsh self-criticisms that hinder one's self-esteem and self-perspective. Unfortunately, abusive systems birth misconceived truths, which make decision-making very difficult when emotionally despondent or unstable. A lack of discretion when speaking or behaving within relationships can rupture a connection, depending on the severity of the act. When assuming that which is misrepresented, biased, or one-sided, one is being judgmental. Sadly, the psychological, emotional, and relational repercussions of harsh judgment can cause serious issues to manifest within. God will judge humankind justly, yet his love, mercy, and grace cover all who believe in Jesus."

Question One Hundred And Fifty-Four
June 3rd

Is it wrong for us to judge our abusers?

Jon: "One of the functions of the Holy Spirit is to 'convict the world concerning sin and righteousness and judgment' (John 16:8). Our ability to discern which actions are right and which are wrong is evidence of God's Spirit working within us. It is good that we are able to recognize when we or those around us are sinning, in that we are motivated to not act sinfully. It is relieving to know that the responsibility to judge others is not ours. And it is comforting to know that said responsibility is in the all-competent hands of an all-knowing and all-powerful God."

Anna: "Evaluating another's behaviors for awareness, understanding, and discernment on how to grieve and forgive one's relational experiences is not misguided or wrong. When one confronts the experiences of the past, not everyone will be able to handle or accept it. When one acts, one must attempt to be ready for what follows, consequences and all. Thoughts of betrayal and feelings of sadness are often left deep within the mind and heart of the abused to wrestle with, scrutinize, or pardon if one so chooses. Truth is truth, however, being human means one does not always judge correctly. It is honorable and good to recognize one's immoral behaviors yet not conclusively condemn one's soul's destination. Release one's pain to God because he knows every heart and his judgment is never wrong."

Question One Hundred And Fifty-Five
June 4th

Because of our abusive backgrounds, none of us feel normal. What is normal, anyway?

Jon: "Normal is carrying out our primary purpose as human beings. And our primary purpose as human beings is to bring glory to God. In Isaiah 43:7, God speaks of all men and women as those 'whom I created for my glory.' Since glorifying God is a spiritual exercise, no one can take it away from us. In other words, because normal is to bring glory to God, it is impossible for anyone to take away from us what makes us normal. No matter what state we find ourselves in, we can always glorify God—and feel normal."

Anna: "Normal's standard models ideals set by a holistic perspective that can be biased. And deviating outside the norm can be the catalyst to mold what is deemed extraordinary. When abused, deprived, and neglected of the fundamentals, ignorance of what is appropriate and tolerable is blurred and misunderstood. Exceptional spirits persevere and abolish what normal represents. From a worldly perspective, what is common can waver with time and trends. Eternally speaking, the goal is to stand out from what the world considers universally ordinary or accepted, and to remain steadfast and set apart. Jesus died for the broken, the wounded, the meek, for sinners, and one's unique-normal can be used to tell others about Jesus."

Question One Hundred And Fifty-Six
June 5th

This question haunts most of us: Why didn't we fight back, run away, or tell someone?

Jon: "God's Word emphasizes that children are to be trained and instructed (see Deu. 4:9; Pro. 22:6; Eph. 6:4). This is because children have absolutely no knowledge of the world. So when children are exposed to harsh environments, they will likely believe that harsh environments are normal. Without the opportunity to compare his or her environment to others, a child will not know that they should or even have the ability to fight, run away, or tell. Emphasizing love and abstaining from harshness, survivors of such environments are uniquely enabled to train and instruct their children in ways others cannot."

Anna: "An abuser twists a child's will to conform to their own. When this child reaches adulthood, the awareness that one's choices play a huge role in one's destiny penetrates one's consciousness. This understanding can be frustrating when delving into the past with a present shift in one's perspective of how one would have done things differently or told someone. When abused young, developmental constraints take hold and one's reality is very much warped into lies, chaos, and disillusionments. Some abusers use scare tactics, temptations, and blatant manipulations to get exactly what is wanted to feed one's nature. Why, you ask? Because one's being was debased, wickedly maneuvered, and stripped of decency and human rights. God knows that a child is not equipped to handle such evil."

Question One Hundred And Fifty-Seven
June 6th

Suddenly, some of us find ourselves stuck in the habit of keeping bad company and maintaining bad behaviors. Can you tell us how we might begin developing good habits?

Jon: "Psalm 51:10 says, 'Create in me a clean heart, O God, and renew a right spirit within me.' God has the power to develop within us a revived inner being: one that desires beneficial habits. And this happens only through faith (see Acts 15:19). It can be difficult to uproot habits from our lives—even self-harming ones. But as we plant new godly habits and see them blossom, we see the old habits as the weeds they are and find less difficulty in plucking them. We plant the seeds of faith as we pluck the weeds of bad habit."

Anna: "Healthy habits and stable friendships are essential and extremely beneficial for maintaining emotional, psychological, and spiritual health. Perpetuations of harmful patterns seem to be instilled within the relationship dynamics of the abused psyche. When harmed on such deep emotional levels by those who were entrusted to protect, immense disorientation of one's self-worth reveals itself in many self-degrading and self-injurious ways. Being completely stuck is a lie and an illusion, but this stifling feeling is all too real, inundating, and often paralyzing. Creating valuable habits becomes less strenuous when one's beliefs align with God's. Faith's discipline takes consistent effort, sacrifice, and the commitment to do what one is created by God to do."

Question One Hundred And Fifty-Eight
June 7th

What does it mean to be spiritually and psychologically free?

Jon: "The enslavement of sin is at least twofold. First, it temps us (see Jas. 1:14-15). And second, it kills us (see Rom. 6:23). But when we place our faith in Jesus Christ, both the power of the allure of sin and the lethality of sin are eliminated (see Rom. 8:1-2). So spiritual freedom is freedom from the enslavement of sin and freedom from the enslavement of spiritual death that sin brings. In his graciousness, God has made this spiritual freedom available for any and all persons (see John 3:16; 1 John 2:2)."

Anna: "One's perception of freedom is rooted within one's beliefs, identity, possibilities, and purpose. Psychological restraint can be interpreted as having apprehensions in one's cognitive processes related to past experiences that interfere with and negatively affect one's behaviors. Twisted perspectives and abuse's restrictions place barriers upon one's existence, set weird expectations, and encourage lies around the ideas of who one should be. This results in being held captive by one's experiences, thoughts, emotions, and perceived limitations. Deliverance from one's flawed nature is overcome through a conscious awareness and decision to surrender one's pride and spiritual independence. Spiritual and psychological freedom is one and the same. One must be willing to accept that lasting freedom is solely found in Christ's life-giving testament of truth, through which one will be truly exempt and liberated for eternity."

Question One Hundred And Fifty-Nine
June 8th

How do we know what our Lord's divine purpose is for our lives when we had parents who did everything in their power to extinguish our true characters?

Jon: "We rely on God to reveal the gifting he has empowered inside each of us, for, 'To each is given the manifestation of the Spirit for the common good' (1 Cor. 12:7). Our purpose in life therefore is not determined by humans, but by God. Job recognized the strong confidence we can have in our divinely appointed purpose when he said to the Lord, 'I know that you can do all things, and that no purpose of yours can be thwarted' (Job 42:2)."

Anna: "Having a solid foundation of character and values, and a definitively rooted identity, is crucial in building and maintaining one's mental health and understanding of one's purpose. When a parent builds an unhealthy, insecure attachment with their child, it can have profound detrimental implications for that child's existence. Their sense of stability, self-esteem, and self-worth are affected, which can cause a skewed perspective of self-purpose. So, if one equates their personal value with how others or abusers have treated them, they will surely be confused and conflicted with who they perceive they are and what they believe they deserve. One must stand firmly upon God's will and promises for one's life and not in the shadow of one's prior experiences."

Question One Hundred And Sixty
June 9th

Do you believe that depression is solitary? That is, do you think that we all feel and express depression differently?

Jon: "Certainly everyone has their own reasons for feeling depressed. We all have different lives and therefore different experiences. But depression is part of the human condition. Everyone at one time or another will experience depression. This unites us. Look how the psalmist expresses his depression: 'Why are you cast down, O my soul, and why are you in turmoil within me? Hope in God; for I shall again praise him, my salvation and my God' (Ps. 42:11). Again humanity is united in that all may conquer depression with God-centered hope and praise."

Anna: "Depression reveals itself distinctly and is complexly contingent upon one's biological and spiritual makeup and development. At times, the symptoms of depression are prolonged in a clear-cut fashion, and in other cases one's feelings and traumas have been so suppressed or neglected that symptoms show atypically and detrimentally. One's discontented state is highly influenced by one's belief systems, perceived strength, identified experiences, and future hopes and present goals. When in the midst of depression's desolation, one may feel completely alone and depleted despite the reality that the expressions of despair and hopelessness are universal and one could seek support. Believers in Jesus, those who have God's Holy Spirit within them, will experience sorrow, yet one's hope and joy is firmly planted and experienced in the Lord."

Question One Hundred And Sixty-One
June 10th

What does it mean to respect one's self?

Jon: "Scripture says that we are fearfully and wonderfully made by God (Ps. 139:14). He implanted within us his own image and likeness (Gen. 1:26). This is how God sees us. We are his wonderful creation. We bear his likeness. And we therefore innately possess admirable qualities. Whether we believe it or not, whether we like it or not, we deserve the respect due to God's progeny. When we see ourselves as God sees us, we respect ourselves. When we acknowledge our likeness to God, we respect ourselves."

Anna: "Positive self-regard, acceptance of one's incomplete nature, recognition of one's value and unique qualities, talents, and divine purpose—all of these exemplify self-respect. The extent to which one honors oneself is a direct reflection of one's personal opinion of self-worth. When contingencies are placed through one's experiences of childhood abuse and external relationship factors, instead of an intrinsic value in who one was simply created to be, psychological discrepancies are forged which enable inaccurate beliefs within one's identity. There is humility and greatness in distinguishing that self-respect derives from the awareness that one was undeniably conceived in God's image, and that without his authority, one would not have breath; the very air in one's lungs comes from God, and reverence toward him is truly loving one's self."

Question One Hundred And Sixty-Two
June 11th

Some of us don't want to refer to God as father. What's wrong with calling God something other than father?

Jon: "There are two authorities that teach us to refer to God as Father: Jesus, and the Bible. Jesus said, 'Pray then like this: 'Our Father in heaven, hallowed be your name' (Mat. 6:9). Hundreds of times, in both the Old and New Testaments, God is referred to as Father or with masculine pronouns. So we refer to God as Father because the Bible and Jesus refer to God as Father. A rejection of the teaching to call God Father is not only a rejection of the authority of Scripture, but a rejection of the authority of Jesus Christ."

Anna: "One's concept of God is affected or formed by one's father figure, primary male influences, and one's family's generational teachings and belief systems. One's overall image of God can be debased by human delinquency and misconceptions, especially when one's parents or masculine role models profoundly disrupt one's sense of security, safety, or value. When abused by a male, or when a father is critical or absent, trust in others and God becomes unsafe, intimidating, guilt-ridden, distressing, and confusing. When God's truth becomes thwarted, one's image of him may become fantasy like, particularly when based upon parental uncertainty and insecurity. God is the Creator and Father of every soul and calling him anything different would be inaccurate; he is one's ideal father-figure."

Question One Hundred And Sixty-Three
June 12th

Many of us spend a great deal of time trying to interpret what other people are thinking. Are we playing God?

Jon: "This depends on the result of the action. Philippians 2:4 says, 'Let each of you look not only to his own interests, but also to the interests of others.' One way of looking to the interests of others is by considering what others are thinking. It takes us out of the realm of self-centeredness and into the realm of other-centeredness. But if the result of our other-centeredness causes inappropriate amounts of anxiety or fear, we've ceased looking after our own interests. In other words, we stay other-centered as long as we don't cause inappropriate harm to ourselves."

Anna: "Human beings have been given incredible abilities. To correctly interpret the motive and root of another's behaviors is valuable, but it may come more naturally to some and should not be manipulated and misused. Having knowledge and applying it appropriately is a gift, but no one, besides God, knows all things. People are complex, and one's cognitions are often influenced by many contributing factors. Minimizing another's intentions, capacity, and depth or treating assumptions as hard evidence is careless. Compassion toward where one has been and the abuses one has endured is critical in having well-rounded understanding. Only God can be God, and even when one tries to comprehend his ways, the way one comes to know his truth is when he so graciously reveals it."

Question One Hundred And Sixty-Four
June 13th

What are the spiritual and mental health benefits of meditation?

Jon: "Joshua 1:8 explains three levels of meditation. In the first level, one makes speaking and thinking passages of God's Word a habitual practice. In the second level, one makes his or her actions accord with the principles affirmed by those passages. In the third level, one begins to prosper and experience success relative to those meditated biblical principles. Remember, Christians do not approach meditation in a dry or robotic fashion. Rather, we fall before God, saying, 'On the glorious splendor of your majesty, and on your wondrous works, I will meditate' (Ps. 145:5)."

Anna: "Living in a chaotic, fast-paced world brings unwanted distractions and temptations that can cause a rift within a person's mental and emotional stability. To stop to rest, and just be can help restore and revitalize one's spirit. Discipline and clarity are key components in obtaining a peaceful state of mind. Christlike meditation principles, such as prayer and reading truth, enable one's faith and heartfelt hope, discipline, knowledge, self-awareness, and wisdom. When a believer meditates on God's Word, the truth of Scripture will not only set one free from bondage, but will heighten one's concentration, personal focus, and give one clarity and peace toward what is truly important and good."

Question One Hundred And Sixty-Five
June 14th

Our abusers were master manipulators. And now, as adults, we still fall prey. Please, can you explain to us how to tell the difference between manipulation and love?

Jon: "Human beings are finite in their knowledge of truth. While God knows everything that is knowable, we only know some things that are knowable. A consequence of having finite knowledge is an inability to always know the intentions of others. Jesus did say, however, that 'every healthy tree bears good fruit, but the diseased tree bears bad fruit' (Mat. 7:17). While we cannot know the intentions of others with certainty, we can make educated inferences based off of the good or bad fruit they produce."

Anna: "Manipulation takes control of one's mind, emotions, and will. To cleverly manage others and situations can be helpful and influential when one's intentions are pure and for the greater, common goal. Manipulation happens in many forms and on many levels. When one is targeted and exploited, the manipulative abuser seeks one's vulnerabilities out. Emotional extortion, dishonesty, and bogus intentions apply to one who takes advantage of other's weakness without remorse or conscience. Love shines through conditioning, because it is truthful. Love has the utmost regard for others, and it protects, especially when one is exposed or defenseless. Love is not control or abuse guised with generosity and remorse. Love is pure and God's love is complete perfection."

Question One Hundred And Sixty-Six
June 15th

For those of us who were not protected by our fathers, what are we to think of Lot, in the Bible, offering his daughters' bodies to the men of Sodom?

Jon: "We are to think that Lot gave a horribly immoral suggestion. A suggestion that was utterly wrong. A suggestion that was neither commanded nor approved of by God (see Gen. 19:8). In fact, the passage shows that the daughters were never harmed. And by God's hand they were able to escape the grievously sinful city (see Gen. 19:16). The offence we take to Lot's suggestion reminds us that we are to never so harm our family. Rather, we are to love and protect them by all appropriate means."

Anna: "When faced with hostility or death, fickle and compromising individuals do desperate and detrimental things. Lot was at times reckless and his beliefs and fortitude wavered in moments of testing. He did not see the full picture, and succumbed to selfishness and fear. Fear gives birth to preconceived notions and affects one's emotions, impulses, and behaviors. It feeds one's anxieties and sheds light upon one's doubts. Lot egregiously suggested bartering and abusing both his daughters' innocence as a means for protection. Fathers should safeguard, yet are imperfect where one's foolishness and mistakes perpetuate to the hearts and spirits of their offspring. Take solace in that from the beginning God is one's heavenly Father, he loves perfectly, and profoundly heals the wounds others create."

Question One Hundred And Sixty-Seven
June 16th

When a great number of us were young, we had to control our home environments because there were no caregivers to maintain order. As adults, we are very controlling of others. How can we stop trying to change the behavior of others?

Jon: "We don't have to stop trying to change the behaviors of others as long as we are doing it for the glory of God. In fact, Jesus *instructed* his disciples to influence others. We are to be salt and light (see Mat. 5:13-16). We are to taste good. And we are to shine in a dark world. If we do these things, others will taste and see their goodness, and be motivated to do them as well. In other words, the best way to effect change in others is to first effect change in oneself."

Anna: "Desiring control, to fix, or change someone, emerges from brokenness. Being stifled and oppressed can bring forth deep-rooted frustrations, anger, and resentments. Feeling dominated or inconsiderately imposed upon will fester serious and unhealthy relationship issues. The behaviors of others are a reflection of their spirit, and not truly linked to another's worth. Control is not love, nor should love be forced due to one's insecurities and fear. Being compelled to promote change takes leadership through modeling what is needed. It is counterproductive to attempt to control one another, because God gave humankind free will yet he set boundaries out of his divine wisdom, protection, and love."

Question One Hundred And Sixty-Eight
June 17th

Most of us are well aware that child abuse and maltreatment can literally damage different areas of our brains. Knowing this, do you really think that healing is possible for these injured regions?

Jon: "God is all-powerful. If God is all-powerful, then he can do anything that is logically possible for an all-powerful being to do. And it is possible that an all-powerful being could heal a damaged area of the human brain. Therefore, it is possible that God could heal a damaged brain. Scripture says that by Jesus' wounds we have been healed (1 Pet. 2:24). Even if we never experience physical healing, the opportunity for eternal healing of our souls is always available through faith in Jesus Christ."

Anna: "When a child experiences stimulus extremes through abuse and neglect, and does not receive the nurturing needed on fundamental levels, changes will occur and one's development can be impaired. One's interpretation of risk can also intensify when one's mind has been negatively impacted by trauma. When early social interactions are built upon psychological manipulations, one's reality and hope becomes uncertain. Through remedial interactions, the brain is stimulated due to igniting and nurturing cell activity through reshaping one's thoughts and emotions via new experiences. The human mind is dynamic and when one's spirit is influenced by God's supernatural presence, healing is obtainable because absolutely anything is achievable with him."

Question One Hundred And Sixty-Nine
June 18th

A number of us keep hearing that we should heal our inner child. This is confusing, as we are adults. Do we have inner children living inside of us?

Jon: "No. Not in a strict sense. God created human beings as singular persons, each of which possess one mind or soul. We are not multiple persons. However, Jesus did say, '... whoever does not receive the kingdom of God like a child shall not enter it' (Mark 10:15). So there is an action we are to carry out in a childlike manner: faith. In other words, adults must believe God as children believe their parents. It is not that we believe in a child inside of us, but that inside we believe like a child."

Anna: "One's inner child is an embodiment of who one was, and what was longed for when young. Its purpose is to acknowledge, process, and validate what was destroyed within or never received, so that one can learn to re-parent oneself at deep levels. This authentic process facilitates self-love, healing, and emotional growth. When innocence is displaced and corrupted, one's true childlike identity is lost. One's inner child truly needs to be found and then set free. God desires for one to have pure faith, a heart full of trust, humility, and dependence upon him; in order to fully experience his love, his Spirit must conquer the psychological and emotional fortress one created to survive one's abusive childhood."

Question One Hundred And Seventy
June 19th

The story in the Bible where Abraham is willing to kill his son, Isaac, is, in some of our minds anyway, a prime example of childhood abuse. How are we to view this as anything different?

Jon: "Passages like these are disturbing (see Gen. 22:9-14). And they stand out because they are so unlike the rest of Scripture. There is another view on this passage, however. As the story goes, a ram was sacrificed in the place of Isaac. And this ram was provided by God. The point is that God gives his people a way out of death. This narrative is a foreshadowing of Christ's death on the cross. What the ram was for Isaac, so Jesus was for all humanity: a substitute who incurred punishment for the sake of others."

Anna: "Acts that supersede explainable norms or have negative associations can be difficult to understand and accept. The Bible's accounts vividly exemplify what true faith, obedience, and sacrifice entail. God is clever, just, and his intention here sends a distinct message for he is forthright and pure. Sacrificing Jesus for humankind's sins is what is reflected here, because he was your sacrificial lamb. An eternity with God is paramount to any tribulation faced on earth, no matter the cost. Following Jesus means authentically giving up one's temporary life and making earthy sacrifices for eternal gain just as he did for you."

Question One Hundred And Seventy-One
June 20th

Some people have told a certain number of us that when they feel their thoughts drifting away, if they hold something in their hand, like a stone for example, the weight of the rock grounds their thoughts. Might there be something to this?

Jon: "Hebrews 6:19 says, 'We have this as a sure and steadfast anchor of the soul, a hope that enters into the inner place behind the curtain...' Hope is an anchor. Its tether connects our inner being to the heaven beyond the curtain of this world. This hope in the gospel is sure and steadfast for two reasons. First, because salvation is guaranteed to the one who hopes in Christ (Eph. 1:13-14). And second, because Christ is invincible. So the action and object of our hope can never be defeated or overcome."

Anna: "Grounding oneself can temporarily bring stability to one's physical state. Using a tangible object or authentic belief to ignite one's senses and validate one's absoluteness can decrease anxiety or disillusions within the moment. However, makeshift tactics are misleading and fleeting. When one experiences trauma, post-traumatic stresses from the incident can arise swiftly and spark visions, flashbacks, and influence or exasperate perceptions and dissociations. Instant gratification, a quick fix, differs from authentic satisfaction, self-security, or emotional and psychological cohesion within one's thoughts, feelings, and core belief system. Bona fide grounding, one's solid foundation and peace, is authentically found in Jesus Christ, where one's infallible identity lies."

Question One Hundred And Seventy-Two
June 21st

If a dog severely injures another dog or a human being, society more often than not kills the dog. But when an adult severely injures a child, they more often than not go scot-free, without punishment. Why is this?

Jon: "Human systems such as government are comprised of men and women. But men and women are prone to err. Therefore, human systems are prone to err. A perfect justice system is impossible. But not for God: 'For the wrongdoer will be paid back for the wrong he has done...' (Col. 3:25). So an adult who severely injures a child will not go scot-free. He or she will be paid back the wrong they have done. We do not depend on a failure-prone system for justice. We depend on a perfectly just and inerrant God."

Anna: "Society is run by flawed individuals who do not wholly possess the same motives and moral compass. When a person is in a position of authority, and casts judgments, mistakes, misuse, or blatant corruption will at some point follow. Justice does prevail, yet more often than not the users and abusers of this world seem to get away with the slaughtering of souls. When a twisted worldview and deceit intertwine, egregious acts flourish and dominate. Humankind desperately needs a shift in perspective. Blessedly, there is assured hope through Jesus, who unfairly suffered and received punishment for all. Take heart, for God sees everything and justice wins."

Question One Hundred And Seventy-Three
June 22nd

We were defenseless as children; but now as adults—for some of us anyway—we decide to no longer be unshielded. Our new motto is: armors on, swords drawn. This fresh image gives us strength to begin to fight for our healing. Can you offer us some encouragement in this regard?

Jon: "Ephesians 6:11 says, 'Put on the whole armor of God, that you may be able to stand against the schemes of the devil.' Evil is poised, ready to strike. But God has not left us defenseless. Truth, righteousness, the gospel, faith, and salvation are our armor; God's Word is our sword (Eph. 6:14-17). While God does supply this wonderful armory, he will not force us to equip ourselves. It is we who must daily *put on* God's armor. The more armor we get on, the less evil will get in."

Anna: "Protectively shielding oneself from negativity is healthy. However, when one's metaphoric sword is constantly drawn because of the past's pain, others could continuously feel attacked, threatened, or that one is on the edge. Living in fight mode will thwart one's opportunity for authentic security and pervade one's consciousness, perspective, and actions. Preparation for life's battles is wise, but this does not mean one is always at the precipice of war. Safeguard one's soul by seeking wisdom. One's protective covering through God's flawless Word is imperative; with swords ready to be drawn, stand firmly in faith, prepare for opposition, while authentically loving others."

Question One Hundred And Seventy-Four
June 23rd

Can some people be so enmeshed in their own pain that they use denial of reality as a defense mechanism?

Jon: "The finitude of man necessitates breaking points. Any such breaking point may well give way to denial. But we must beware the nature of denial. It is akin to the nature of lying. As one lie may lead to more lies, so too may one denial of reality lead to more denials of reality. To support one denial, one must erect another denial. And another. And another. We can begin to accept our reality when we recognize that, in Christ, God knows everything about us—past and present, good and bad—and accepts us."

Anna: "One will attempt to survive by unconsciously developing metaphoric stone walls to defend against unwanted emotions to avert from the discomforts of reality. When it becomes automatic to escape or reject real-world truths by not acknowledging or minimizing reality, one's patterns of suppression and avoidance increase within their emotional experiences. The dismissal of anything painful, within the moment, may help one cope, but it will be short-lived and have long-lasting consequences if not addressed. Eventually, those painful feelings will emerge unconsciously, psychologically, emotionally, and relationally. Denial of one's reality will lead to a disillusionment of one's expectations and role within the circumstance. God can powerfully heal, but one must emotionally surrender and be real with where they truly are."

Question One Hundred And Seventy-Five
June 24th

Does God choose our parents for us?

Jon: "Acts 17:26 says, '[God] made from one man every nation of mankind to live on all the face of the earth, having determined allotted periods and the boundaries of their dwelling place...' God's omnipotence and sovereignty over humanity is clear throughout Scripture. However, he does not override human free will and choice: '... choose this day whom you will serve...' (Jos. 24:15). So, God is sovereign over a universe in which the free actions of our ancestors led to the uniting of our parents."

Anna: "People are free to do what they choose: good, bad, or indifferent. When following one's own will as opposed to the will of God, one is choosing to serve one's flawed human nature. Serving one's self in brokenness, psychological and emotional turmoil, or greedy ambition tends to lead to dysfunction within one's being, choices, and relationships. This state of mind and existence requires a change in beliefs, perspective, and approach. Everyone makes choices, as simple or as complicated as they may be. God's Spirit and will leads those who surrender to his authority, so that his divine hand is directing their gifts and choices. Others follow their own will, so even though their choices may have been outside of God's initial plan, he will graciously adapt and use it for his glory."

Question One Hundred And Seventy-Six
June 25th

For many of us, we grew up in immoral homes, with no clear sense of what is right and what is wrong. Can you give us please a transparent definition of sin?

Jon: "No reasonable person denies the reality of moral law. Rape and child abuse are always objectively wrong, while love and forbearance are always objectively right. The existence of supernatural moral law necessitates the existence of a supernatural moral lawgiver. The supernatural standard of morality, then, is God. So, failing to meet God's standard of morality is sin. The Bible defines sin in this way: '… whoever knows the right thing to do and fails to do it, for him it is sin' (Jas. 4:17)."

Anna: "Humankind was born with an intrinsic need to understand right from wrong. However, when living amid a fallen world, this message becomes misrepresented. The understanding of sin seems to have different components: one's knowledge, one's moral awareness and conscious accountability level, and judgment. One's character is important to recognize when identifying immorality. To weigh this with one's social, personal, and spiritual identities, one's upbringing, core values, self-concept, and concept of God will help one understand why one sins in the way that they do. When the baseline of what is good has been corrupted by abuse, wrong can appear somewhat right and what truly is right was not fully taught. Sin is destructive, deceptive, and abusive; it opposes God and your heart's truth."

Question One Hundred And Seventy-Seven
June 26th

We know that Jesus was an extremely influential teacher. But, how do we know that the Bible is true?

Jon: "Christians know the Bible is true because they believe in Jesus, who taught from the Old Testament (see Mat. 4:4, 7, 10, 5:17, 12:40, 13:19, 19:4-6, 22:29, 23:35, 24:37-38; Mark 13:19; Luke 24:27). Jesus maintained that Scripture is imperishable (see Mat. 15:18) and unbreakable (John 10:35). He gave authority to the apostles (see Luke 9:1)—who confluently wrote the New Testament with the Holy Spirit—and claimed the Holy Spirit would remind them of everything he said (see Mat. 10:19-20; John 14:26)."

Anna: "Human nature is tainted as one has experienced within their family's dynamics and relationship conflicts throughout life. Human beings need much guidance in many ways. Psychology's focus is: self-awareness, self-esteem, self-image, self-worth, self-actualization and so forth. Interestingly, God's mission is saving humankind from evil and itself. From a sound perspective, logic, discernment, and wisdom need to be applied in regards to understanding biblical truths. If Jesus is real and the Bible is indeed accurate, then the Holy Spirit must be real. This is how one knows the Bible is true: the Holy Spirit empowers a new nature to manifest itself within the believer's soul and spirit. This experiential truth in correlation with the God's accurate Word and one's faith-based experiences solidifies that the Bible has been written and inspired by God."

Question One Hundred And Seventy-Eight
June 27th

A great number of us are told that we need to be patient with our healing process. What does this mean?

Jon: "Psalm 27:14 says, 'Wait for the LORD; be strong, and let your heart take courage; wait for the LORD!' Patience isn't an end in itself. It produces other things. Namely, it produces a means for God to implant within us new strength and courage. And oftentimes this is exactly what we need. We can become weak and discouraged from injury. So it may be helpful to think of patience not as a singular virtue, but as a bridge to God-wrought strength and courage. We need patience *because* we need strength and courage from God."

Anna: "Healing is a challenging and inspiring journey that has deep valleys and splendid peaks. When grieving the abusive traumas of the past, time is needed, yet does not wait. Patience entails withstanding one's burdens with self-compassion, self-forgiveness, and self-respect, especially when one perceives to fall short of any standard. Patient endurance does not mean one will not feel, have overwhelming days, or not currently struggle because of their abusive childhood. It means that one will conquer their pain by not giving up. Interestingly enough, the sufferings of life are what breathe meaning into one's existence. Authenticity and self-love are truly needed within one's restoration process. Patience means faithfully living life with a humble understanding of one's humanness, as God so graciously does."

Question One Hundred And Seventy-Nine
June 28th

Somewhere in the Bible it says that anyone who curses or strikes his or her mother and father will be put to death. How is this relevant to us today?

Jon: "Capital punishment is a worldwide reality, one on which different political entities take different stances. The theocratic laws in Old Testament Israel were tentative and lasted only for a time. The church today is not a political entity. Regardless, Leviticus 20:9 and 18:21 explain how this specific law was only relevant to a child who exhibited continuous egregious rebellion. It was not for a one-time slip-of-the-tongue. Interestingly, the law may have only served to demonstrate how seriously God takes sin and the sacredness of the parent-child relationship. For there is no biblical record of this law ever being enforced."

Anna: "To wish evil upon or physically abuse another is connected to one's inability to emotionally regulate one's concept of love and retaliation, and one's cognitive reasoning and problem-solving skills when triggered. Mistreating another without dignity and respect, as one has experienced, detrimentally manifests. In an atmosphere where contempt thrives and multiplies insidiously, angry or even violent tendencies brew. Being punished with death is extreme, but happens to stop intolerably vicious behaviors. Today, the relevancy represents actual and spiritual death if one lives their life hurting, abusing, or even killing. These behaviors show that one is living outside of God's will, yet his grace covers all who believe, confess, and truly repent."

Question One Hundred And Eighty
June 29th

Scores of us feel completely disconnected from God. Will you please tell us how we can build a bridge to him?

Jon: "This is one of the most glorious truths about Christianity, namely, that even though there is no possible way for man to build a ladder or bridge to God, God has already built the bridge for us through Jesus Christ. In other words, Jesus is the bridge to God. 1 Timothy 2:5 says, 'For there is one God, and there is one mediator between God and men, the man Christ Jesus…' The only building left for us to do is the building up of our faith (Jude 20). For, while it is Christ who grants us access to God, it is faith that grants us access to Christ. Faith therefore is the toll to cross the bridge of salvation."

Anna: "A connection with God is founded upon truth, faith, respect, humility, authenticity, vulnerability, and the identification of and value in one's intrinsic needs. Detachment appears to be safe and uncomplicated when one's abusive relationships consistently brought misery and sorrow. This inaccurate belief and temporary defense creates more problems than it solves because, ultimately, psychological separation does not fix the issue. In order to construct anything one must have a solid understanding of how and where to lay one's foundation. Building upon God's love, his Word, and making the daily decision to engage in a genuine relationship with Jesus is one's confident bridge of faith."

Question One Hundred And Eighty-One
June 30th

**Many of us have heard that Satan is the god of this world.
Is this true?**

Jon: "Only in one narrow sense. Namely, in that people *make* Satan their ruler by 'following the course of this world, following the prince of the power of the air, the spirit that is now at work in the sons of disobedience' (Eph. 2:2). But Satan is a created being, an angel who disobeyed God (see Rev. 12:9). He is finite in power and, like all created beings, under God's absolute sovereignty (see Job 1:1-12). And we are unafraid of Satan because when we submit to the true God, we may 'resist the devil, and he will flee from [us]' (Jas. 4:7)."

Anna: "A god, whether consciously idolized or not, is glorified by those who follow a false agenda. Satan has this unbelieving and abusive generation within his grasp due to his deceptive influence upon the fallen and broken world. He has been given reign over the earth but knows that his time is limited. His parasitic evils temporarily sustain from God's creation because his doom is inevitable. Satan knows he will lose, but desires to take whomever he can down with him, especially those who have a warped sense of identity due to maltreatment. God has jurisdiction over the universe, but because of Satan's rebellion, righteous maneuvers were made so that humankind would be saved through the belief, death, and resurrection of Jesus Christ."

Question One Hundred And Eighty-Two
July 1st

Can you offer us some words that can help us to feel invincible?

Jon: "Left to our own, we are not invincible, for 'all flesh is like grass and all its glory like the flower of grass. The grass withers, and the flower falls...' (1 Pet. 1:24). We are finite in strength, finite in wisdom, and finite in time. In Christ, however, we can say, 'I can do all things through him who strengthens me' (Phil. 4:13). When we place our faith in Jesus Christ, we are indwelled by God's Holy Spirit. If God is invincible, and he resides in us, whom shall we fear?"

Anna: "Comprehending the definitive truth about one's purpose and the meaning of life would make anyone feel special and somewhat powerful. Having understanding with truth's perspective enables the mind and heart to be at peace. When one truly believes, one is victorious simply by faith, and one will beat death. God is indestructible, and to be in his favor and a member of his chosen kingdom, one will overcome when faithful and dependent upon his Word. No matter what life may bring, the suffering one endured, one's heavenly destination is untouchable through faith. There will be redemption for one's pain. Invincibility, then, equates to obtaining eternal life. When one believes in Jesus, eternal life is one's gift so graciously given by God. One is invincible through faith."

Question One Hundred And Eighty-Three
July 2nd

Why should we forgive those who hurt us?

Jon: "God commands us to forgive others (see Mat. 5:44; Eph. 4:32; Col. 3:13). And it would be hypocritical to not forgive others when we expect and receive forgiveness from God (see Mat. 18:33). Moreover, if we are not forgiving, God will not forgive us (see Mat. 5:7, 6:14). But the central reason we forgive others is because the reality that we have been forgiven is greater than our hatred for those who offend us. The grandeur and gloriousness of our redemption in Christ Jesus is a million times more impactful than our resentment toward others. Redemption defeats resentment."

Anna: "For psychological, emotional, relational, and spiritual freedom. A mind and heart full of disapproval and blame can lead to cruelty, condemnation, self-righteousness, and delusions regarding one's true character. Choosing to forgive is a beautiful example of humility, honor, and inner peace. Mercilessness can bind one to the past; can trample upon one's existing and future relationships, and parades around a negative demeanor and misaligned spirit. This saying is heard all too often: forgiveness is not for the other person, but for one's self. This fundamental egocentrism is not only disheartening but contradicts and opposes forgiveness' wonderful and selfless nature. Naturally, when one forgives grace's blessings are implanted and reaped from deep within yet true forgiveness is not self-centered. Forgiveness sets the stage, it defies the odds, it combats evil, and when Christ-centered it reflects God's Spirit and his divine mission."

Question One Hundred And Eighty-Four
July 3rd

Why do some of us intentionally cut, hit, burn, bite, and/or scratch our bodies?

Jon: "Temptation leads to such action. Many may not know that Jesus was often tempted. Hebrews 4:15 says, 'For we do not have a high priest who is unable to sympathize with our weaknesses, but one who in every respect has been tempted as we are, yet without sin.' In other words, Jesus understands exactly what we are going through. He knows exactly how to get through it, and he wants to show us how to get through it. Therefore, we may come confidently to him and find grace and mercy in our time of need (Heb. 4:16)."

Anna: "Sadly, self-mutilators are in a personal hell, a mind-boggling torment that one feels the urge to release the deep-rooted pain self-malignantly. Self-harm is a tangible manifestation of one's distressing and depressive thoughts. Acting out is common for survivors of abuse because one's needs and emotions were unmet, taken advantage of, or blatantly disregarded so one acts out of anguish and self-hatred. The tortured soul is spiritually afflicted, and without Jesus, self-love, and loving support, authentic healing will be difficult. One's body was created to be a powerful vessel not to be marred by one's own hands. When one succumbs to impulses and temptations to purposefully hurt oneself, the evil one's lies have gained ground. Rebuke what is sinister in the mighty name of Jesus, for one is precious and assuredly loved by God."

Question One Hundred And Eighty-Five
July 4th

Most of us are well aware that child abuse is generational, that if the cycle is not broken in one generation, it will continue to the next. In terms of breaking this cycle, is it best to keep family secrets?

Jon: "While revealing secrets unnecessarily is slanderous (see Pro. 11:13), there are times when confession brings healing (see Jas. 5:16), and sharing lightens our burden (see Gal. 2:6). If we are troubled emotionally, spiritually, or mentally, it is to our benefit that we seek good counsel from the wise and qualified. The psalmist reveals where to find free counseling from the God of heaven: '… your servant will meditate on your statutes. Your testimonies are my delight; they are my counselors' (Ps. 119:23-24)."

Anna: "Generational dysfunction embedded within physical, sexual, and psychological abuse is soulfully tragic. When dealing with abuses, secrets are not far behind. Sadly, hidden truths and mental illness build upon one another. Children through emulation learn behaviors, whether negative or positive. Abuse's secrets and self-medication unfortunately grip one's hands as a false-comfort-system. When one has limited grief's movement, will not confess their heart-changing experiences, or release the emotions associated, suppression, devaluation, invalidation, numbness, and dishonesty with who one truly is occurs. The authentic acknowledgment of one's family secrets is therapeutic because unrevealed truths are like invisible chains that hold one back and spiritually bind. True freedom is found in God's righteousness and God's truth."

Question One Hundred And Eighty-Six
July 5th

In the Bible, Lot has incestuous relations with his two daughters. What are we to make of this?

Jon: "Actually, as the story goes, it is Lot's daughters who take advantage of Lot (see Gen. 19:30-38). They caused him to become so drunk with wine that he was unaware of what they did to him. Although the daughters' intent was to preserve their family's offspring, this of course is to be taken as a horribly immoral act. One which was not commanded or approved of by God. This story demonstrates the perils of drunkenness and the atrociousness of incest. And moreover, it attests to the Bible's responsibleness and loyalty to reporting events accurately."

Anna: "Desperate intentions and skewed perspectives cause people to act perversely when they otherwise would not. When Lot had sexual relations with both his daughters on two separate occasions, he was inebriated. When one's psyche is altered and open to influence, one's physical body enlivens and one's emotional state can be deceptively swayed. Incest, to most, is unfathomable to act upon, yet happens in the shadows of the world's homes. Intimacy and sex differ due to one's concept of connection and morality. The effects of sexual abuse and incest are spiritually devastating because living with the shame and secrets bring havoc upon one's identity and worth. The Bible accounts people's behaviors whether immoral or just, but what is penetratingly clear is humankind's desperate need for God's mercy, grace, and love."

Question One Hundred And Eighty-Seven
July 6th

Incest destroys its victims. Too many of us have difficulty experiencing pleasure, disturbing thoughts haunt us daily, and we have a propensity to stay in abusive relationships. (And this is just a very, very short list of incest's devastating reach.) Given this, in the Bible, why did God permit incest?

Jon: "The Bible is not a fairy tale. It is not fiction. It is history and law, prophecy and poetry, biography and epistle. When the Bible describes historical events, it recounts those events accurately. Since most of history is a recounting of the actions of mankind, and mankind is sinful, much of history will describe sinful actions. But the telling of a morally reprehensible historical event does not make the teller morally reprehensible. We mustn't shoot the messenger. Moreover, God's permission of evil is neither his commanding nor his approving of evil. Man is free to act according to his will and will suffer the consequences of defying God's."

Anna: "Those who act upon incest are psychologically confused, emotionally craven, and have twisted falsehoods that become perverted truths. Incestuous behaviors are a reflection of one's soul and one believing that the lure of what is forbidden is just too much to withstand, that it is natural or normal. Dysfunction is carried out through selfish choices, and when Lucifer fell, he changed the world's trajectory. God allows every able being to choose one's destiny, but he does not agree with one's sin, nor is he to blame."

Question One Hundred And Eighty-Eight
July 7th

Some of us are proud of the fact that we don't need help. We have already won the battle for control of our souls and spirits. Thoughts?

Jon: "It is good to overcome obstacles in life. But as the proverb goes, 'Pride goes before destruction' (Pro. 16:18). Scripture even says that God *opposes* the prideful (Jas. 4:6). How is it that pride brings destruction and opposition from God? To receive salvation, one must acknowledge their powerlessness to save themselves. Namely, they must acknowledge their inability to remove their own sins or reach God. These two things are only achievable through Christ (see John 14:6). Refusing to acknowledge this, the prideful bring downfall and separation from God upon themselves. Let us boast then never in our own doings, but only in what God has done in and through us."

Anna: "One's perception of control can be very different than one's reality. Abusive experiences can manipulate a learned helplessness within a person. Though persevering despite one's feelings of inadequacies can help one overcome obstacles, it can also be misleading when behaving from a mode of overcompensation to self-protect. Serious misconceptions and emotional stress manifest when one is attempting to have authority over something that is not theirs. The Holy Spirit needs access to gain mastery of one's mind through free-willed surrender because it is in the midst of combat; the battle is not yet finished, nor is one's mission yet complete, so please, humbly and earnestly continue on."

Question One Hundred And Eighty-Nine
July 8th

For those of us who are trying to know the truth of all the spiritual and psychological theories to choose from, how do we know which ones to pick?

Jon: "The abuse of a child, say, is always wrong. One's opinion is irrelevant as to whether or not child abuse is wrong. It is always (or, objectively or categorically) true that child abuse is wrong. Therefore, we want to choose a spiritual worldview that affirms that child abuse is always wrong. This means that every worldview that says child abuse is right, or that child abuse is not wrong, or that it is neither right nor wrong, is an incorrect spiritual theory. Such worldviews we ought to not choose. Rather, we ought to only choose a spiritual worldview that accurately corresponds to reality."

Anna: "Different psychological theories can be applied circumstantially and inter-dependently upon one's endured trauma, belief system, emotional capacities, personality traits, and behavioral issues etcetera. Logical and appropriate methods integrated with accurate conceptualizations of one's past can enable progression in one's current functioning. Ideologies within psychology and spirituality have played a critical role in understanding human development, behaviors, identity, and resiliency within the context of abuse. When worldly approaches negate biblical truths or deviate from one's Christian compass, red flags have been raised. One must choose based upon truth. The Bible reveals that Jesus is one's entrance to eternity; in this, there is no discrepancy. Foremost, seek God through his Word's knowledge."

Question One Hundred And Ninety
July 9th

Churches. They should be institutions of safety. But some of us were molested by a certain number of our clerics. Help?

Jon: "Churches should be institutions of safety because churches are made of people, and people should facilitate safety for one another (see Eph. 4:1-6). But people are not perfect. People do not always do good. And some people do a great deal of evil. Therefore churches will almost inevitably harbor some danger. But this applies to every institution comprised of persons. The difference between the church and all other institutions is that the true body of believers will one day reach heaven where there will be no mourning, no death, no tears, and no pain (Rev. 21:4)."

Anna: "It is hypocrisy when love's purpose should be at the core of one's congregation, yet it is debased by a leader's destructive behaviors and perverse cravings. How is one to trust the church again when one's experience was utter betrayal by traumatic abuse that caused tremendous suffering, self-hatred, and confusion? Sadly, in every institution there are forms of corruption and misrepresentation. All people cannot be trusted, all churches are not safe, and this is rapidly becoming more obvious due to the heedless evolution of human behavior and prophetically depraved times. No matter one's beliefs, humankind has been chosen by God to help carry out his plan. Delinquency is inevitable, yet its ramifications are profound when the one who does such evils professes the Lord's name."

Question One Hundred And Ninety-One
July 10th

Because of childhood abuse, some of us cannot maintain healthy relationships. What can we do?

Jon: "A home can be an intimidating structure to maintain. For, multiple tools are required either to fix, build, or renovate any one portion of the home. But how many tools are required to maintain the structure of a relationship? Galatians 5:14 says, 'For the whole law is fulfilled in one word: "You shall love your neighbor as yourself."' Love is the multi-tool of relationship. It can fix, build, or renovate any portion of its structure. Much less intimidating are relationships knowing we need not master a thousand tools but one."

Anna: "In order to truly change, one's beliefs, mindset, and behaviors need to positively progress toward truth. When abused, healthy communication and conflict resolution seem like unreachable skills to grasp, let alone practice or master. When navigating and maintaining relationships, the stakes increase for the need to successfully regulate one's emotions, which enables the transmission of healthy resolutions. Traumatic experiences often create defensive, reactive, or impulsive behavioral tendencies because one is simply confused on a basic relational level: one's feelings were not protected, nurtured, explained or explored lovingly. Through the restoration of one's thoughts and belief-systems, one will transform, and this will extend to one's relationships. Authentic connection, God-breathed intimacy, requires genuine expressions of one's heart and soul while nurturing one's relationship with Jesus."

Question One Hundred And Ninety-Two
July 11th

What is truth?

Jon: "Truth is what *is*. It is whatever accurately corresponds to reality. Statements about the world around us and the things and people inside of it are either true or false. And they are true or false depending on whether or not they accurately correspond to the way things actually are. Jesus made the ultimate truth claim. He said, 'I am the way, and the truth, and the life. No one comes to the Father except through me' (John 14:6). Here Jesus not only equates himself with truth, but reveals the most significant truth concerning humanity: Salvation is only attainable through him."

Anna: "Within a relational context, one's truth is often determined by what one believes, which is not always an accurate measure of the truth. Abuse's message is deceptively inaccurate, yet one's perceived beliefs about the abuse they endured can positively affect or negatively alter their life. However, one's belief-systems are powerful and do indicate when something may be completely right or very wrong. The minimization of one's personal truth, one's abusive childhood, is a problematic way to exist. Experiences and emotions cultivate one's quality of life yet biblical truths are what should drive and motivate one's purpose. In the end, divine truth will obliterate all lies, the enemies' temporary craft, and truth will prevail. Truth always is regardless of one's perception; it does not waver. Jesus is truth, sacrificed for humankind's gain, proven through God's Word, God's truth."

Question One Hundred And Ninety-Three
July 12th

Many of us cannot say no to other people's requests of us.
Why do we feel so guilty about denying their wants?

Jon: "It is good to meet the needs of others when appropriate. It is Christ-like. But it is also Christ-like to say 'No.' Peter once approached Jesus early in the morning. He told Jesus that a crowd was looking for him. But Jesus said, 'Let us go on to the next towns, that I may preach there also, for that is why I came out' (Mark 1:38). Jesus couldn't stay in Capernaum. He was limited in his human nature and therefore had to move on to other towns to continue his ministry. Being limited, we too must sometimes say 'No' to requests made of us."

Anna: "When boundaries have been crossed to feed another's psychological, emotional, or physical appetite, one's understanding of love becomes biased: one's self-conceived role based upon abusive experiences is interpreted that one must please others. Codependence utilizes blame and has the ability to make a consoling act unhealthy, because the behavior is often feeding selfish motives or uncomfortable feelings. Within enmeshment, anxieties will rise due to an insecure identity. Ambivalence regarding one's value places high importance upon the opinions and behaviors of others. This imbalance fuels guilty thoughts, which then corrode one's confidence. God has a masterful boundary system and when one's identity is truly found in him, one will learn to lovingly say no."

Question One Hundred And Ninety-Four
July 13th

Most of us feel like we have taken all the punishment that we can stand. Having said that, somewhere in the Bible it says that God will punish one generation after the next. Does this mean that we are to expect more punishment?

Jon: "It is right to punish wrongdoing. Our judicial systems are predicated on this reality. And we sense a need for justice when we are wronged. Scripture says that God visits the iniquity of every generation who hates him (Ex. 20:5). So we should expect consequences for our wrongdoings before God. But the passage doesn't end there. The Lord says, 'but showing steadfast love to thousands of those who love me and keep my commandments' (Ex. 20:6). Inasmuch as we should expect consequences from God for wrong actions, we should expect steadfast love from God for keeping his commands."

Anna: "Consequences for breaching boundaries are crucial because if they did not exist the repercussions would be irreversible. Dysfunctional behaviors have natural and painful penalties and the chain reactions of abusive conduct affect everyone, all around, to certain levels and degrees. What one does, the way one treats others, and the messages planted within one's psyche, oftentimes transcend the good-centered truth of why humankind exists. Abusive and destructive behaviors will manifest self-induced psychological, emotional, physical, and spiritual punishments. The coming generations will have the opportunity to believe in Jesus, yet humankind will face God for everything that has been done."

Question One Hundred And Ninety-Five
July 14th

We pray and our prayers go unanswered. Why?

Jon: "1 John 5:14 says, 'And this is the confidence that we have toward him, that if we ask anything according to his will he hears us.' This passage highlights that prayers must be in accord with God's will. In other words, our prayers will go unanswered if we pray for something that does not accord with God's will. But this doesn't discourage us from prayer. Rather, we have hope knowing that God's perfect sovereign plan will be better than our own. For, '[God] is able to do far more abundantly than all that we ask or think' (Eph. 3:20)."

Anna: "One's spiritual foundation and raw motivation for prayer is most certainly weighed, understood, and resolved accordingly. The unanswered prayer can sting one's pride, bring disappointment to one's ideas, challenge one's motives, and agitate insecurities of feeling discounted or undeserving when one's interpretation is narrow-minded. Prayer can be an antidepressant and decrease emotional imbalances within one's spirit. When meditating and praying, the brain is activated and re-shaped on neurological levels, which promotes spiritual rejuvenation. Prayer reveals one's faith, one's hopes and inner peace, which reduce one's fears, anxiety, and stress levels. There is hidden value when God works within one's prayers, always; his plan is most excellent, he knows exactly what one needs, and he will adjust, or not, according to his glorious purpose."

Question One Hundred And Ninety-Six
July 15th

Many of us did not know our biological mothers and fathers. They may have been taken away from us for a number of reasons: addictions, adopting us out, mental or physical illnesses. Will we meet our real mothers and fathers in heaven?

Jon: "Often in the Bible, it is said that those who have passed are gathered to their people (see Gen. 25:8; Num. 20:24; Judg. 2:10). After the death of his newborn child, King David said, 'I shall go to him, but he will not return to me' (2 Sam. 12:23). Moreover, on the Mount of Transfiguration, Jesus and his three apostles recognized Moses and Elijah though they had been dead for centuries. In heaven, we will gather with and recognize our loved ones."

Anna: "The continued grief one experiences when abandoned due to abuse or neglect is a deep process that will not lead to immediate healing, or be completely understood overnight. When one does not know where one comes from or has not experienced others who are a reflection of their genetic makeup, a piece of their earthly identity will be sadly unresolved. Now, depending upon the pull one has to seek out their family and connect with them, this will affect one's individual identity development, identified worth, self-statements, and self-beliefs. Embrace that one's true identity is found in Christ and one's gifts and purpose are reinforced through God's Word and Holy Spirit. Every soul that believes in Jesus will reunite in heaven."

Question One Hundred And Ninety-Seven
July 16th

What does a *call to action* mean?

Jon: "A *call to action* is an encouragement to do something. James 1:22 says, 'But be doers of the word, and not hearers only, deceiving yourselves.' It is pointless to read God's Word without putting it to use. The words of Scripture must make the journey from head and heart to hand and foot. Reading the Bible is only half of the way. So the Christian who only goes half of the way is only a halfway Christian. The Christian who goes the full way is a full-way Christian. Not wanting to deceive ourselves, we ask, 'Am I a halfway Christian, or am I a full-way Christian?'"

Anna: "Have you felt the alarm go off within your soul to do something, to rise up, and to move toward a more fulfilled purpose? That is and will continue to be your call to action: a specific, productive, response follow-through toward your mental, physical, and spiritual well-being. This movement could entail forgiving yourself, processing the abuse, grieving what cannot be changed, attempting to mend what has been broken, or simply taking steps toward acceptance and surrender. What one truly values, where one's gifts reside, is where one will be authentically called to flourish. One's faith should produce actions that help, encourage, protect, and bless others. Christians are called by God to move, to diligently take action led by the Spirit, to boldly help accomplish his will."

Question One Hundred And Ninety-Eight
July 17th

What does it mean to have a healthy pride?

Jon: "Scripture virtually always sets pride in a negative light. At least pride of self. The author of Proverbs calls those who boast in self an 'abomination' (Pro. 16:5). So if we must boast, we ought to boast in others. Healthy pride therefore is pride with a trajectory that is away from the self. But God says in Jeremiah 9:24, 'let him who boasts boast in this, that he understands and knows me...' God delights in our delight of him. He is pleased when we are pleased in him. The healthiest pride therefore is pride with a trajectory that is toward God."

Anna: "Opportunities arise when one delights in who they were created to be and what they were created to do, because one's mind, heart, and behaviors unite with purpose. Pride based upon external factors or an air of cockiness masking one's insecurities is off-putting because one's interactions are not genuine or meaningful. Confidence is not feeling superior or more worthwhile than others. With assurance, humility and tact should not trail, but should instead gracefully accompany one's value system and motives. Healthy pride is not self-importance or arrogance; it simply has hope in one's divine identity. Acceptance with who one is, belief in who one is striving to be, and a humble remembrance of where one has so desperately been is budding self-regard. One's security, one's enjoyment, and one's dignity lies assuredly in Christ."

Question One Hundred And Ninety-Nine
July 18th

Most of us believe that anyone suffering from mental health issues should be offered all that humankind has learned about healing the soul, body, and spirit from both biblical and psychological perspectives. What can we say to those who disagree with us?

Jon: "Psalm 34:8 says, 'Oh, taste and see that the LORD is good!' Those who do not believe that the Bible should be offered to the suffering have simply not tasted the Bible. We can look at food. We can smell it, touch it, and talk about it. But until we take a bite and chew, we can never know whether or not it tastes good. We can look at the Bible. We can even read it. But until we allow its truths to descend from our mind to our heart, we will never know whether or not it tastes good."

Anna: "One could say that wanting to understand, heal, and grow is quintessential for the human experience. However, it is understood that meaningless information or secular head-knowledge can take one away from the simple, yet profoundly life-changing theological truths that are pertinent for establishing, maintaining, and developing emotional strength and mental health. Humankind is flawed and frequently takes an alternate route rather than the course intended for authentic healing and lasting transformation. People were given incredible minds to learn, discover, process, and problem solve. Understanding truth is imperative and one should discern which psychological perspectives align with God and his Word."

Question Two Hundred
July 19th

Many of us socially isolate ourselves because we are afraid of being rejected. Can you offer us a *baby step* which we can take toward interacting with others?

Jon: "Responsibility and duty tend to affect strength and boldness in one's actions. The Lord said to Joshua, 'Have I not commanded you? Be strong and courageous. Do not be frightened, and do not be dismayed, for the LORD your God is with you wherever you go' (Josh. 1:9). It is not that God is with us because we are bold; it is that we are bold *because* God is with us. We have the prestigious duty to rely on his infinite strength."

Anna: "Understanding one's fear of rejection is a good place to begin. To withdraw and socially isolate oneself can go hand in hand with feelings of inadequacy. Self-imposed isolation with a false perception of safety can cause negative self-internalizations of others and perpetuates self-rejection. Humankind was not created to be strictly alone. However, to meditate in solitude for rejuvenation purposes is vital for one's psychological and emotional health. A false pretense of security when isolating because of minimized anxiety can have interesting effects on one's social development. When that false pretense turns into denial of one's basic needs and emotions, quality of life decreases. Knowing one's true identity, recognizing one's purpose in Christ, and seeking out resources that nurture fellowship and social acceptance will help one take steps towards social interaction."

Question Two Hundred And One
July 20th

Letting go: the ability to quit the bitterness held in old habits and hurtful people. Why are some people simply not able to let go?

Jon: "The strategy for doing away with bitterness may not be obvious. In the book of Acts, Peter encounters a magician named Simon. Seeing that Simon was entrenched in bitterness he said to him, 'Repent, therefore, of this wickedness of yours, and pray to the Lord that, if possible, the intent of your heart may be forgiven you' (Acts 8:22). Doing away with bitterness has less to do with *quitting* certain actions and more to do with *starting* certain other actions. Prayerful repentance is the light that scatters the shadows of bitterness."

Anna: "Bitterness spears through positive intentions and has the power to destroy relationships. Living in, replaying, and allowing oneself to be stuck in the past will only create devastating emotional, psychological, and behavioral cycles of regret. Letting go is not always simple, black, or white. This process can emerge from defeat, anger, confusion, resentment, and deep-rooted pain. It is not a final destination; it is a daily, conscious decision to conquer life within acceptance and love. When addressing the past while moving forward, an attitude of celebration is important to have. To be thankful one has been freed from one's mental and emotional chains are truly a gift. Those who cannot let go are struggling to surrender to God's Holy Spirit by allowing him to transform one's soul."

Question Two Hundred And Two
July 21st

How do we make peace with our hellish pasts?

Jon: "God's Word says, 'And we know that for those who love God all things work together for good, for those who are called according to his purpose' (Rom 8:28). All of us have committed terrible actions or have had terrible actions committed toward us. Some of those actions seem irredeemable. For those who act in accordance with his will, however, God graciously and irrevocably brings about something good from those actions. You can look back over your past and know with certainty that God will manifest good from every moment."

Anna: "Making peace with the abuses of one's past does not mean one is minimizing what took place or that it is wrong to hate the evil that was done. Having an understanding of why immorality exists and that it was not included in God's initial plan is fundamental in understanding his character and living within his peace and framework of love. One of the many beautiful attributes of God is that he has been gracious through the forgiveness of humankind's transgressions: past, present, and future. All one must do is believe in Jesus, repent, and have a relationship with him. Making peace is dependent upon understanding truth and that one is free through Christ. Knowing that one's belief in Jesus leads to an eternal life in God's presence hopefully helps one make peace with their hellish experiences, one's present purpose and future glory."

Question Two Hundred And Three
July 22nd

Many of us have developed food disorders, such as bulimia, anorexia, and overeating. Can you offer us some words that might help us stop these destructive eating patterns?

Jon: "We are not our disorders. Our identity is not found in them. Our identity is found in God. And Romans 8:37 says, 'we are more than conquerors through him who loved us.' God has implanted within us an identity that is *superior* to that of conquerors. Even more, this implantation is no emotionless event for God. He does so because he loves us. Our disorders don't love us. They seek to destroy. So we turn not to our disorders, but to a God who loves us and who works to triumph in our lives."

Anna: "The perceived urgency for control in an unruly world, and the desperation for support when living within a detached family system have severe repercussions. The pressure to meet unreachable ideals takes its toll on those who do not feel worthy or loved. When one attempts to master their emotions upon one's own strength, overcompensations and disorders arise. Consuming support through destructive behaviors only creates more problems. Overindulging or restricting food instead of eating for nourishment develops from one's yearnings to alleviate uncomfortable feelings from one's abusive experiences. Seek God's comfort and faith-based support because he created one with the inherent desire for truth, acceptance, and love; when these components are missing, one seeks out love independently of God."

Question Two Hundred And Four
July 23rd

How does one repent?

Jon: "Many times we sin because we are not satisfied in God. We look to other things in life to satisfy our needs. So we can think of sin as a turning away from God. Repentance is the opposite. It is turning away from our sin and back to God. Peter said in Acts 3:19, 'Repent therefore, and turn back, that your sins may be blotted out.' So genuine repentance is not only a turning of oneself back to God, but also a turning of the knob which opens the door through which enters the forgiveness of God."

Anna: "True transformation will not stand its ground without genuine repentance. The confession of wrongdoing, to recognize where one has gone wrong and to truly have a change of heart, is regret in its process. Abusive people wield and exploit the concept of remorse, trust, and forgiveness. Their cycle is fickle, yet predictable, because 'sorry' is often said, convincing words of harmless intent often follow, and their actions and words can be deceptively loving and blatantly harmful all in the same notion and day. The confusion this creates is unbearable and devastating. Repentance starts with divine conviction and is followed with sincere remorse and then sincere action. A believing and confessing heart accepts atonement from God through Jesus Christ and is truly made clean through one's belief and taking action in faith."

Question Two Hundred And Five
July 24th

Some of us are in such deep spiritual and psychological pain that we want to commit suicide. Is it acceptable in this regard to take one's own life?

Jon: "You are not alone. Deep turmoil of the soul is part of the human condition. Even the authors of the Bible had similar struggles. In fact, about one-quarter of the psalms are expressions of pain and despair. In these times of darkness, it may be helpful to spend time in the light of the Word of God. And his light shines brightest in his Son. Jesus said, 'I am the light of the world. Whoever follows me will not walk in darkness, but will have the light of life' (John 8:12). Though darkness now surrounds us, God promises, 'Light dawns in the darkness' (Ps. 112:4)."

Anna: "Giving up is not the answer to one's problems. It may momentarily alleviate the pain and emotional stress one feels, but the outcome is irreversible and the consequences are deep. Wanting to escape one's suffering is instinctively normal. However, feeling unusually ensnared and in such anguish that one is convinced that there is no other way out is spiritual deception. In this mindset a lack of insight and understanding of one's worth, what is truly possible, and what is doubtlessly at stake have overtaken one's hope. When taking one's life into one's own hands, one's purpose is precipitously cut short, and God's power is disallowed to actively move, heal, and transform."

Question Two Hundred And Six
July 25th

What is a lie?

Jon: "We lie when we immorally and intentionally deceive another. So there is nothing immoral in keeping secret a gift for a friend. Nor is there anything immoral in keeping one's opinion to himself or herself when it might be offensive to another. It is the immorality of a statement that makes it a lie. Proverbs 19:5 says, 'A false witness will not go unpunished, and he who breathes out lies will not escape.' Whatever the unbeliever intends to avoid in this life by lying will be replaced by a punishment far worse in the next; whatever the believer intends to avoid in this life by lying will be replaced by a lessening of reward in the next."

Anna: "When one lies, it serves a conscious and subconscious purpose. Whether to keep or boost the family's reputation, to appease interpersonal relationship issues, or to increase the perception of one's worth, people lie. In the moment or thereafter, dishonesty can alleviate or increase one's negative emotions in attempts to convince oneself or another that things are not what they appear to be. A lie is an illusion, a temporary gratification, and a diversion that deprives one's spirit of authenticity and purity. A liar has been deceived on such essential levels that the distortions in their world and disunions within their soul's identity have been deluded. A deceptive tongue has been polluted by one's human nature and evil's ploys. Surviving childhood abuse and the lies it creates deeply affect one's soul. God is truth; seek him. He heals and disproves all lies."

Question Two Hundred And Seven
July 26th

In the Bible, it says that he who beats small children against a rock will be blessed. How can this ever be?

Jon: "Psalm 137 is a lament over the atrocities and sufferings Jerusalem had endured at the hands of the Babylonians. Namely, how the Babylonian army took Jewish babies and dashed them against rocks. In verse nine, the psalmist says that whoever re-pays with equity this action committed by the Babylonians will be happy or blessed—a sentiment we too might feel if placed in similar circumstances. Notice too that it is not God who makes this statement, but the lamenting psalmist. God does not approve of the psalmist's request, but does approve of his honest com-munication in prayer."

Anna: "Man-willed behaviors and utter atrocities have been doc-umented throughout history. Reality is reality whether condoned or not. Human nature is most definitely temporal yet one's mo-tives and decisions will negatively affect a lifetime if one so lets it. A standard set for exact retribution has evolved through time. A guideline to repay an act with its direct counter no longer is law, but justice is sought accordingly. Psychoanalytic questions, issues, and behaviors are detected within Scripture and con-fronted just like today, including abuse and murder. God does not condone the physical abuse of anyone, let alone children, yet from the beginning he has been completely honest about man's experiences and the deep repercussions that sinful behaviors have on one's spirit and soul."

Question Two Hundred And Eight
July 27th

What does it mean to reflect?

Jon: "We can think of reflection as sincere meditation or contemplation. God's Word teaches at least two key characteristics of reflection. Psalm 119:15 says, 'I will meditate on your precepts, and fix my eyes on your ways.' The first characteristic of reflection is fixation. Aimless thought is the enemy of reflection. There must be a focus or centrality to what we are reflecting upon. The second characteristic is godly content. Fruitful spiritual reflection needs at least in part to be composed of God's precepts and ways. The goodness of our reflection is proven when it gives rise to action."

Anna: "Healthy reflection encompasses all aspects of one's existence. Introspection leads to self-awareness and promotes self-enrichment when one is truly willing to be authentic and assess one's self and experiences. One's self-concept may differ from another's perspective of who one has been and the impression one has made. Deep contemplation takes time, effort, and sincerity. When self-reflecting, be careful of harsh self-scrutiny and self-condemnation. Reflection does not mean one focuses on the negative, it means one acknowledges the pain balanced with truth, to hopefully forgive and heal. Reflection is a powerful tool used for understanding, insight, clarity, and preparedness with the prospect to learn from one's past abuse and lay the foundation for change. One of the many goals of a Christian should be to emulate Christ: to reflect on and embody his nature with a sincere heart."

Question Two Hundred And Nine
July 28th

So many of us don't trust our own opinions; so we don't give them. Does this make us appear weak?

Jon: "Proverbs 30:5 says, 'Every word of God proves true; he is a shield to those who take refuge in him.' We find refuge in God's Word. We are secure in it. If we aren't sure of our opinion, we can err toward God's opinion. And this is hardly erring. For God's Word is never wrong. It is an invincible shield we can take up at any moment. It is a stalwart fortress of truth no enemy can overtake. Even if we are weak, God is strong. And our weakness can give way to God's strength."

Anna: "Lacking confidence may lead to not believing one's intuitions or speaking up when truly necessary. Self-regard affects one's self-esteem, and indecision manifests from insecurity and doubt. When a child's opinions are not valued and criticized, that child can develop an inferiority complex, which leads one to subconsciously filter their self within an experiential frame. A child negatively internalizes an adult's words or behaviors when they communicate that one is unimportant, less than, or bad. If one's self-conception is rooted in mistrustful moments, and one is living based upon these faulty experiences, one will undoubtedly have delusive beliefs, which illuminate one's perception of being weak. Everyone's nature is frail. Only God's indwelling Spirit within the believer can truly perfect one's essence and give one unconquerable strength."

Question Two Hundred And Ten
July 29th

If we dig deep enough, will we find most all of the psychological theories developed by humankind in the Bible?

Jon: "While the Bible is not a psychology book, it is surgically precise on how humanity received its psyche, how humanity ruined it, and how they may redeem it. God is mind. Made in his image, we have mind. And while sin did not utterly destroy our mind, it did injure our cognitive faculties with the greatest damage done to our knowledge of God. By grace, however, God begins to reverse this damage when we place our faith in Jesus Christ (see Phil. 4:19). Sin doesn't necessarily *cause* psychological dysfunction. Sin *allowed* it to enter the world long ago."

Anna: "Within psychology lies the unconscious, and within biblical teaching one's fallible mind can be affected by the unseen. The way one thinks affects one's behaviors, which is accurate, and the Bible is clear in that the believer must hedge one's soul against unrighteousness, because this will affect one's spirit and actions. However, salvation is not found in the human psyche, the gateway is Christ. The human paradox is that one's humanness is dysfunctional, yet when a believer, one's flawed nature can manifest God's perfection. This truth can be completely overwhelming, yet it is truly fantastic and amazing. The psychological theories are not in the Bible but some principles can be connected with biblical truths. The Bible was written through God's innovation and should foremost be valued above the theories conceptualized by humankind."

Question Two Hundred And Eleven
July 30th

How can we have more compassion for those who abused us?

Jon: "Jesus said in Luke 6:28, 'bless those who curse you, pray for those who abuse you.' And he would put these words into action most clearly when, from the cross he had been nailed to, he prayed for his murderers. He prayed not only that they would be forgiven, but he prayed in their defense, saying, 'for they know not what they do' (Luke 23:34). This scene is both tragic and beautiful. The tragedy is in the hands of the abusers, but the beauty is in the hands of the abused. And the beauty comes when the abused prays for his abusers."

Anna: "Everyone has a story, everyone has a soul, and abusive perpetrators are no different. The abused and neglected have experienced loss from disadvantageous to tragic that some develop a viewpoint of no return. When one is persecuted and forced to endure a loveless existence, this creates a destroyed self-perception and many turn around to treat others in the same way. This is the harsh reality of abuse's effect. Having empathy toward another, even abusers, and yet not enabling or accepting their abusive behaviors is a conscience-forward way of being. Opening compassion's door, pushing through fury's fire and walking into love takes courage, forgiveness, and strength. The compassionate heart does not forsake, and yields to move despite the unfairness of life's hand. Choose to love deeply and faithfully serve the Lord with tenderness."

Question Two Hundred And Twelve
July 31st

What is paranoia?

Jon: "Many biblical figures displayed mental conditions associated with paranoia. For example, Cain demonstrated severe jealousy and unwarrantedly believed he was being treated unfairly (see Gen. 4:1-9). King Nebuchadnezzar demonstrated extreme self-importance with irrational anger and distrust (see Dan. 2:1-13, 4:30). These are common characteristics with varying degrees that affect many men and women. Along with receiving appropriate medical advice, we trust that God's power is at work through our weaknesses (2 Cor. 12:9) to bring from them some good (see Rom. 8:28)."

Anna: "Paranoia, which is sorrowfully enslaved to unsoundness and fear, can cause intense relationship conflicts that brew condemnation. When other people's intentions are constantly skewed or perceived as malicious, trust is continually destroyed with every assumption or mental and verbal accusation. Having cognitive processes where reality is altered, irrational, and extreme causes one to feel like the world is heartlessly and defiantly against them, which feeds the savage cycle of danger, suspicion, and emotional disorganization. Deranged cognitive processes which lead to unusual behaviors can and will push a person that much further away from what one longs for within a healthy and sanctified existence. Being afraid is at the root of paranoia and will attempt to detour God's protective peace. God's love transcends when one chooses to abide in his Spirit's essence, hope, and rest."

Question Two Hundred And Thirteen
August 1st

Some of us sense danger even when in a peaceful environment. How can we learn just to enjoy the peace?

Jon: "Jesus said in John 16:33, 'I have said these things to you, that in me you may have peace. In the world you will have tribulation. But take heart; I have overcome the world.' Peace is not found in an environment. Peace is found in a person. Namely, in the person of Jesus Christ. By nature the world is always a source of tribulation, while by nature Christ is always a source of peace. As we enjoy more and more the person of Christ, we experience more and more his peace."

Anna: "One's instincts and a keen awareness of one's surroundings are advantageous for protection. However, one's perception can be exaggerated when one has endured an abusive environment. A hyper-arousal of one's senses affects the body, psyche, and emotional processing which signals for one to make decisions regardless of an inaccurate baseline. This response to a perceived stressor can affect one on many levels. One's alert system could be discerning another's negative mood or noticing someone's aggressive tendencies but this does not mean one is always in immediate threat. Seeing the truth is a gift, yet consistently reacting upon paranoia or the possibility of trouble is fear-based, anxiety driven, and spiritually taxing. Exercising faith and being grounded within one's true identity will bring guidance, guardianship, and wisdom when danger is self-induced, avoidable, or legitimate."

Question Two Hundred And Fourteen
August 2nd

As children, many of us were told not to tell others about our abuse or we and/or our loved ones would die. Now as adults, and with that threat gone, what's the point of sharing our stories?

Jon: "2 Corinthians 3:3 says, '… you are a letter from Christ delivered by us, written not with ink but with the Spirit of the living God, not on tablets of stone but on tablets of human hearts.' We are living epistles. Living letters from God. And he wants to use our stories to direct people to himself in a similar way to how he uses books of the Bible. While this is a great blessing, it is also a great responsibility. Namely in that we must not only share our stories, but share them such that maximum glory and credit is attributed to Christ: the Author and Perfecter of our faith (Heb. 12:2)."

Anna: "Secrecy, silence, and threats of foreboding are abuse's ruse. Sharing one's story allows for personal freedom; it enables psychological and emotional release, self-expression, and builds the platform for social interaction, acceptance, and transformation through one's vulnerabilities and pain. The point is to unchain oneself from bondage, to liberate one's cognitions, emotions, and fears, to grieve and testify to others. God has accounted for Jesus' suffering, false accusations, betrayal, death, and glorious resurrection for humankind's gain, so that one will have palpable proof and the opportunity to experience his saving grace through one's faith."

Question Two Hundred And Fifteen
August 3rd

How can we guard our inner beings?

Jon: "Matthew 6:22-23 says, 'The eye is the lamp of the body. So, if your eye is healthy, your whole body will be full of light, but if your eye is bad, your whole body will be full of darkness...' The quality of content we allow to pass through our senses dramatically influences our inner being. The more worldly content we expose ourselves to, the more worldly our inner being will be. The more godly content we expose ourselves to, the more godly our inner being will be. We guard our inner being by not letting unhealthy worldly content pass through our senses."

Anna: "One's inner being, one's soul, is guarded by one's spirit and mind. When one's thoughts are negative, inaccurate, or misleading, one's very essence, one's cognitions, emotions, and behaviors are adversely persuaded. Sadly, many people psychologically manipulate their self through distorted core beliefs and false self-perceptions, which are subconsciously and consciously connected to one's human nature and dysfunctional experiences. Protecting one's self, graciously covering one's soul with truth, wisdom, and productive action, will preserve one's daily existence and purpose-driven future. One's inner being can be complex yet when nurtured through what truly matters, the simplicity of contentment is attainable. To guard one's being, one must believe in Jesus and depend upon God's shielding Spirit, his unwavering Word, his wisdom, and impenetrable love."

Question Two Hundred And Sixteen
August 4th

Regarding suppressed memories, some of us have read that God will only reveal them to us if and when we are ready. Is he protecting us?

Jon: "Isaiah 40:31 says, 'but they who wait for the LORD shall renew their strength; they shall mount up with wings like eagles; they shall run and not be weary; they shall walk and not faint.' Life is full of unexpected events. And oftentimes we are unprepared. But if we wait for and trust in God's timing, he will make us strong when the unexpected happens. We take comfort in knowing that although there is no guarantee that we will be ready, God is always ready."

Anna: "Self-protective measures occur at the subconscious and conscious levels. One's traumatic experiences may be relived through memories and can repetitiously taunt one to no end when one's awareness of the wherewithal they truly possess has not fully been discovered. An innocent child cannot emotionally handle or differentiate one's being from the abuse. Therefore, suppressing one's traumas to reduce the overpoweringly negative feelings happens naturally and defensively. Yet, never addressing one's painful experiences and the continual minimization of feelings will detrimentally affect one's soul. God's ways are well-defined, yet the depths of his protection will not fully be known until all truths are completely exposed; everything God has done or will ever do is to protect his precious children so that one might live with him gloriously for eternity."

Question Two Hundred And Seventeen
August 5th

If we are angry people, wouldn't it be good for us to take up an activity, like boxing for example, to relieve some hostility?

Jon: "This may address the effects of anger. But it will not address the cause. James 4:1 says, 'What causes quarrels and what causes fights among you? Is it not this, that your passions are at war within you?' Relief will come to those struggling with anger who take up godly activities. For these address the state of the inner being where the cause of anger lies. James continues to suggest that desire and covetousness are likely causes of anger. The key is not to rid oneself of desire, but to redirect it away from worldly things and toward God."

Anna: "Anger is healthy, adaptive, and telling when one's emotional response is processed, understood within one's experience, and promotes change. Anger manifests from deeper feelings and when unaddressed becomes hostile and destructive. When one identifies with being angry, one's underlying issues have penetrated through to strongly influence one's character. Redirecting and expressing one's feelings, where emotional release is met, can truly invigorate and heal one's angry spirit. The pressures to emotionally maintain within a perceived acceptable framework can limit one's vulnerability and psychological growth. Aggression is not of God's Spirit, but born from a fallen nature. The therapeutic extrication of one's traumatic experiences can and will move one closer to God and who he created one to be."

Question Two Hundred And Eighteen
August 6th

Some of us are going to change our affiliations with people who are no good for us: gangs, drug dealers, and toxic people. Isn't this a smart idea?

Jon: "Deuteronomy 22:10 says, 'You shall not plow with an ox and a donkey together.' Why? The ox will pull forward while the donkey stands still, forcing the ox to make fruitless circles around the donkey. This is a perfect illustration of the believer's union with an unbeliever. It is not that we do not have interaction with unbelievers. It is that we must not yolk or bind ourselves to them in ways that hinder our walk with Christ (see 2 Cor. 6:14). Every disconnection from the world is a connection with heaven."

Anna: "One's perceived needs are necessary to understand because they lay the foundation to one's motivation. To associate with a specific culture or subculture within society is connected to one's self-concept, perceived identity, and self-worth. Affiliation with any group has implications and effects for one's mental and physical health because certain associations coexist with different behavioral patterns and lifestyles. For example, the individual who hangs out with drug users is more likely to use or abuse substances and engage in riskier behaviors due to one's environment and the impact mind-altering substances have upon one's moral code and efficacy. So yes, let go of toxic affiliations and affiliate with God's family. When one's identity is in Christ, one has been made righteous through divine affiliation."

Question Two Hundred And Nineteen
August 7th

We want to learn to be more assertive in getting our needs heard and met in a manner that is both genuine and respectful. Can you help us?

Jon: "Jesus says in Matthew 5:37, 'Let what you say be simply "Yes" or "No"; anything more than this comes from evil.' Notice Jesus' emphasis on speech. Namely in its quality and in its simplicity. First, our speech must be of high quality. We speak only humble truth. Second, our speech must be of low quantity. We use as little words as possible to convey only the core of our message. We are fully confident knowing that our high quality and low quantity of speech is certified by Christ himself."

Anna: "Within an abuser's controlling ways and tyrannical mentality, one's voice gets muzzled, shunned, and one exists within an internal dialogue to keep one's opinions locked away. This is a stifling reality to live, feeling as if one needs to break free to just be heard. Within dysfunctional relationships, when one is not safe, clear boundary setting is often futile because one cannot make sense of another's ambivalent and nonsensical ways. Self-awareness, addressing one's desires, and processing one's emotions effectively lead to productive communication and nurturing oneself apart from and within relationship. The ability to express one's thoughts comes from conviction and self-confidence. To lessen one's indecision and uncertainty, one must stand firm upon God's Word, his promises, and purpose uniquely chosen for one's life."

Question Two Hundred And Twenty
August 8th

What is virtue?

Jon: "A virtuous life is one filled with moral integrity and good works. 2 Peter 1:5 says, 'For this very reason, make every effort to supplement your faith with virtue, and virtue with knowledge…' First notice that virtue must be supplied with knowledge. Coming to know what is and is not virtuous requires a lifetime of learning. Second, notice that virtue is subordinate to faith. It is by faith in Christ that we gain true access to God and our virtue attains cosmic significance (see Rom. 5:1-2). Without faith, a thousand years of good works is accomplished in vain (see Gal. 2:16)."

Anna: "Virtue is righteousness and one's vices destroy one's virtue, and one's personal integrity enables one's behavioral patterns. An abusive environment breeds mental and emotional weaknesses, immoralities, and addictions, which teach one to cling to vices and not one's intrinsic values and virtues. When honorable relational systems are not modeled through healthy behaviors and interactions, negative messages are internalized, matched, and then projected. Bad habits stem from low self-respect, self-worth, and self-esteem, not from truth. When negative seeds are planted within one's psyche and being from one's parents, family, environment, and worldly norms, generations of dysfunctional misfortune and devastation follow. One's heart reflects one's virtue and one's virtue reflects one's integrity. One's character in Christ will illuminate one's virtuous soul when leading a life controlled by the Holy Spirit."

Question Two Hundred And Twenty-One
August 9th

Many of us have so little. What's wrong with coveting what others possess?

Jon: "The tenth commandment forbids coveting what is not ours. Coveting is dangerous because, unlike the other commandments regarding human-to-human interaction, coveting occurs within the inner being. In other words, no one but God sees us covet. Knowing no one will object to our inner sins, we continue in them. Given enough time, we can become callous to those hidden sins. And untamed, hidden sin usually evolves into more devastating, outwardly transgressions. If even the apostle Paul once struggled with 'all kinds of covetousness' (Rom. 7:8), we ought to destroy our covetousness before it destroys us."

Anna: "To unrightfully crave magnifies one's dissatisfaction within. Desires are inborn yet an unfulfilled soul consumed with wanting more creates a self-centered, discontent perspective. One's greed or possessions can become a replacement for what one never received as a child. To envy another for who they are, what they have, or what they have accomplished can stir up self-destructive cognitions, beliefs, and aspirations. Covetousness can turn into jealousy or begrudging behaviors. Illicit desires, at their core, are faulty and impair one psychologically and emotionally. Immorality shows up in so many forms whether subtle or accepted by mainstream culture. God calls the believer to be thankful and content. When immersed in Christ, one will fathom and yearn for what truly matters."

Question Two Hundred And Twenty-Two
August 10th

What is kindness?

Jon: "Jesus said in Luke 6:35, 'But love your enemies, and do good, and lend, expecting nothing in return...' He used the word *enemies* on purpose. He said *expecting nothing in return* on purpose. Because kindness is not easy. It requires us to ignore the impulse to hate our enemies and keep everything for ourselves. This means that we are most kind when we desire most not to be, but still do good. We must ask ourselves whom we least desire to be kind toward. Only when we show *this* person love and generosity does God say that we are kind."

Anna: "Kindness is ingrained yet can be suppressed or unlearned. Abusive people manipulate and sprinkle kindness amidst the cruelty, which is very confusing and frustrating. Thoughtfulness stimulates positive emotions and one's internal chemistry is affected. Niceness is often equated with trust. However, when kindness is superficial, deceptive, or does not have depth, discernment toward one's motives must be weighed. Many will misuse or not appreciate one's kindness. Being considerate and compassionate are not frailties, they are beautiful qualities to embody, and pleasing to one's soul. If one's heart desires to be treated pleasantly, but by what means? A need for acceptance can manipulate one into codependency. Jesus was courageously kind and still confident in truth. He did not shift his beliefs or behaviors for anyone because he served God and him alone."

Question Two Hundred And Twenty-Three
August 11th

What is sloth?

Jon: "The slothful are those able to work who are reluctant to do so. And this reluctance leaves the soul empty. Proverbs 13:4 says, 'The soul of the sluggard craves and gets nothing, while the soul of the diligent is richly supplied.' There is something about work which fills one's inner being with rich contentment and accomplishment—two things the human spirit craves because we were created to crave them (see Eph. 2:10). Left ignored, these cravings may fester into depression and guilt. But we are motivated to work knowing it will bring not only monetary riches but heavenly riches as well."

Anna: "An idle mind is an idle body that stands still and misses opportunity. Laziness is a deceptive ploy, a mortal issue that affects one's soul and behaviors. Sloth takes advantage of sadness, which manifests in mind, body, and spirit. One's will, when succumbed to one's dysfunction and internal chaos, changes one's beliefs and self-direction. When motivation diminishes due to many factors of one's abuse, life's circumstances, or relationship issues, one's goals are suppressed and pushed aside. Sloth is a vice, an excuse, and a self-fulfilling prophecy to fail because that is what one was expected to do anyway, right? God created humankind with the liberty to accomplish his purpose, to use one's talents toward a miraculous mission. Do not let deception keep one idle, for when one does nothing, evil has more opportunity to flourish."

Question Two Hundred And Twenty-Four
August 12th

What is diligence?

Jon: "Diligence is determined hard work. Colossians 3:23 says, 'Whatever you do, work heartily, as for the Lord and not for men…' Hard work is not for money—though money may be acquired through it. And hard work is not for status or success—though status and success may be acquired also through it. Hard work is done for God. This is because men and women are highly susceptible to idolatrize their work and serve it rather than God. For those who loathe work, if we serve God through our work, even the most bothersome task becomes sacred and meaningful."

Anna: "A negligent upbringing can crush diligence or have it fight for one's existence. When desires spark interest and goals are set, diligence carries plans out and drives it home. Perseverance uplifts one's character, self-confidence, self-worth, and reflects the unseen heart. Dreams come to life through one's hopes and actions, and one's determination is a product of one's internal processes and self-beliefs. Abuse can create irrational cognitions, a distorted self-perspective, and when fueled by deceit one's emotions become downtrodden, and lethargy can subtly creep in. Persistent laziness causes psychological and emotional pain because it opposes one's purpose. Inactivity deactivates one's soul and suppresses one's gifts. The Holy Spirit gives abilities so that one will be equipped, hardworking, embodying a strong will that seeks God, leads by example, and tells people of Jesus' gift of salvation."

Question Two Hundred And Twenty-Five
August 13th

What is greed?

Jon: "Greed is the excessive desire to acquire more than one needs. Jesus said in Luke 12:15, 'Take care, and be on your guard against all covetousness, for one's life does not consist in the abundance of his possessions.' The guard is stationed at his post because the enemy attacks at any moment. Greed is such an enemy. It assaults us daily and without warning. So we must stand guard over our inner being lest it be infiltrated. May our desire for the things of the world ever wither as our desire for the things of God ever expand."

Anna: "Exorbitance reflects one's innermost desires and a greedy frame of mind lacks depth. One's pride can get in the way of so much because selfishness breeds subtle and obvious self-distortions. Within abuse, self-centeredness and greed coincide because wrongdoing does not care about whom it destroys and takes what it desires. Dysfunctional behaviors impose disappointments and unconscionable messages upon its victims, which create a perceived deficiency from deep within. This cycle creates a futile hunt because now the survivor yearns for what was taken and now seems to be lost. This craving, such overpowering compulsions, creates a deep neediness, a lust if you will, to appease the pain. The believer is called to be satisfied because one has been given the answer, Jesus Christ, the one whose Spirit will appease one's soul and truly gratify one's life."

Question Two Hundred And Twenty-Six
August 14th

What is charity?

Jon: "Charity is the giving away of one's possessions. Hebrews 13:16 says, 'Do not neglect to do good and to share what you have, for such sacrifices are pleasing to God.' There are two points here. First, charity is not to be neglected. The Christian has a responsibility to give to those in need. Second, charity is worship. We venerate and glorify God when we give to others. Moreover, if we are unable to part with our possessions for godly causes, we show that we do not own them; they own us."

Anna: "Survivors of abuse experienced malevolence in many ways. The continual imposition of ill intent through maltreatment changes one's idea of trust. Doubt will often spark feelings that another's compassion is negatively motivated or that one feels sorry for them. Acknowledging one's circumstance as unfair is very different than treating someone as if they are completely dependent upon one's assistance. When extending a helping hand, one's reasons should be sincerely weighed. One's environment does not equate to one's worth and one should not be looked at or categorized as a charity case. Generous acts, when self-appeasing or from selfish ambition, attempt to conceal impure motives and underlying insecurities. Graciousness invites generosity and a giving spirit is comforting, infectious, and inspiring. Kindness stems from love, empathy, and compassion. A forthright and generous heart extends past one's behaviors and penetrates another's soul. Give humbly and graciously in Jesus' name."

Question Two Hundred And Twenty-Seven
August 15th

What is temperance?

Jon: "Temperance is self-restraint over indulgence. 1 Corinthians 9:25 says, 'Every athlete exercises self-control in all things.' Here Paul compares the Christian to an athlete. The athlete abstains from too much food or drink or idleness for the sake of performing well in their sport. The Christian too must often practice moderation for the sake of performing well in their faith. Our desires must not rule over us; we must rule over our desires. And we are motivated to practice temperance knowing our reward in heaven is an eternal glory beyond all comparison (2 Cor. 4:17)."

Anna: "Temperance is the ability to control one's lusts, desires, unhealthy behaviors, and the wisdom to understand the value and significance of doing so. Disorganized environments create one's needs to feel in control even when one is choosing to do uncontrollable and pleasurable things. Addictive behaviors, impulses, and emotional reactivity all stem from dysfunction's intemperance. Gluttony, substance abuse, and self-indulgences develop from psychological confusions and deficiencies within emotional regulations and behavioral processes. One's cravings symbolize what one truly needs. When one becomes lonely and longs for comfort, attention, and emotional support, then one may go overboard with instant gratification to subdue one's isolated and painful feelings. God desires one to yearn for what is upright because it will bring light to one's life; the indulgently sinful things of the world will become more and more unappealing when the Holy Spirit leads."

Question Two Hundred And Twenty-Eight
August 16th

What is chastity?

Jon: "The chaste abstain from sexual immorality. And many believe they have accomplished this when they keep themselves from sinful physical actions. However, Jesus said in Matthew 5:28, 'But I say to you that everyone who looks at a woman with lustful intent has already committed adultery with her in his heart.' We must not only abstain from sinful actions, but sinful thoughts as well. Sinful action almost always begins in the mind. So when we take control of our thoughts, we significantly lessen the likelihood that more damaging physical sin will occur. We must be chaste in body and mind."

Anna: "Chastity is keeping one's purity balanced within the confines of moral goodness, shielding against sexual immorality while following soulful truths. The negative effects abuse has on one's concept of intimacy, one's pleasure threshold, one's sexual mentality, and one's self-esteem can be detrimental. To give away one's virtue through temptation, or to be pressured or forced into performing demeaning acts, affects one's mind, emotions, self-image, self-worth, and relational attachment impulses and defenses. Lust controls one's flesh and one's flesh can profoundly reflect one's choices. The world thrives upon its appetite for excitement, pleasure, gratification, emotional escalation, and the illusion of self-comfort. Satan solicits sexual deviancies to bring one's soul down to his hellish level, to accomplish his evil schemes, and because he knows the effects they have on one's being: it flames serious disconnection from God and deceptive shame."

Question Two Hundred And Twenty-Nine
August 17th

What is wrath?

Jon: "Wrath is extreme anger. And it may be helpful to consider two kinds of wrath: God's wrath, and human wrath. Human wrath is always sinful. Jesus said in Matthew 5:22 that 'everyone who is angry with his brother will be liable to judgment.' Notice that mere anger potentially qualifies us for judgment. Therefore extreme anger will qualify us for extreme judgment. God's wrath on the other hand is always righteous. His perfect justice and holiness guarantee that his anger—however extreme—is always justified. It is comforting to know that God's wrath is only poured out with just cause."

Anna: "Anger, when fueled by injustice, needs wise conduct to withstand. Abuse and wrath can be one and the same yet they can differ dependent upon one's intent and following behaviors. An abusive person's temper stems from deep within, and when emotionally escalated, the inability to manage the rising frustrations are dangerously fueled onto another. Anger fuels vengeance and one's anger can turn into hatred and malicious action. When harsh and abrupt wrath is what one witnessed and knew as a child, one's perception of acceptable reactivity is skewed. One's image of God is reflected within one's home, and when abusive behaviors are prevalent, one's concept of God would seem to reflect the same. God loves, yet any wrath he has is justified because his anger is righteously directed at sin, not the sinner, whom he created and deeply loves."

Question Two Hundred And Thirty
August 18th

What is patience?

Jon: "Romans 8:25 says, 'But if we hope for what we do not see, we wait for it with patience.' Notice how Scripture connects patience with hope. Patience involves hope. In other words, patience is not only a willingness to endure. Patience is expectation. And we don't put our expectation in receiving whatever it is *we* desire. We put our expectation in that God will allow to happen whatever *he* desires. This kind of patience will always produce fruit because God's will is always fruitful."

Anna: "Patience is bearing one's life graciously. Patience eases one's impulses, will transform one's thought processes, and will affect one's intent and behaviors. The world's ways are not virtuous and one's honorable deeds will not necessarily be accepted or valued. Even when one is walking along the humble and patient pathway, one may be rejected for simply having wisdom and peace of mind. To endure one's pain, self-inflicted or not, is strength of heart and abiding in one's purpose. Knowing what one is capable of and continually pressing on despite one's mistakes is patient perseverance. Maintaining composure under pressure or in hurtful situations shows an ability to suffer long and displays faith and character. Endurance and self-control will enable one to listen and hear from the Lord to accomplish his will. One's fortitude comes from God, empowered by his Holy Spirit, who will develop one's patient mentality, with his divine hope, measure, and wisdom."

Question Two Hundred And Thirty-One
August 19th

What is narcissism?

Jon: "Narcissism is sin. Proverbs 16:18 says, 'Pride goes before destruction, and a haughty spirit before a fall.' Pride, or satisfaction in one's accomplishments or self, is not necessarily bad in itself. Rather, pride is a trigger emotion that can lead one into spiritual danger. Narcissism then is a morally reprehensible state of over-advanced pride. All of us, however, have at one time sinned in thought or deed and therefore have no right to such pride, if any at all. Jesus Christ was the only perfect person—committing no sin—and yet he did not act narcissistically, but instead gave himself up unto death for the sake of others."

Anna: "Narcissism is satisfaction's quest through self-importance. When a person is self-focused, self-absorbed, arrogant, or obsessed with their self-image, they fall into the category of having narcissistic tendencies or traits. Narcissistic people have the propensity to think only of themselves and lack empathy for others. This can cause deep confusion, rejection, and codependence within those the narcissist knows. Loving oneself, taking care of oneself, and valuing oneself is not narcissism. Putting oneself on a pedestal above others and being so self-absorbed that one cannot see straight or acknowledge another's presence and pain, creates serious problems within relationships. God desires for humankind to esteem others just as one esteems themself, but to be humble, caring, and selfless in the process."

Question Two Hundred And Thirty-Two
August 20th

What is humility?

Jon: "Philippians 2:3 says, 'Do nothing from selfish ambition or conceit, but in humility count others more significant than your-selves.' A bloated ego is the enemy of humility, always bringing rivalry and conceit. Pride and pomp never fit the humble. It is modesty and meekness that clothe them. And Christ wore these better than any. Coming down from heaven, he dwelt among and loved the very men that would crucify him. He not only washed dirt from their feet, he washed sin from their hearts. Such is the power of humility."

Anna: "Awareness of what one is prone to, an understanding of one's psychological limitations, and a realistic perspective of one's flawed nature shows humility. When one understands their limitations of self-will, and weighs unreachable with accom-plishable ideals grounded in biblical truth, one has a realistic per-spective. Humility's scope exposes another's pretentions, yet an unassuming heart will continue to be strong and respectful to-ward one in difficult, extremely provoking, or abusive situations. Humility is not weakness, nor is submission not standing up for what is upright. One's spirit becomes exalted through humility's power. No one epitomizes perfection and to act as such is inau-thentic. When one walks in truth and strength, one has humbly surrendered to God's will. Through his Spirit's conviction, dis-cernment, and love, one's pride can be guarded and kept wisely out of reach."

Question Two Hundred And Thirty-Three
August 21st

People keep calling some of us sadists. What is a sadist, anyway?

Jon: "A sadist is one who derives pleasure from the suffering of others. Sadism is especially dangerous precisely because of its incorporation of pleasure. Since pleasure is immediately gratifying, we are given the illusion that whatever we are doing is good. But suffering and pain are degradations of what God created as good. And any willful participation in the degradation of what God created as good is sin. Sadism therefore is sinful. This reminds us to pause and reflect on the sources from which we derive pleasure. If any of those sources depose what is good, we do well in deposing those sources."

Anna: "A sadist is gratified through misery that is not their own. Ruthless preoccupations consume the sadist and one's thoughts involve dishonoring others. A possible allurement toward violent cognitions, abusive acts, and a blatant disregard for another's value underlie or surface forcefully. Sadistic tendencies are a reflection of one's deep-seated emotions, desires, and lusts. When a person is severely abused, one can fuel the maltreatment into twisted projections and manifestations. Extreme cruelty and perverse fantasies stem from negative experiences and psychological and emotional bondage. Sadism is from Satan himself, so do not be fooled; it is not of God, it can be debauchery, which is in complete opposition of what is healthy and good: remember, one is forgiven, spiritually reborn, and set free through faith in Jesus."

Question Two Hundred And Thirty-Four
August 22nd

Don't these two statements contradict one another? God will punish those who abuse children. And, if one believes in Jesus Christ, they will be saved.

Jon: "God is perfectly just. He will always bring the right punishment for every sin. But those who believe in Jesus Christ are not punished (see Rom. 8:1). That's the point of the gospel—the good news. But that doesn't mean that their punishment is erased. On the contrary, their punishment is placed on Christ. In this way, God is both the just and the justifier (Rom. 3:25). Because Jesus is God, his sacrifice is of infinite value. It can atone for all sins ever committed by humanity. Nothing will stop God's love from reaching those who love his Son."

Anna: "One's deliverance is not contingent upon one's actions, nor is the extent of one's punishment a culmination of how little one is loved. One can believe in Jesus, yet still sin and coincidentally reap what one has willfully done. Abusers may or may not be punished observably. However, the retribution for the choices made have many possible aftereffects within the psychological, physical, and spiritual domain. One's behaviors are not an indicator of one qualifying for salvation, yet do demonstrate the spiritual enslavement one is in. God's grace saves; it is a divine gift that is not deserved. Human behaviors are grievously filled with contradictions, however, God is most definitely not."

Question Two Hundred And Thirty-Five
August 23rd

Most of us regret our lost childhoods and the horrible repercussions from not having them. Is there a way to stop regretting this?

Jon: "The apostle Paul struggled with regret (see 2 Cor. 7:8-10). His first letter to the church at Corinth left the congregation extremely grieved by their actions. This grieving, however, ultimately led the Corinthians to godly repentance. Seeing this, Paul's regret turned into rejoicing. He saw the good that came from his grief. This task is by no means easy. But when we prayerfully consider what good has come from our grief, we invite God's omnipotent Spirit to help us replace our regret with rejoicing."

Anna: "Human beings do not have the ability to change the past, which makes regret a natural reaction that comes from wanting protection from the outcome of painful circumstances. Where regret begets regret is when mourning becomes darkness, resentment, or obsession with what one has experienced, never had, or desperately wants. These fixations create a cycle of dissatisfaction, bitterness, and secondary victimization that turn one's present state into a nightmarish sequel of reliving the past and enabling one's present demons. To move forward, embody acceptance, forgiveness, and gratefulness daily. God naturally restores what is damaged but one must choose to pardon; stop residing within negativity and surrender one's heartache to the Lord, so that one's discontented essence may be renewed through him."

Question Two Hundred And Thirty-Six
August 24th

Why are some people sexually attracted to children as opposed to seeking someone their own age?

Jon: "Some of our proclivities are a product of our upbringing, environment, genetics, and so forth. Bluntly, we cannot help but be sexually attracted to whomever we are sexually attracted to. But remember, humanity brought sin into the world. And sin has negatively affected the world, including human sexuality. So it is very likely that our sexual desires will be marred by sin (see Rom 1:18-21). But the urge to do anything immoral does not give us the right to do it. Sometimes we have to forsake our desires in order to love God and follow his commands."

Anna: "Sexual deviances are truly creating confusion within the minds and hearts of many. A perceived low self-efficacy and delusional thinking within intimate relationships are just a few factors that could push one into having a nonconforming sexual appetite toward young children. Just like any impaired behavioral process, one's beliefs and cognitions are notably misaligned. Perceptions are powerful and when influenced by antisocial tendencies and psychopathologies, one can come to believe and think almost anything, even ruminate and act upon their sexual attraction to children. The Word of God warns against those who destroy innocence, and for those who have survived sexual abuse, he understands one's pain; Jesus died for all, and believers can powerfully intercede through prayer for those who are deeply lost and in need of a savior."

Question Two Hundred And Thirty-Seven
August 25th

When some of us were only children, we received gifts of food, drugs, money, housing, alcohol, affection, and cigarettes. At first, we thought that these offerings were given to us out of love but later understood that they were just a way to get us to have sex with one or more people and nothing more. We were tricked and exploited. Weren't we?

Jon: "Yes. Unequivocally. And in these types of circumstances, it was not your fault. Nevertheless, God's Word clearly condemns bribery (Ex. 23:8) as well as extramarital sex (1 Cor. 6:18). So we see at least three wrongs committed here: one on the part of the gift receiver, and two on the part of the gift giver. The gift receiver is guilty of extramarital sex. And the gift giver is guilty of both bribery and extramarital sex. Even though both are guilty, both are still capable of receiving God's mercy and forgiveness through faith in Jesus Christ (Acts 13:38). May we never be tricked into believing God will not forgive us, especially when at the deception of another."

Anna: "Being tricked is accurate because a molester's tactics are immoral and manipulate complexly. When grooming, the child molester strives to desensitize and deceptively condition by breaking down the child's natural defenses so that the perverse behaviors appear unsuspicious. A secure bond, credibility, then privacy are the initial goals and most molesters are very patient and go to extreme measures to cover their tracks. A child is highly susceptible to trickery, but God is not, for he knows all; justice and truth prophetically prevail."

Question Two Hundred And Thirty-Eight
August 26th

Many of us were abandoned by our parents/caregivers. And now as adults, we believe that our loved ones will abandon us as well. Can you help us?

Jon: "People will leave us. They will come and go. If not for any other reason than that they or we will pass away. But Deuteronomy 31:8 says, 'It is the LORD who goes before you. He will be with you; he will not leave you or forsake you.' God will not come and go. He has been with us since we were born. He is with us now. And through faith in Jesus Christ, he will always be with us (see John 3:16). Therefore we may abandon the thought that we will ever be abandoned by God."

Anna: "Abandonment can affect one so deeply and recurrently that the thought of truly trusting others seems too scary. Within trauma, abuse, or desertion, an inconsistency with another's constancy persists and a deficit in tolerating extreme feelings toward a particular, temporary caregiver, or lack thereof, is internalized and projected within relationships. To be neglected when love should endure empowers internal ambivalences and apprehensions toward one's value within connection. When left behind or given away, an unconscious cycle of self-sabotage may ensue to fulfill and affirm one's worst fears. Human beings can heartlessly forsake one another, which is truly demoralizing. Hold tightly to God's promises because he loves completely and has adopted believers into his family and kingdom."

Question Two Hundred And Thirty-Nine
August 27th

The Fifth Commandment tells us to honor our father and mother. How do we honor fathers and mothers who abused us?

Jon: "The author of Ephesians observes that this commandment is the first with a promise: 'that it may go well with you and that you may live long in the land' (Eph. 6:2-3). We honor our father and mother for their God-given responsibility to raise us well. If parents choose to abuse their children instead, they are in sin — and sin is not honorable. Children are commanded to honor their parents that it may go well with them, not that they may be abused."

Anna: "Honoring a parent who has abused you does not mean one remains enslaved by their dysfunction nor does it mean being permanently or completely submissive to an abusive parent's authority. One can honor oneself and others through compassion, understanding, forgiveness, and yet still enforce and keep healthy boundaries established in truth and love. To set personal limits with an abuser with the intent to protect and heal one's self is not wrong. Rebuilding broken bridges for someone who has completely demolished your trust can only be done through surrender, along with psychological, emotional, and spiritual transformation. Faith in Jesus and God's Holy Spirit can truly restore what humankind has broken, yet without God, true and divine honor is not accomplished."

Question Two Hundred And Forty
August 28th

Most of us believe that love is an action verb. For example, the mother who stands by and does nothing while her children are being beaten by her husband does not love her children. Correct?

Jon: "Jesus said in John 13:34, 'A new commandment I give to you, that you love one another: just as I have loved you, you also are to love one another.' So we are commanded to love *like* Jesus loved. And Jesus loved through all that he was able to do. He cared for the sick and the destitute. He washed the feet of his disciples. He suffered torture and death for the sake of others. A mother's inaction to protect her children when she *is able* to protect them is not showing love. But a mother's inaction to protect her children when she *is not able* to protect them neither demonstrates nor disproves her love."

Anna: "Sadly, some people do not love well, yet their inabilities can teach life-changing lessons. Human love is deficient, a reflection of one's spirit and conscience, which propels one's thoughts, emotions, and behaviors. One's capacity to love can fluctuate, grow, and vary dependent upon one's mindset and what is at stake. Fruitful love requires action, patience, grace, kindness, forgiveness, and truth. When abuse disrupts the family unit because the dynamics have shifted within the abuser's control, one's faith and genuine desires may somewhat retreat to simply survive. Love is beautifully deep and fully capable yet human beings underestimate its power. Unfortunately, human love can cower when needed most. However, God's love will transcend any occasion when consciously honored."

Question Two Hundred And Forty-One
August 29th

Some of us have family and friends who were also abused in childhood. These people remain very emotionally immature and don't believe that they need help. Do you have any words of advice?

Jon: "God's Word is clear that no one is perfect (Rom. 3:23). There is not one person who is without sin. And since God is perfectly holy, these sins keep us from his presence (Isa. 59:2). The thing we need most—to reach God—is the one thing we need most help in. For it is impossible for us to do this on our own (John 14:6). We need Christ. He is who connects man to God. So if we can demonstrate that one is not perfect, we prove their need for Christ."

Anna: "When exposed to consistent abuse one's brain chemistry may change and one's emotional development may get arrested within continuous defective cycles and subconscious processes. After trauma one's identity becomes somewhat distorted. One's cognitive intelligence may be subtly stunted in correlation to one's maturation and emotional regulation abilities. To regress to one's insecure, vulnerable state is somewhat instinctual and needed to soothe and appease what has been psychologically and emotionally lost. Yet, not addressing the abuse's aftermath is disruptive to one's emotional stability, healing, and growth. Everyone needs assistance, which is why God created humankind: to have fellowship with and the support of one another, and to establish and relate an enthroned awareness of one's dependence upon him."

Question Two Hundred And Forty-Two
August 30th

If one was never taught what a sin is—take worshiping false idols, for example—why would they be called a sinner if he or she didn't know any better?

Jon: "Romans 2:6-16 shows that human beings have God's law written on their hearts. We possess a conscience that either accuses or excuses our thoughts and actions. So morality is spiritually instinctive. Everyone has an understanding of good and bad, right and wrong. But the passage also shows that a person will be judged based on how they respond to their moral understanding. God will not punish someone for something they did not know was wrong. He will judge everyone based on what moral knowledge has been revealed to them in nature and conscience."

Anna: "Whether one is aware of certain truths or blindly influenced by their environment, every human being commits immoral action and therefore is a sinner. Now, being 'a sinner' is attached to such deep, negative connotations that one can simply feel unworthy and damned for just being alive. The psychological effects of sin's truth, disconnected from one's divine purpose, are calamitous to the human soul and spirit. However, sin's misfortune has triumphantly been overthrown. The unveiled beauty of it all is that God truly has resolved what sin has created, which is why he sent Jesus to die for humanity, to resurrect and conquer death, so that through belief one will be saved from inevitable transgressions."

Question Two Hundred And Forty-Three
August 31st

Is it true that truth is never the enemy?

Jon: "Truth is simply what corresponds to reality. What makes something true or not is whether or not it accurately portrays how the world actually is. Truth is emotionless in this way. It is we who have emotions toward the truth. We may like the truth, or hate it, or be indifferent toward it. But truth is never these things. For example, if the truth is that someone is hostile toward us, it is not that truth that is hostile toward us, but that someone. The truth regarding the enemy is not the enemy; the enemy the truth is regarding is the enemy."

Anna: "One can use truth for evil, to divide, to conquer, and to manipulate or abuse. For example, one may deliver the truth with such malice, disdain, or derision that the messenger's motives twist the truth and shine a crooked light upon the information's authenticity. The truths behind one's childhood abuse have attempted to employ damaging psychological processes, yet one has the capability to overcome. Misleading or ambiguous messages can merely be bait to hook its prey and watch one's demise. Truthfulness can be powerful and has the ability to revolutionize and advance one's psychological and emotional intelligence, one's foresight, and purpose in life. Honesty is a precious gift when applied genuinely and personally. The truth of God's news brings forth an abundance of divine blessings to those who truly receive it."

Question Two Hundred And Forty-Four
September 1st

Many of us who are serving jail time were abused as children. Is there any hope for our futures?

Jon: "Jeremiah 29:11 says, 'For I know the plans I have for you, declares the LORD, plans for welfare and not for evil, to give you a future and a hope.' There has never been nor will there ever be one moment where God is not thinking about you. He is thinking about you right now. And all he wants for you and your future is peace and hope. If we are ever uncertain about our future, we can remember that God is certain about it. And if we are ever without hope, we can remember that God hopes in us."

Anna: "Most definitely. Realistically, one's abusive inflictions will affect one's mentality and behaviors. Even though the stigmas of incarceration echo beyond every jail cell's walls into the minds and hearts of others, a humbling reality check at one's most broken has the potential to transform one's life. When easily accessed temptations have been stripped away, and one is left to simply sit with who one has become, humility, reflection, and holy-assessment can thrive. Jail is a consequence for one's actions but not a definitive benchmark for one's value or future success. In fact, it can be the precursor needed to truly shape one's destiny. When at one's most desperate place, God can work within one's soul, and through faith, one's future will be anointed by God's righteous hand."

Question Two Hundred And Forty-Five
September 2nd

A great number of us have heard that God doesn't give us more than we can handle. Is this true?

Jon: "1 Corinthians 10:13 says, 'No temptation has overtaken you that is not common to man. [God] will not let you be tempted beyond your ability… he will also provide the way of escape, that you may be able to endure it.' God will never put us in a situation where we are forced to sin. If we were forced to do something immoral, it would not be sin, for we had no choice. In situations where we do have a choice, however, our free will guarantees that we can always deny sin. God does not keep us from sinning; we must keep ourselves from it."

Anna: "Suffering is universal and not an indicator that one is unloved. Assumptions and stigmas can unconsciously attach to personal or family burdens, which stew shame and a negative self-identity. There are different forces working against one within moments of hardship and tribulation. Testing through psychological and physical pain is evil's advocate and could take one out if one opts to surrender to the deception and lies. Making the distinction between the causes of one's trial and maintaining a faithful and discerning heart is critical to withstand life's difficulties. God fully grasps one's capabilities and perceived strength when under fire. He knows one's limits and sees one's will. Wholeheartedly trust and seek him, especially when facing adversity."

Question Two Hundred And Forty-Six
September 3rd

Some of us grew up witnessing such satanic rituals as incest, murder, orgies, voodoo, witchcraft, bestiality, black magic, cannibalism, sexual torture, human sacrifice, and the drinking of blood. Now as adults, we are doing these things ourselves because we believe that Satan is stronger than God. And he is. Do you know this?

Jon: "God's Word confirms the existence of Satan (see 1 Pet. 5:8). But it also confirms that Satan is limited in power and even able to be resisted (Jas. 4:7). This is because Satan is, along with the rest of creation, a created thing under the sovereign control of God. Satan is not all-powerful. God is. Satan is not all-knowing. God is. Satan is not everywhere at once. God is. And the fact that Satan can be resisted when we submit ourselves to God demonstrates that we are stronger than him."

Anna: "Satan has worldly dominion and his influence should not be minimized, yet his power is limited and will be obliterated. Satan lies and so does the abuse he fosters. He is evil and the misrepresentation he delivers is heartbreaking. His ammunition is aimed toward one's soul and purpose. He is skillful, treacherous, and has a legion of fallen angels, demons, who do his misdeeds. Know these things yet do not fear, for one has God's Spirit and power, and Satan knows his fate. Intercede through prayer and pursue God's Word, his knowledge, and ask for protection through one's faith in Jesus, one's shelter, one's hope."

Question Two Hundred And Forty-Seven
September 4th

Even after hearing that God doesn't put an end to child abuse because he gave humankind free will, a number of us remain atheists. And if this means that we are going to hell, well, we'll feel right at home. How can you refute this?

Jon: "Hell by definition is a place where one cannot feel at home. So to say that one will feel at home in hell is a contradiction. It is tantamount to saying two plus two is five. It is a false statement. This is because the phrase *at home* means 'comfortable', whereas *hell* means 'a place of torment.' There is no comfort in a place of torment. There is therefore no comfort in hell. The person who believes that they will be comfortable in hell is either mistaken about the definitions of these words or they are using them in a nonstandard idiosyncratic way."

Anna: "Touché, living through an earthly hell could lead one to conclude that one deserves nothing more than what was experienced. The reality of suffering is troublesome for most and abuse undoubtedly changes one's interpretation of self-worth and self-purpose. God choosing to not control humankind's behaviors can be frustrating and perceived to be counterproductive, but one just does not understand his methods. Free will has created immorality; however, God is always good, always just. He cannot be anything contrary, which is why he sent Jesus to die and then breathe again so that abuse could be reconciled."

Question Two Hundred And Forty-Eight
September 5th

Some of our mothers didn't like the idea of being submissive to their husbands and boyfriends and this idea caused our mothers to mistreat them. Does the Bible teach women to submit to men?

Jon: "Ephesians 5:22 says that women are to submit to their husbands. But that one verse is followed by eight verses of orders that the husband must obey. He is commanded to love his wife, sacrifice himself for her, read Scripture with her, provide for her, cherish her, and devote himself completely and only to her (25-33). In other words, he is to treat her as Christ treats his church. It would be hard not to consider this kind of leadership a blessing and submission to it desirable."

Anna: "Women are not called to submit to every man nor are women inferior to men. Submission is not a standard set without limits or to be applied without context. When married, men and women have biblical roles within the household for different purposes tailored towards building a functional and fulfilling relationship. These specified duties should not be confused with women being treated as less than men or to condone abuse of any kind. To comply does not mean rejection of oneself, because a nonresistant devotion is a blessing especially within a divinely unified marriage. Every human soul is equal in the eyes of God, man and woman alike, and he requires both to submit to one another with humility, grace, respect, sacrifice, dedication, and love."

Question Two Hundred And Forty-Nine
September 6th

Are we being abusive to our children if we teach them to believe in other religions besides Christianity?

Jon: "If Christianity is true then teaching someone to believe otherwise would be eternally destructive. For it is only through faith in Christ that one can be saved (John 14:6). So keeping someone from Christianity literally keeps them from salvation. But this does not mean that we are to keep ourselves from learning about other religions. In fact, it is our responsibility as Christians to be able to defend our faith when the need arises (1 Pet. 3:15). And understanding the basic tenets of other religions greatly helps us do so."

Anna: "To mislead a child from one's calling by practicing a false religion will psychologically and emotionally affect that child in impactful ways. However, ignorance in comparison to blatant mockery holds a different weight within one's awareness, motives, message, and mission. Confusion is different than denial, and to impose one's disbelief onto a child is somewhat heartless and unfair. Giving directives to deny or disrespect Christ dependent upon what is said, implied, or alluded to, is relevant because the effects can change the course of one's destiny. To teach a child to oppose their intrinsic needs, one's very existence, by renouncing their one and only savior, will have natural and spiritual ramifications. Denying the truth is self-injurious and believing what is untrue has the ability to profoundly handicap one's soul."

Question Two Hundred And Fifty
September 7th

What do we do if we have no positive role models to identify with?

Jon: "In 1 Corinthians 11:1 the apostle Paul says, 'Be imitators of me, as I am of Christ.' He did not say *imitate me*. He said *imitate me, as I am of Christ*. Only some of Paul's actions were Christ-like. So Paul says to copy his actions inasmuch as they copy Christ's. This is because Jesus' actions are always perfect. He is the one and only person whose every action is emulatable. He is our perfect role model who will never leave us wanting. We rejoice in that we have access to not only Jesus' life and teachings in the gospels, but to Jesus himself in prayer."

Anna: "Having positive influences help form one's character, attitude, ethics, and values throughout early development. To build upon a foundation of immorality and devastation negatively shapes one's self-perceptions and worldview. When a child identifies with their abusive parental figure or family member, one unconsciously and consciously personalizes and materializes their traits on some level. Identification with others happens throughout different stages of life and can be adaptive or destructive depending upon one's experiences, unmet needs, support system, and level of awareness and self-efficacy. One must differentiate oneself from others' negative and damaging behaviors and not model themselves after them. Wholeheartedly remember: one's true identity and worth is found solely in Christ and his loving and perfect example."

Question Two Hundred And Fifty-One
September 8th

Being abused as children has left a number of us ignorant in terms of what to teach our own children. What are some lessons that we ought to teach them?

Jon: "First: Place your faith in Jesus Christ. The other two will not work unless this is done first. Belief in Jesus gives this life and the one after infinite significance and value. It guarantees eternal salvation. Second: Love God with all your heart, soul, strength, and mind. There is nothing that can overcome you when your entire being is devoted to the Lord. He has good and hope planned for your life. And third: Love your neighbor as yourself. We were made for communion. And when we practice with one another the gifts God has given us, heaven is manifest on earth."

Anna: "Despite maltreatment, humbly live out one's dignified purpose. Care for one's mind, body, and spirit; confidently complete one's race. Honor others with one's thoughts, words, behaviors, even when undeserved or unappreciated. After all, that is grace. Have immovable faith in Jesus but allow oneself to grieve when abandoned, betrayed, misunderstood, and broken because the Lord knows what one endures. Choose to love, and do not let anyone's evil dim one's light; courageously and remarkably shine. Be persistent in life and hold tightly to biblical teachings and promises with wisdom and the Holy Spirit's might. Most importantly, put God first daily, because his love is most powerful, and permanently withstands."

Question Two Hundred And Fifty-Two
September 9th

Between the ages of five and eighteen, millions of us were child laborers. We were forced to work in such industries as mining, fishing, tourism, agriculture, and manufacturing. Does the Bible endorse slavery, of any kind?

Jon: "The institution of slavery recognized in the Bible, namely the Old Testament, is nothing like the race-based slavery of the American antebellum south where men, women, and children were forced against their will to serve and work for their captors. The Bible unambiguously condemns that kind of slavery. Slavery permitted in the Bible, however, was used by willing participants vocationally to earn a respectable living for themselves and for their family when their only other option was poverty. And there were many rules that protected the interests and rights of slaves. Most notably, they were to be treated fairly and granted freedom at every year of jubilee."

Anna: "The young are targeted due to a lack of awareness, a power deficit, and the physical inability to protect themselves. Sadly, inexperienced bodies become exploitable commodities when predators selfishly inflict their immoral agenda. When oppressed through enslavement, one's innocent essence can be temporarily stripped from one's being. Slavery is unjust and has been maximized for social stratification and power. Many accounts of human captivity through duplicitous behaviors are documented. Slavery is not endorsed, promoted, or justified; it is recorded to show that the world is flawed and how desperately one needs Jesus, the answer to one's soul's salvation."

Question Two Hundred And Fifty-Three
September 10th

Some of us are free from such feelings as anxiety, depression, and dissociation. Can these disorders return?

Jon: "It is not impossible that former challenges return to us. And this is exactly what happened to the apostle Paul. He says in 2 Corinthians 12:7 that a messenger of Satan continually returned to harass him. This was difficult. But he recognized that the harassment from the returning messenger was to keep him from becoming conceited: a benefit that far outweighed a life void of harassment. So although a returning challenge may be difficult, God may have good reasons to allow such a return. We can be hopeful and even excited if and when we encounter a returning challenge, knowing that God will bring a benefit from it that would not have been unattainable without it."

Anna: "Freedom from one's cycle of self-persecution, one's uncontrollable emotions, and the prolonging of symptoms is relieving, empowering, and often short-lived when one becomes prideful or solely self-reliant. One must understand where one's true and lasting strength lies and where the unforeseen battle occurs. One's mind can be evil's playground when not rooted in unadulterated truth. Mental or emotional snares, confusion, hopelessness, and one's fears can resurface when one's weaknesses have been exposed through immorality's reopened door. One's issues are impelled through one's will. Consistently draw upon God's strength, because one's true nature is patiently waiting; ask the Holy Spirit to transcend one's flesh and afflictions in Jesus' name."

Question Two Hundred And Fifty-Four
September 11th

If God's plan is to save humankind from itself and psychology's aim is self-actualization, is there a therapeutic middle ground here?

Jon: "If we consider that God's aim for humankind is that it come to know him more fully, and that the aim of psychology is to study something created by God—namely, the mind—then there is no tension between God and psychology. When one studies a created thing, one comes to know more about the creator. So when one studies the mind, which is created by God, one comes to know more about God. Therefore there is then no ground between God's aim for humankind and psychology, because the two are one and the same. God wants us to know more about him, and psychology allows us to do so."

Anna: "Within one's life-quest there is much to cover. From a humanistic standpoint, one has basic needs at different levels, and when unmet, misunderstood, or conditional, one's foundation is unstable yet one's power is one's will. From a Christian perspective, when one's true identity and purpose is unknown or misrepresented, one's intrinsic needs will be undiscovered and one will not live out their purpose fueled by Christ. Building oneself up is vital for one's mental health, but without truth's application, one cannot truly reach greatness separate from God. Self-actualization is paradoxical if one is not rooted in Christ; there is no middle ground where eternity is concerned. To reach one's God-given potential, self-actualization must materialize through God's will."

Question Two Hundred And Fifty-Five
September 12th

Can you give some advice to those of us who continue to see our victimizers, knowing full well that after we see them we will be miserable?

Jon: "While one may have some awareness of being abused by their partner and/or parents, they may also experience some joy, love, security, and nostalgia with them. In other words, all the good things that come with a bad relationship can easily obscure one's ability to see that the relationship is bad. Which may be why the proverb says, 'Like a dog that returns to his vomit is a fool who repeats his folly' (Pro. 26:11). The offensiveness may be meant to sober us up. The grossness may be meant to unobscure our ability to see that what our victimizers are doing to us is gross. And this simple realization may commence our departure from the relationship."

Anna: "Child abuse can be soul binding, and misery can be involuntary. Yet, when past traumas continually manifest personal despair, one has limited their capacity. With no intention to minimize one's legitimate pain, at some point one must choose to not let the past control one's present. Not confronting the abuser's behaviors inhibits one's freedom, and avoidance only strengthens abuse's effects. Facing the truth, addressing one's dysfunctional tendencies, and setting personal boundaries are necessary. Allowing the enemy to pervade one's life brings personal despair. Deliverance and protection through prayer are obtainable, and one's delight can be restored."

Question Two Hundred And Fifty-Six
September 13th

What can you say to we more mature survivors who just now want to share our stories of abuse, but feel there is no time left to reap the benefits of doing so?

Jon: "Abraham and his wife, Sarah, all their lives desired to have a child together. But he was ninety-nine. And she was ninety. How could *they* conceive a child? Indeed, they felt there was no time left to experience that joy. However, the Lord appeared and told Abraham and Sarah that they would have a child in one year's time. They both laughed out loud in disbelief. But the Lord was gracious and kept his promise. Isaac was born the following year. So if God wants to do incredible things in our lives, more than we can imagine (Eph. 3:20), the only hindrance may be our own disbelief."

Anna: "If one desires to tell one's story, then do so. Keeping quiet, shortchanging oneself, or allowing the past to deflect one's opportunity is letting one's abuser continue to control one's identity and purpose. One's greatest pains, one's tragic experiences, will be salvaged for good but one must choose to let it. When one's spirit is prompted to step out in faith, to speak when one would usually stay quiet, and to move when one desires to stand still, revelations are at work. Allow God's will to move through you, to validate, comfort, and empower others to no longer cower, and to righteously persevere."

Question Two Hundred And Fifty-Seven
September 14th

Many of us watched our fathers and stepfathers beat our mothers. We tried to rescue them by putting our bodies between our fathers and mothers, trying to deflect the blows onto ourselves. Now as adults, we are constantly waiting for someone to rescue us as we tried to rescue them. Can you help us?

Jon: "Humanity was in desperate need of rescuing. And it seemed that nothing could do the job. How could we possibly pay the price for our sins? How could anyone avoid the penalty deserved for wrongs committed? Just when all hope seemed lost, Jesus was born. He came to our rescue. He lived a sinless life so that we might finally inherit the righteousness necessary to be with God. And on the cross he deflected the blows that we deserved onto himself. The wait is over. It's been over for more than two thousand years. Believe in Jesus Christ, and be rescued."

Anna: "Disentanglement from the past's web takes more than one's flawed attempts to save. One can experience genuine support from others, but legitimate restoration is found in God's Spirit through belief in his Son. When a victim survives to become a protector, one may turn into an adult casualty if not truly aware of one's codependence. One's earthly fantasies for deliverance may be realized when one's expectations are drawn from the correct source. Salvation rescues one from the world's abuse and the enemies' lies; true deliverance is in Christ, humankind's divine defender."

Question Two Hundred And Fifty-Eight
September 15th

Could studying spiritual truths and psychological theories help us to compensate for our abusive childhoods?

Jon: "There is no way for us to go back in time and change the past. However, God's truth can change us now. It can recover our lost relationship with the Creator of the universe. Moreover, Jesus affirms in John 17:17 that we can be sanctified by God's Word. We are made holy and set apart when we study God's truth. Where can we find this truth? In the Bible. It is in the Bible where we can gain that which is more precious than whatever might be gained from ten thousand childhoods. In believing this we do not make less significant our childhoods, but we make more significant God and his Word."

Anna: "Counterbalancing by striving to overcome, rising above, or becoming knowledgeable and successful can temporarily offset one's pain but will negatively compensate when one's motives are falsely perceived. When one tries too hard, there is an imbalance, which will manifest mentally and emotionally. One's painful experiences can turn into one's shortcomings when unaddressed, suppressed, or avoided. Rectifying one's abusive childhood, conquering one's demons, and living one's passions do not just atone for the past, they honor one's identity and purpose. There is only one superior truth that leads to eternal life, which is through Jesus Christ, the savior of the world; an eternity with God is what truly redeems one's childhood abuse."

Question Two Hundred And Fifty-Nine
September 16th

Some people, for whatever reasons, are spiritual and psychological stressors for us. Many times at events, these people cannot be avoided. As we are trying to bring more calm to our souls and not more turmoil, can you please give us some advice that we can adhere to before we go to the function?

Jon: "This kind of question is telling, namely, that this person who causes us stress is someone we should not be around. At least not yet. There may come a time when reconciliation occurs. Until then, however, if there is someone we are not ready to be around then we should not put ourselves in situations where we will encounter them. Or else, we're setting ourselves up for catastrophe. If an encounter is unavoidable, we have two options, reconciliation or accommodation. We can either reconcile our differences with this person face to face or else we have to make accommodations to avoid them."

Anna: "Anxiety and fear grab hold of one's experiences and crush one's fulfillment. Negative expectations fuel unhealthy cognitions. Insight into why one reacts due to a triggering scenario can teach one how to handle emotionally difficult situations. Mental preparation that feeds emotional perspective wisely anticipates and adjusts with spirit-driven discipline. When another's essence is not of God's Spirit, social interactions are mismatched and may become uncomplementary; the truth's light will gleam upon what is not, and spiritually preparing oneself for this reality is life-changing."

Question Two Hundred And Sixty
September 17th

As we have discussed, we are highly aware of the traumas that our childhood sexual molesters bestowed on us: shame, anxiety, insomnia, distrust, depression, powerlessness, low self-esteem, suicidal thoughts. While we are learning to manage these difficulties, we cannot get over the fact that our molesters disabled our minds. Is there hope for us?

Jon: "Even if it is true that our minds have been impaired, there is always hope for healing and recovery. Isaiah 41:10 says, 'fear not, for I am with you; be not dismayed, for I am your God; I will strengthen you, I will help you, I will uphold you with my righteous right hand.' Why should we not fear? Because God is with us. Why should we not be sorrowful? Because the almighty God is our God. We bring our impairments to him because he is a God who makes it his business to provide for those who are in impaired."

Anna: "Sexual abuse attempts to destroy one's perceived purity, can shift one's beliefs, and distort one's identity development because its very nature opposes one's honorable worth. And sadly, often a lack of relational security, interpersonal threats, and rejections lead to a higher susceptibility toward false beliefs and re-victimization. A malleable mind, when traumatized or neglected, can affect one's personality and behaviors yet hope is never lost. When one's fundamental view of human relationships was built upon mistrust, exposure to disorganization within one's thoughts can prevail without God's truth, faith, and the Holy Spirit's power, comfort, and peace."

Question Two Hundred And Sixty-One
September 18th

Is teaching children that hell is a real place child abuse?

Jon: "If hell is real, then telling them it isn't real is child abuse. There are one of two destinations for all men and women. Either we will 'go away into eternal punishment,' or 'into eternal life' (Mat. 25:46). The place of eternal punishment is what is frequently called *hell*. Everyone needs to know of the reality of hell the same way every child needs to know what will be the consequences of his or her punishable actions. When a child knows the potential consequences of their actions, they have the ability to choose whether or not they want to commit those actions and receive those consequences. We are thankful that God has given us fair warning about the consequences of choosing not to believe in Jesus."

Anna: "A child's mind cannot conceptualize complexity, so the information given combined with one's approach is crucial for healthy development: adaptive comprehensiveness and appropriate applications. Teaching a child that hell exists is not abusive, however, misrepresenting their abilities within the context of free will plants falsified seeds into that child's spiritual perspective. Through abuse, a child is taught that they are unlovable, unworthy, or going to hell because they are bad. This is spiritual misuse. Hell is real, yet a child should be schooled on God's abundant grace through Jesus' sacrifice and that heaven is where God has truly called one to be."

Question Two Hundred And Sixty-Two
September 19th

This makes no sense: that some of us were taken away from our abusive parents only to be placed into a cruel foster care system. Is humankind really that overwhelmed that it can't take proper care of its children?

Jon: "The list of perfectly executed endeavors on which mankind has embarked is a short one. But this does not mean that we do not continue to care for afflicted orphans, an endeavor James 1:27 calls 'pure' religion. True to his character, God considers the purest religious act one that seeks after the betterment of one's suffering neighbor. It should be no surprise that the human race, which defiles virtually everything it touches, is not able to perfectly execute the most undefiled act of religion. However, there should be no other act of religion we exercise more effort to accomplish than the betterment of those in need."

Anna: "The system, just like the world, can be cruel and unfair. Children should be protected, at all costs, yet due to vulnerability and powerlessness are often pushed aside or punished. Dysfunction, selfishness, and a blatant disregard for others have consumed many souls. When children undergo rejection, and are then exposed to a corrupt system that mentally and emotionally destroys, the dignity one perceives to have left is crushed and one is profoundly changed. Do not forget: God did not relinquish one amidst the nonsense nor will he turn his back on any who reach out to Jesus."

Question Two Hundred And Sixty-Three
September 20th

Can you explain the difference between a panic attack and an anxiety attack?

Jon: "Just before his crucifixion, Jesus prayed on the Mount of Olives. Luke 22:42 says that Jesus knelt down and prayed, 'Father, if you are willing, remove this cup from me. Nevertheless, not my will, but yours, be done.' The passage continues saying that Jesus was in so much 'agony' that 'his sweat became like great drops of blood falling down to the ground' (Luke 22:44). The Greek for *agony* could be translated *anxiety* or *terror*. In any case, Jesus understands feelings such as anxiety firsthand. We come to him when we are anxious because he is able to sympathize with absolutely anyone; whether we are anxious about a new job or because we know, as Jesus did, that death is near."

Anna: "Within anxiety's commotion and confusion lie panic attacks and panic disorder. Excessive worry and significant behavioral changes rule over one's life when one's anxiety becomes disordered. Anxiety affects one's mind and body because of the apprehensions held toward what is expected. Severe panic is an emotional interpretation, which affects one's cognitions and responsiveness. A person can be anxious or have anxiety throughout the day without having a panic attack. Panic and anxiety attacks are similar yet the distinction is made when recurrent anxiety persists into a panic disorder. As fear starts to pervade one's thoughts, emotions, and behaviors, God's Spirit requires preeminent control; pray for God's peace and assurance."

Question Two Hundred And Sixty-Four
September 21st

For those of us who have always felt detached from our bodies, can you give us some idea of what it feels like to be inside of a healthy body and mind?

Jon: "The feeling that ought to be most prevalent in the person who possesses both a healthy body and mind is love. This love must extend toward three objects. The first object is *God*. Remember, a tree is only as good as its roots. We become rooted in God, the highest good, when we love him with all our heart, soul, strength, and mind. The second object is *others*. The love we receive from God is not meant to be kept to ourselves but shared with others. The third object is *one's self*. We love ourselves appropriately and biblically when we do things with our mind and body that bring glory to God."

Anna: "Detachment strategies are developed to self-protect. When one disconnects, one has been somewhat tricked into feeling secure. Human beings thrive when safely connected within authenticity and free to communicate with honesty, not when in continual self-preservation mode and isolative processes. Being in tune with one's reality, having the ability to identify the reasons behind one's behaviors, to genuinely understand the weight of one's purpose, nurtures one's psyche, self-worth, and enables spiritual transformation. A healthy soul values humankind, is connected within relationships, and not only comprehends the irreplaceable value of one's eternal destination, but puts it into action."

Question Two Hundred And Sixty-Five
September 22nd

Is this right? We cannot be truly reconciled with someone who does not admit that he or she abused us, does not seek our forgiveness, and does not show remorse.

Jon: "It may be that in some relationships there will never be full restoration. People are free to make decisions according to their will. Some people will choose to refuse to do what is necessary to bring them reconciliation with another. But our focus ought to be chiefly toward reconciliation with God. For we need this perilously more than we need reconciliation with our fellow man. While our separation from our neighbor may cause distress in this lifetime, separation from God will cause distress for all eternity. It is only when we are in Christ, believing in him, that we are reconciled unto God. May we never refuse to seek this reconciliation."

Anna: "Thankfully, reconciliation and forgiveness are not dependent, yet a refusal of either can bring much heartache. Forgiveness starts within and plants seeds toward reuniting, even when undetected. One can settle issues within their soul despite another's viewpoint or behaviors. However, restorative reconciliation takes two willing individuals upon common ground, for a mutual purpose. Choosing to forgive with hopes to reunify is living within a spirit-driven perspective. When a relationship restores, it is a sweet victory covered with grace and mercy. To be reconciled by God means belief and repentance collide and orchestrate a beautiful relationship with Jesus Christ, one's savior, one's friend."

Question Two Hundred And Sixty-Six
September 23rd

Plenty of our bodies have healed from being physically abused while our minds remain injured from being verbally abused. Why are we unable to heal from the hurtful words used against us?

Jon: "At least immediately speaking, physical abuse yields physical injury while psychological abuse yields psychological injury. Physical injuries can be looked at. They can be touched. You can apply ointment and gauze to them. Psychological injuries aren't this way. They can't be looked at or touched or given ointment. Due to the limits of the hard sciences, we can't know the full extent of psychological damage. We can think of hurtful words as depth charges dropped into an opaque black sea. In the same way that we have little idea what damage the explosives will do, we have little idea of the extent of damage hurtful words cause. This is why spiritual and psychological counseling is so vitally important. And over time, if the injury is not too severe, the pain will subside."

Anna: "The lasting effects of abuse can be difficult to reform, yet the outcome of one's rehabilitation is dependent upon one's deep-seated beliefs, determination, and spiritual wisdom. Cruel words have the ominous ability to adhere to one's consciousness without invitation when entrapped within insecurities and fears. Having difficulty recovering from another's words is contingent upon accepting those words as truth. Healing progresses when having a doubtless awareness of one's worth and purpose. With God, inability and impossibility do not exist."

Question Two Hundred And Sixty-Seven
September 24th

Are we born knowing the difference between good and evil?

Jon: "Romans 2:15 says that people 'show that the work of the law is written on their hearts, while their conscience also bears witness.' So unless someone is either born without full capability of their cognitive faculties or has somehow had them hindered later in life, everyone has a conscience that bears witness to God's law. This includes his moral law. Furthermore, that there are objectively wrong actions such as child abuse and objectively good actions such as charity demonstrates that there must be an objective-moral-lawgiver. This of course is merely another name for God. Even the one who believes that God doesn't exist because of the evil in the world is admitting the existence of moral law which consequently proves God's existence."

Anna: "As one matures, good and evil become more apparent, yet the human condition often fights against what is virtuous. The experiences through one's family and social systems form one's conceptions and beliefs. When a parent is behaving badly, yelling, screaming, raging, threatening, or hitting, what is highly destructive sadly becomes normal and this confusing existence muddles one's outlook. The understanding of what was intended becomes biased when one's identity and the context of their existence was built from extreme negativity. Truth is instilled deep within one's soul, yet one must choose to believe in Jesus through God's Word and Spirit, to spiritually discern between evil and good."

Question Two Hundred And Sixty-Eight
September 25th

As adult survivors of childhood abuse, what does the cross symbolize for us?

Jon: "The cross is the symbol of the death Jesus Christ was subjected to but ultimately conquered. There is a paradoxical dual nature to the cross. On the one hand, the cross was an instrument of torturously agonizing pain. Although his body was inflicted with many lacerations and stabbings resulting in great exposure and blood loss, it is understood that he ultimately died from asphyxiation. The macabre nature of the cross is a perfect picture of the macabre nature of sin and its consequences. On the other hand, the cross represents Christ's miraculous resurrection from death. For adult survivors of childhood abuse, the cross reminds us that in Christ there is always hope of restoration after suffering."

Anna: "Symbolism is a powerful tool used to reach the mind, emotions, and will of the receiver. For many, burdensome feelings, deep and projected shame, humiliation, ridicule, incessant violations, and cutting rejections are a few but hefty examples of what abuse epitomizes. The cross represents an interesting dichotomy of unjust suffering, sacrifice, selflessness, forgiveness, hope, salvation, and freedom; a torture device brutally endured for all of the world's sins, past, present, and future. Perfect love and one's hopeful promises were completed through the beloved cross. Adult survivors can take refuge in the fact that Jesus experienced wretched abuse from human hands, yet he adores humankind still, and graciously died for every soul, and truly fathoms one's afflictions."

Question Two Hundred And Sixty-Nine
September 26th

Why is it so hard to accept the truth of what happened to us?

Jon: "Sometimes we equate an affirmation of an event's historicity with an affirmation of the event itself. In other words, we believe that when we validate that an event *took place*, we are validating the event itself. But this isn't true. Historicity and morality are two separate things. So we can affirm that an event took place without affirming that what took place during the event was right or wrong. For, the rightness or wrongness of an event has nothing to do with whether or not the event took place. This is not easy, but it may be that affirming merely that a difficult past experience happened is the first step toward restoration."

Anna: "Abuse influences one's integral boundary system and the aftermath of spiritual violations causes great psychological, emotional, and behavioral distress within the survivor. The ability to manage reality grapples with one's inability to mentally adapt, process, express, and grieve one's emotions. Being innocently trapped within dysfunction's walls, and enduring torment by the very same people that should protect one when confused or afraid, creates denial, detachment, withdrawal, and often delusional thinking within the survivor. When affected beyond one's understanding turns into doubting one's innate value over acknowledging the reality of God's amazing love, one has allowed other people's behaviors and twisted projections to define one's worth."

Question Two Hundred And Seventy
September 27th

Being abused as children has left many of us so self-absorbed that we seldom see ourselves as being in the wrong. But, the more we think about it... No one can always be in the right. Do you agree with us?

Jon: "There is only one being who is always right: God. Moses says in Deuteronomy 32:4, 'The Rock, his work is perfect, for all his ways are justice. A God of faithfulness and without iniquity, just and upright is he.' God does nothing wrong. It is his nature to do everything right. This is not so with human beings. It is our nature to err. In the same way God cannot be anything but perfect, we cannot be anything but imperfect. So when we think we are without fault we lift ourselves to God's status—which is pride—making us not only factually but also morally wrong."

Anna: "Imperfection is bound to human nature, so no one is always right. When naiveté, immaturity, and self-doubt dilute one's perspective and emotional development, projection, deflection, or inflexibility will direct and weaken one's relationships. Insecurities will distort the truth by allowing one's past victimizations to morph into present issues through negative misinterpretations. Emotions can be powerful and misleading when one's identity is rooted in one's traumatic experiences. When being wrong for merely existing is imprinted upon a child's soul one will unconsciously fight back. Ask God to reveal one's truth for understanding, humility, and self-awareness."

Question Two Hundred And Seventy-One
September 28th

As you are well aware, we have experienced great sorrow and not felt much joy. Can you then describe to us what joy feels like?

Jon: "Often Scripture connects joy with faith. 1 Peter 1:8 says, 'Though you have not seen him, you love him. Though you do not now see him, you believe in him and rejoice with joy that is inexpressible and filled with glory,' and Romans 15:13 says, 'May the God of hope fill you with all joy and peace in believing...' Notice the link? It's not bad to want joy. Whether you've felt it or not, we all want joy and God wants to give it to us. But the necessary condition of obtaining joy is belief. When we believe in Jesus Christ, the Son of God, we are promised to be brimming with wonderfully unspeakable joy."

Anna: "Internalizations of external factors will certainly affect one's mood. Abuse projects destructive messages sadly endorsed by one's thoughts, emotions, and behaviors. Happiness is often equated to self-satisfaction and temporary desires that do not sustain one from within or forever. A somber disposition can form through negative experiences, which is then conceptualized and ascribed to one's identity. Joy is freedom established in goodness. Sorrow dwells upon inflictions caused by others yet joy urges one to emotionally rejoice despite them. Incomparable elation is supernatural, spirit-driven, which is embodied and assuredly expressed within one's thoughts, will, and presence. Unexplainable joy manifests through God's Spirit and is truly known when faithfully living within his love."

Question Two Hundred And Seventy-Two
September 29th

Do you think that if child molesters knew how deeply they were hurting their victims that they would stop?

Jon: "It is hard to imagine that a person who is fully aware of the damage abuse has on a child would willingly abuse a child. In another sense, one wonders how anyone who has not experienced child abuse could ever understand what it feels like to have experienced such a traumatic event. In any regard, we want to affirm that the abuser is fully responsible for their actions. They have the choice to carry out or to not carry out abuse. It may be that a child abuser never knows how significantly they have harmed their victim, but that does not diminish how significantly they are to blame for inflicting that harm."

Anna: "Some would stop, and dismally, others would not. Child molesters are mentally, ultimately spiritually ill to the extent where their moral boundaries have been maligned for insidious purposes. These souls desperately need a deliverer due to the psychological, emotional, and sexual bondage they have succumbed to. One's psychopathology can spread wide and one's mindset is influenced either by righteousness or by darkness. One must choose what is right because it is screaming from deep within. When delivered through Jesus Christ, when one surrenders to conviction and repents, one's spirit and mind progressively transform, and one can truly have an awareness of the damage one has enforced upon others and themselves."

Question Two Hundred And Seventy-Three
September 30th

As you know, we have had our share of bad news. When people speak of Christ and the good news, most of us know who Christ is but what is the good news?

Jon: "The bad news is that our standing before God is that of a sinner. The good news, or Gospel, is the message of the means by which we may change that standing of sinner to sinless. 2 Thessalonians 2:14 says, 'To this he called you through our gospel, so that you may obtain the glory of our Lord Jesus Christ.' So the good news is that we have a means of obtaining the sinless standing before God the Father that Jesus Christ has. How relieving and satisfying it is to know that we need not struggle after the impossible feat of attaining for ourselves sinlessness. It is good news indeed to know that through faith we may have Christ's."

Anna: "Bad news seems to be a recurring reality for those who have survived extremely dysfunctional environments. When one feels unlovable, invaluable revelations can be difficult to understand. Continually experiencing unfortunate circumstances does not mean one is undeserving of good, but sadly this misconception is tragically believed. Another's behaviors are not a reflection of one's significance or potential; it is a candid manifestation of their spiritual state. The good news is God's kingdom through Jesus Christ, who died for humankind's sins; belief in Jesus leads one into eternity."

Question Two Hundred And Seventy-Four
October 1st

A majority of people do not like to be told what to do. And as adult survivors of childhood abuse, we are extra sensitive to taking orders. Will we ever stop feeling as though someone is trying to take our power away?

Jon: "Being a Christian is not about relying on one's own power. Being a Christian is about relying on God's power. This ought to make Christians experts in relinquishing power. This doesn't mean that we allow everyone and anyone to control us. That would surely spell disaster. It means, however, that we must become so accustomed to allowing another, namely God, to take control that we are able to allow another beside God to take control when appropriate. In other words, taking orders from proper authority is easy for the Christian because he or she so easily takes orders from God, the Ultimate Authority."

Anna: "When one's will is persistently forced to obey or serve another, one's loss of autonomy may turn into a defeatist perception that brews resignations toward one's concept of power and love. When given orders, being controlled, and unfairly taking another's emotional projection, it is hurtful and frustrating but should not be the measure of one's significance. The hope is that one's view will shift when the understanding is reached that intrinsic value and purpose cannot be taken, but only given away. One must choose to not be powerless anymore. The believer has access to God's infinite might through his Holy Spirit, given to all who believe."

Question Two Hundred And Seventy-Five
October 2nd

For those of us who were sexually molested as children, why do many of us feel so much loneliness as adults?

Jon: "The reasoning might go something like this: *I was severely abused by another or others in the past. I never want to be abused again. Therefore, I will stay away from other people.* In summary: *If I stay away from people, I cannot be hurt by people.* The problem is that isolation is also harmful. It is best to get involved with a safe Christian community. Remember, we were made in the image of God. And God is triune in nature—Father, Son, and Spirit. We were made to live in community. While it is true that when we are out of community we suffer, when we are in community we excel."

Anna: "Sexual abuse creates a void within one's existence that cannot be quenched by self-protecting through isolation. One may have understanding and encouraging people in their life, yet will still feel an isolative despondence that cannot fully be appeased. The heartache caused by molestation not only affects one's psychological and emotional framework but it directly changes one's self-image and sexual character. This loneliness is created from a confused and severed identity, which enables relational detachments, and overwhelming feelings of social apprehension and separation. When loneliness and deception seeps into one's soul, know that with God, one is truly never alone."

Question Two Hundred And Seventy-Six
October 3rd

Those of us who were sexually molested as children and who grew up preferring same-sex relationships will, more than likely, never know if we were born gay or if we were forced gay. Would you agree?

Jon: "It is hard to say if everyone who has been abused as a child will ever know the cause of their sexual affinity. Perhaps they *do* know. Perhaps they don't. Perhaps they *will* know. Perhaps they won't. Regardless, if one finds him or herself inclined toward one sex or the other, what can they do? One cannot force oneself to be inclined toward what they are not already inclined toward. It is not as important to focus on *who* a person is attracted to as it is to obey what God commands we do with that attraction. Who we are attracted to is nobody's business except ours and the Lord's."

Anna: "Suffering through sexual violations and defilements from the same or opposite sex causes deep-seated damage. One's induced needs, revulsions, or impulsions toward a specific sex become more complex and driven through one's dysfunction. Manipulations become falsified beliefs, unhealthy desires, and self-protection creates defensive dissociations and unhealthy attachments. 'Forced' implies one's lack of will, yet the perceived push one feels to act due to dysfunctional circumstances has a strong, spirit-based coercion where deception thrives. Live according to God's Word so that one stands firm in his truths and more personal disorientation is not created."

Question Two Hundred And Seventy-Seven
October 4th

When we were little, some of us were sold into child pornography and prostitution to satisfy the global demand to have sex with children. The adults who sold us lined their pockets, and in that exact moment suffocated our spirits. Why was money more important than our well-being?

Jon: "1 Timothy 6:9-10 says that the desire for and love of money causes temptation, harm, ruin, destruction, evil, loss of faith, and strife. These are all antithetical to what we assume we will gain with money. We think life will get easier, better, more full. But does life get easier, better, and more full for the children forced into this industry? Does life get easier, better, and more full for the person who grows old having made money from selling a child into pornography or prostitution? That guilt alone is deadly. And there will be a reckoning for such things—in this life possibly, in the next absolutely."

Anna: "Money could never be more important than your being because one is and always will be priceless to God. Selfishness, financial gain, and power drive individuals to lead a life of doing unspeakable things especially when their moral compass is perverted by evil's ambitions. Pervasive, unethical behaviors will radically dilute one's conscience, and one's intended purpose will become thwarted. Abnormal has become common and what is right is rarely seen. Yet, justice prevails, and words cannot depict how precious children are to God."

Question Two Hundred And Seventy-Eight
October 5th

A number of us have friends who were also abused as children. They often mention that they suffer from flashbacks. Will you explain a flashback to us?

Jon: "Scripture does not make many words about flashbacks. The word never occurs in the Bible. It is reasonable to assume that Paul suffered from intense disturbing memories of his past. For, before he became one of the greatest evangelists of all time, Paul was a persecutor of the church. Acts 22:4 reveals he not only threw both men and women into prison but he ordered their deaths. How did Paul cope with these memories? In Philippians 3:13, referring to his past, he says he strains forward to what lies ahead. For Paul, the remedy—at least in part—was to expend great energy in considering the prize of eternal life we inherit in Jesus Christ."

Anna: "Flashbacks are unforeseen, unpredictable, and attack one's senses. Intrusive remembrances of abuse push one to defensively dissociate, and cognitively and emotionally implant oneself within another time and space. Reliving trauma is frightening because within a flash, one's reality, one's security, is tampered with. When one survives difficult circumstances, anxiety and fear often increase due to a believed lack of control. Traumatic stress does not just disappear; it lingers in relentless ways, and often is suppressed or avoided due to one just trying to survive. Amazingly, with God's Spirit and power, one can address and grieve the traumas of one's past."

Question Two Hundred And Seventy-Nine
October 6th

What does it say of people who go to church and then go home and abuse their children?

Jon: "There is an obvious disconnect in such a person provided that the church he or she attends is not the issue. Any Bible-teaching, gospel-believing church will likely create an environment, both spiritual and physical, where such behavior is categorically forbidden. But when the church service is over, we don't leave the lessons of Scripture in the pew. They don't stay behind. They come home with us. They come to work with us. They come into our conversations. They come into our arguments. They come into our anger. And they change us (see Heb. 4:12). Anyone, therefore, who goes to church only to come home and abuse their children has left the lessons of Scripture in the pew."

Anna: "Hypocrisy is rampant, especially with churchgoers, yet the sting and twist of it all destroys perceptions, beliefs, and lives. The messages one relays with every blow and degrading word shapes the mind and heart of the individual affected. When a belittling, disparaging, professed God-fearing person creates spiritual confusion through oppressive control, emotional conquest, or psychological games, their church's so-called god is not appealing to the one who has been unjustly abused. Humanity has been gifted with free will and should not exploit this honor. It is truly disheartening that many proclaim God's name yet act like the devil himself; imposters will be exposed."

Question Two Hundred And Eighty
October 7th

A lot of us understand that through Christ, God has forgiven our sins. But from what source can we draw in order to forgive ourselves?

Jon: "Forgiveness has to do with one who is *wronged* and one who is the *wrongdoer*. And the wronged is the one who deserves forgiveness from the wrongdoer. So how can one be both the wronged and the wrongdoer? They can't be. What's happening here is that one is pronouncing over oneself condemnation when it is not one's place to do so. It is God's place to do so. But if one is in Jesus Christ, as Romans 8:1 says, then they are not condemned. And the only way to be condemned is to not be in Christ. But God is the one who condemns. So it is God from whom we seek forgiveness, not ourselves."

Anna: "The shame messages that transpire within abuse can overpower one's self-regard. After the emotional, psychological, or physical beatings cease, subconscious self-hatred sadly continues. Beating up oneself is what one knows to emulate, and this plays out within one's dysfunctional thoughts, behavioral patterns, and abusive relationships. Forgiveness and grief are unique processes, which require patience, acknowledgment, understanding, surrender, and mercy. Humankind exists through God, so he is one's ultimate resource for support, answers, strength, and healing. The power and exoneration of his Holy Spirit is unparalleled, which pristinely counsels the willing believer so one will experience forgiveness through God's love and grace."

Question Two Hundred And Eighty-One
October 8th

Can you speak to us about the devastating effects that divorce can have upon children?

Jon: "The passages that condemn divorce are many and spread across both the Old and New Testaments (Mal. 2:16; Mat. 19:6, 9; Luke 16:18; 1 Cor. 7:10-11). And in Matthew 19:8, Jesus reminds his listeners that divorce is 1) because of hardness of heart; and 2) opposite God's will for married men and women. But God's will for married men and women is for them to be fruitful and multiply (Gen. 1:28). In other words, God's will for marriage is linked to the bearing and raising of children. So whatever is good for the marriage is good for the children. Conversely and unfortunately, whatever will cause rupturing in the marriage will cause rupturing in the children."

Anna: "Divorce alone is difficult to overcome but when abuse conjointly disrupts the family, serious complications and attachment issues can arise due to stress and division. Trust is often abolished, confusion is flamed, and the child is left to process difficult questions alone because the thought of being a burden is too much to tolerate as self-blame begins. Another devastation is that an abuser can detrimentally affect a child through deceptive programming and lies, which divides the child from the other adult, known as parental alienation. This causes great psychological and emotional pain. The family was intended to mirror God's love, and when it does not, the effects distort one's identity and spiritual foundation."

Question Two Hundred And Eighty-Two
October 9th

From an earthly perspective, we shed our tears in silence and isolation. Indeed, while our parents and/or caregivers did not comfort most of us, we were wondering if, perhaps, God might have heard our cries?

Jon: "How important are our sufferings to God? Psalm 56:8 says, 'You have kept count of my tossings; put my tears in your bottle. Are they not in your book?' We have vague and fading memories of our late-night stirrings of the soul. God has them numbered. We have heedlessly wiped away all our tears on handkerchiefs and sleeves. God has them in bottles. We will forget most of our experiences. God has them written down. So we can have assurance that however much importance we put on our sufferings, God puts more. Our cries are never made in silence, but always in the presence of God."

Anna: "A life built from abuse often feels lonely and demoralizing because one's inner plea for love and acceptance lingers from the neglect and apathy. When a child is not heard or validated, those unmet needs turn to self-pity, self-loathing, and attempts to self-soothe turn into self-protection and emotional or physical seclusion. Seeking solace through others can be misleading, exhausting, and disappointing. Humankind was created to be in authentic connection with the greatest dependence upon the one who sustains all. Without a doubt God heard and continues to hear one's cries and he truly desires to supernaturally love and comfort you."

Question Two Hundred And Eighty-Three
October 10th

While some of us realize that abuse has left us more vulnerable than most, we have heard that one of the reasons we may become so hurt by certain people is because we want to be considered so important to them. Could this be?

Jon: "If this is so, it may be time to calibrate the amount of respect we grant mankind. I am not suggesting that we begin to respect people less. Indeed, we are called to love our neighbors and consider them more significant than ourselves (Phil. 2:3). What I am suggesting is that we begin to respect God more. We must ask ourselves, 'For am I now seeking the approval of man, or of God? Or am I trying to please man?' (Gal. 1:10). When we consider God more important than man, we naturally seek his approval rather than man's. More attention for God leaves less for man."

Anna: "One's sensitivity toward others can develop from the rejections one faced, which turns into desperately needing approval to deem oneself as simply tolerable. Security and abuse are polar opposites, thus leaving its survivors feeling invaluable, dehumanized, and unworthy. Vulnerability and emotional reactivity differ and, when extreme, the tendency to express them disproportionately and impulsively greatly increases. Most people equate self-worth with how others treat them. This reasoning is fundamentally flawed. Worth derives from God, whose words spark life, and proves humankind invaluable therefore created from his everlasting love."

Question Two Hundred And Eighty-Four
October 11th

How do we go about finding a mental health care provider who we can trust with our stories and feelings?

Jon: "Scripture cannot tell us which health provider to choose, but it tells us the way to go about choosing one. In Acts 17:11 the people of Berea were said to be of more noble character than others because of their relentless eagerness in examining the Scriptures. There is a relevant principle here. When considering any proposition or option in life, it is considered noble by God's Word to investigate such things with determined enthusiasm. It will not be enough to glance momentarily at our options. And this is especially true when considering who will be an acceptable confidant. It is likely that the health care provider will only be as excellent as our search for one is."

Anna: "When asked or inspired, many will share the life-changing experiences they had with a counselor or clinician, because it enables the continual freeing of one's bondage and plants seeds of hope within another. What one is not aware of, one cannot grab onto. Be inquisitive, ask others, seek out referrals, research, and wisely use one's resources. Discernment with persistence is a great recipe to push psychological and emotional transformation. Foremost, seek God and ask him what to do, for he will lead one into one's divine will. Seek godly counsel and through truth measure one's spirit, and confidently move in Jesus' name."

Question Two Hundred And Eighty-Five
October 12th

A great number of us keep hearing that Christ paid the price for us on the cross. If he paid the price, why do we still feel completely indebted to our childhood sorrows?

Jon: "Because we sin before a perfectly holy God who is perfectly just, we ought to be punished (see Rom. 6:23). Jesus offered himself on the cross to take that punishment we deserve (see 1 John 2:2). Genuine faith in Jesus accounts his sacrifice to us; meaning we no longer deserve punishment (see Rom. 8:1) and obtain access to God (see Heb. 10:19-22) who has the power to take away our sorrows (see Mat. 11:28). While punishment for sin is *immediately* removed upon placing one's faith in Christ, the sting of painful memories is not—not yet. But it most certainly will be in heaven (see Rev. 21:4; Isa. 25:8, 35:10)."

Anna: "Just the thought of eternal glory, if only for a moment, can bring one pure bliss. Yet, even when given the key to one's existence, living life does not become effortless or completely casual. Oftentimes it will become that much more grueling because of one's awareness, and the raw reality that unwanted secular movement can crush one's being if not suitably discerned and protected. When one's innocence has been disturbed, one's self-security and self-worth were impeded upon. Even though Christ has risen and those who believe are saved, one still has to face reality's cruelty, persecutions, and childhood's grief."

Question Two Hundred And Eighty-Six
October 13th

A number of us have a hard time getting out of our own heads. It is almost as though the abuse causes us to look at everything from our very battered points of view. As a result, we are often told that we need to be more objective. What does this mean?

Jon: "Objective thinking relies on facts. Not on feelings, prejudices, or biases. It relies on what is outside the person or outside the mind. In other words, when thinking objectively, we become more influenced by what is external than by what is internal. And as we come into contact with truth, we allow it into our minds without reacting emotionally to it. Of course we should always evaluate truth claims, testing to see whether or not they are in fact true. Once discovered that something is true, we accept it, and decide what is best to do with it."

Anna: "An objective state is not swayed to form partial opinions, conclusions, or have drawn-out reactions dependent upon one's emotions. A battered mindset impairs one's vision, cripples one's belief system, and manipulates one's thoughts, which influence action. Objectivity with wisdom and discernment is a powerful combination. The humility to be unbiased, to remove oneself from the scenario and not take things personally is a tremendous gift in preserving one's relationships and mental health. Jesus objectively sacrificed for humankind, he died for every soul, and not for those he believed deserved it more."

Question Two Hundred And Eighty-Seven
October 14th

Putting aside our parents' rejection of us when we were children, some of us now hear that if we are rejected by others it is an opportunity to learn something about ourselves. Do you agree?

Jon: "Christians aren't promised constant acceptance by their peers. In fact, Jesus promised the opposite (see Mat. 10:22). Rejection will come. But Luke 6:22 says, 'Blessed are you when people hate you and when they exclude you and revile you and spurn your name as evil, on account of the Son of Man!' This is the God we serve: When others hate and exclude us, he blesses us. When others revile and spurn us, again he blesses. We come face to face with rejection and we do not flinch because we know that it will only result in our blessing."

Anna: "All circumstances present an opportunity to discover, self-reflect, and grow. However, being rejected, especially when unwarranted, is difficult to not take personally within the moment. Nonacceptance strikes at one's core, as if one's very essence is excluded from being valued. Human behaviors are compelled by a source, and understanding this is necessary because the root of what drives another's decision to shun can be persuaded by the unseen. The rejection of a soul is misguided and evil as proven by Jesus' persecution. What drives one's motives comes from either the Spirit of God, evil, or one's flesh acting upon one's spirit's influence."

Question Two Hundred And Eighty-Eight
October 15th

Societies have a way of establishing gender norms—rules for how we should look and behave. For example, some societies train boys that they should grow up to dominate their partner and girls should grow to be the submissive companion. How are we to function in such a society where being sexually molested as children has left men feeling shamefully passive and women painfully aggressive?

Jon: "To know how to move forward, we look back to where we come from. Genesis 1:27 says that God created mankind, male and female, in his own image. Both genders have been made to reflect God. That means that our purpose, regardless of gender, is to shine godliness. We do this with our words, and our thoughts, and our actions. That is how we are to function. Therefore, as we move forward, we fix our attention on God's Word and his Son Jesus Christ. These sources are our only hope in helping us discover who we truly are."

Anna: "Molestation influences one's beliefs which stir confusions before one has the ability to properly discern deception from truth. Gender taboos, prejudices, and socialization trends imposed upon the sexually abused leave individuals cornered to internalize negative impressions as opposed to nurturing one's indigenous individuality. The stereotypes and shame associated cause deep pain. Designed roles and natural inclinations toward gender and identity have been set by God for protection, structure, to uplift relationships—not to enable confusion, humiliation, or rejection."

Question Two Hundred And Eighty-Nine
October 16th

Some of us were wondering if it would be helpful to know: Do thoughts evoke feelings or feelings evoke thoughts?

Jon: "We know that emotions such as anger or sadness can easily affect our thoughts. When we are angry, say, we tend to think angry thoughts. But what about the other way around? Can thought affect feeling? Philippians 4:4, for example, commands us to rejoice. But how do we rejoice when we don't feel joyful? Is Philippians 4:4 implying that we sin when we don't feel like rejoicing? No. Remember, Romans 12:2 says that we are transformed by the renewing of our mind. So Scripture understands, so to speak, that the content of our thoughts will affect our feelings over time. To significantly move our feelings one direction, we must deliberately move our thoughts that direction first."

Anna: "Cognitions influence emotions at different rates and levels. Thoughts are powerful and can manifest different sensations and emotional reactions. Different symbols translate into language and evoke connections. The mental formulation of images and concepts can trigger one's emotions, yet one still chooses to act upon them. Negative thoughts will transcend one's emotions and affect one's mood. One's spirit can infiltrate another's territory when allowed, through insecurities, low self-esteem, emotional reactivity, and limited awareness. Thoughts and emotions do affect each other, and one's words can have a serious impact on others. Be kind, and protect one another with what one thinks, says, and does."

Question Two Hundred And Ninety
October 17th

A lot of us are told that one of the best ways to heal ourselves is to become silent. But we fear silence—we had to conceal our ruinous secrets in the silence of our youth and quite simply do not know how to imagine silence as restorative. Can you help?

Jon: "Restoration and healing can come through silence when silence is appropriate. Consequently, there are many ways in which silence can be restorative. We can pray in silence. We can read God's Word in silence. We can choose to remain silent when we know our words will be hurtful. But silence can also be damaging. Isaiah 1:17 says, 'learn to do good; seek justice, correct oppression; bring justice to the fatherless, plead the widow's cause.' What might not be so obvious about this passage is its application to the self. Sometimes we must pursue restoration for ourselves and this may mean speaking up."

Anna: "When silence is meant to hide, to cower in fear, to not say anything or one will pay, one's existence is smashed to feel null and void. Feeling unloved and alone seems too natural and overwhelming to sit with. Chaos, like one's childhood environment, unsettles one's soul and spirit. The thought of appreciating stillness, desiring time alone, will take a rebirth where divine perspective thrives. To be still, to bask in God's love and peace, to rest in righteousness, truly reflects one's mindset, heart, and faith."

Question Two Hundred And Ninety-One
October 18th

In what ways is Christ an example of spiritual and psychological health?

Jon: "In every way; and he is an example in every way because he never sinned (see John 19:4; 2 Cor. 5:21; Heb. 4:15; 1 Pet. 2:22; 1 John 3:5). This means he made all of the right choices. With this optimum spiritual state attained, Jesus' psychological state was not marred by sin. In other words, his mind was not affected by sin. But for all his perfection, he still experienced great and deep spiritual and mental anguish. So we do not lose heart when our souls and psyches ache. Rather, we look to Jesus and learn that his ability to abide through spiritual and mental anguish was to make his singular priority to do the will of God (Luke 22:42)."

Anna: "Jesus acted upon his convictions in truth and love, with wisdom, discernment, grace, and soundness of mind. He meditated, prayed, and rested from personal, worldly, and spiritual demands. He retreated from distractions, to fellowship with God, to seek clarity, counsel, and comfort. The certainty and tenacity he embodied regarding his eternal will and the unwavering understanding and commitment he had to his consecrated purpose is the epitome of mental and emotional health. Christ lived humbly and genuinely valued fellowship with others. His way of being aligned with God's laws, which ruled his thoughts, intentions, and actions. One's psychological and spiritual well-being, must be rooted in truth, in Jesus Christ's perfection, in order to truly be revolutionized."

Question Two Hundred And Ninety-Two
October 19th

To help us heal, would it be beneficial to not only tap into our spirituality—to how we choose to continue to strive for peace and harmony in all aspects of our lives—but also to study some theology, the nature of God?

Jon: "Exceedingly beneficial to any person is remaining obedient to God's will, and there is arguably no better way to know God's will than to understand God himself. This does not mean that we can ever fully comprehend him. It means that understanding God's will for our lives is directly correlated to how well we know him. The more we know about him, the more we know his will. The more we know and carry out his will, the more peace and harmony will fill our lives. But this will only come about if our theology makes it into our hearts and our hands."

Anna: "One's spirituality, living led by God's Holy Spirit, is critical to one's psychological, emotional, and physical well-being when established in biblical truths because not all information is accurate. Coping with everyday circumstances takes a distinct strategy. Life's blueprint is found modeled within the Bible. God's character and spiritual principles were written to prove humankind's purpose through faith for one's teaching, conviction, comfort, and personal application. God's unveiling wisdom, his boundary system, his grace and forgiveness are all beautifully embodied within Scripture. Human nature only survives through God's nature. His Spirit's nature is miraculous and only understood through an authentic, loving relationship with Jesus."

Question Two Hundred And Ninety-Three
October 20th

Do you think that it would put us more at ease if we were to envision Christ going into therapy with us, walking with us into a counselor's office, and/or sitting beside us during an online therapy session?

Jon: "Jeremiah 23:24 says, 'Can a man hide himself in secret places so that I cannot see him? declares the LORD. Do I not fill heaven and earth? declares the LORD.' There is nowhere where God is not. He is present everywhere, or *omnipresent*. One of the great implications of God's omnipresence is that God *is* wherever we go. Therefore, we do not have to envision Christ going with us anywhere because he already is wherever we are. He is God and simply *is* wherever we go. This also means that there is nothing hidden from God. We ought to be aware, therefore, that we are accountable for all of our actions."

Anna: "Positive associations connect to one's memories and ignite pleasant thoughts and emotions, which motivate and encourage one's attitude and decisions. Visualizations, projecting one's desires and seeing one's ideals consciously creates one's reality within a secure and hopeful net, a perceived safe space where one can allow for vulnerability and self-expression. Having faith is imperative for one's psyche as taking initiative is when making life-changing decisions. As a believer, the Holy Spirit resides within, and bringing Jesus and his love to life is not only helpful but a gift that will bring comfort."

Question Two Hundred And Ninety-Four
October 21st

Whether or not we choose to bare our tortured souls to God, a friend, or a counselor, or all of the above, what are the therapeutic benefits of confession?

Jon: "In Acts 19 we see a story of revival in the city of Ephesus. A man possessed by an evil spirit had overpowered seven men who were the sons of a Jewish high priest named Sceva (Acts 19:14). The possessed man wounded the seven sons and caused them to flee from the house naked. When the people of Ephesus heard this, they turned from their ways toward Christ and confessed their sins. Immediately after this 'the word of the Lord continued to increase and prevail mightily' (Acts 19:20). Spiritual revival comes after confession. God will increase and prevail in the lives of those who confess their sins."

Anna: "To admit, release, and be absolved from one's bondage is relieving and comforting in that one does not have to continually suffer secretly and alone. To acknowledge one's faults, to confide in someone, to reveal one's hidden self, one's abusive experiences or ways, is self-emancipation and loosing dysfunction's grip on one's soul. Submission acts upon revelation and confession allows surrender to be nurtured. Authentic freedom occurs when one's eyes, mind, and heart have been opened to truth, and then one acts upon those truths. Honesty within admission, and a sincere movement toward God, is when one's fears decrease, and one's faith blossoms."

Question Two Hundred And Ninety-Five
October 22nd

There are those of us who are continually asked when are we going to have our own children. Quite frankly, we are afraid that we will abuse them as our parents and/or caregivers abused us, that we're simply not good enough for the role. Thoughts?

Jon: "If it is true that we genuinely feel that we would abuse our children if we were to have them, then we should certainly not have children. This doesn't have much to do with whether or not we are *good enough* to have kids. It has to do with whether or not we *should* have kids. Therefore, we should not have children if we would abuse them. Now let's shift focus. It is vastly more important that we consider the children more than ourselves. Our concern must be less for our own desires and more for the safety and well-being of our children."

Anna: "Abuse permeates through generations when ignorance, selfishness, and pride take precedence over truth, humility, sacrifice, and hope. Awareness, pure intent, and the will to flourish is a recipe for success when one's beliefs are founded upon virtuous truths. It takes courage to admit one's fears, faults, and face the obstacles that one must destroy to not perpetuate destructive patterns. When dysfunction is implanted within one's soul it needs to be removed so that one's mind, heart, and spirit can truly transform. When given authority, the Holy Spirit will lead and shape one's character."

Question Two Hundred And Ninety-Six
October 23rd

What does it mean when someone says to us to not hide our spiritual lights?

Jon: "In Matthew 5, Jesus says that believers are 'the light of the world' (Mat. 5:14). He argues that in the same way a city located on high ground is visible, so too the believer's light shines before others. This is a powerful statement. Jesus isn't necessarily saying that we must work harder to *make* our light shine. He's saying that a believer's light *will* shine. By nature a believer's faith is apparent to those around her in the same way a city's light is apparent. Lights are made to shine light; faith is made to shine God's glory. The faith we have in Jesus Christ will by nature motivate us to good works which direct others back to him."

Anna: "Hiding one's authentic self and keeping secrets is sadly second nature to those who have experienced rejection. When dysfunction casts a shadow upon one's soul, darkness settles in and dominates. At times, any glimmer of one's hope appears distant, unreachable, and this affects one's thoughts, emotions, perceptions, and purpose. Disbelief, walking in shame, succumbing to adversity's deception, believing that one is utterly alone will suppress one's intrinsic value. One's spiritual light is one's testimony of faith and one's truth can and will illuminate the world. Believe that you are God's precious child, divine royalty, a purpose-driven being graciously chosen to embody God's marvelous light that shines bright from within."

Question Two Hundred And Ninety-Seven
October 24th

Even though a number of us are fully capable of taking care of ourselves, we have no problem whatsoever letting others wait on us, pay for us, and pretty much steer the course of our lives. But suddenly, we are beginning to hear these people say that while they are responsible to us, they are not responsible for us. What does this mean?

Jon: "This means that we are in an unhealthy relationship. Not only are we taking advantage of others, but those others are arbitrarily and inconsistently contributing to and therefore validating our advantage taking. We take, and sometimes they validate. We take, and other times they invalidate. This is confusing and begs for strife. If we are taking advantage of someone we should cease doing so immediately. It someone is gift-giving under the façade of charity only to become angry with the person they've given to about that gift, they should cease doing so immediately."

Anna: "What drives one another is very important to uncover when desiring a relationship with a dependable boundary system. A person with a victim mentality craves an enabler, a comforter to appease one's whims and deregulating emotions. An immaturely need-based connection, rooted in codependency, lacks differentiation and independence. Love entails support, provision, grace, but trust—without wise and constructive confines—will not thrive. Human beings were created to love within authentic connection. Ask and allow God to truly fulfill one's needs so one can flourish within relationship."

Question Two Hundred And Ninety-Eight
October 25th

Does God appoint each of us a guardian angel to watch out over us?

Jon: "We don't know. There is conjecture over Matthew 18:10, 'See that you do not despise one of these little ones. For I tell you that in heaven their angels always see the face of my Father who is in heaven.' If there are *appointed* angels, then Matthew 18:10 would only show that children have them. But this doesn't necessarily mean that we don't each have an appointed angel. Again, we just don't know. We simply have to say that Scripture is silent on the issue. Of course, it is not silent as to whether or not angels exist (see Ps. 68:17; Heb. 12:22, 13:2; Rev. 5:11). They do. But where Scripture is silent, there we should be too."

Anna: "Humanity has been given the knowledge and resources to seek out protection and take responsibility for one's will. The Bible does not speak of assigning each believer a guardian angel, yet without question, angels adhere to God's orders to protect his people. One's faith, God's Word, the Holy Spirit and God's angelic army are one's fortress. Angels help those called to live righteously, however, one is the steward of one's thoughts, beliefs, and actions. Learning to surrender one's pain over to the Lord will spiritually preserve. God's heavenly hosts, his divine messengers and protectors exist; his mighty warriors, his celestial soldiers, veiled and unseen, are awaiting and ready to assist you in battle."

Question Two Hundred And Ninety-Nine
October 26th

Does one's self-esteem, whether high or low, drive the human spirit?

Jon: "The westernized world is addicted to self-esteem. Our society promotes self and promotes the promoting of self. We are out for number one, and society is okay with that. In fact, society advises it. Advertising and media operate on pleasing the ego and its desires. It's all about self and if you're not promoting yourself, you're going to fall behind. It is in this sense that self-esteem does drive the spirit. But this is antithetical to Scripture. Christianity cannot be properly lived out by someone who allows self-esteem to drive them because Christianity is about being driven by the Holy Spirit: 'For all who are led by the Spirit of God are sons of God' (Rom. 8:14)."

Anna: "One's attitude toward self affects one's will. Human behaviors are driven by one's soul and spirit. One's spirit affects one's soul, and one's soul is founded upon one's purpose, which emerges from one's belief systems. One's spirit can be steered by lies, negativity, or cruelty, which warp one's mission and causes low self-worth. Abusive environments create an unlovable existence, which changes one's trajectory. Demonic spirits, whether indwelling or influential, are real and thrive within lowly, oppressed, dysfunctional environments, which suppress one's essence. When one's spirit is authentically connected to God's power, his Holy Spirit, one will truly esteem others through oneself and be driven by love's purpose and one's eternal glory."

Question Three Hundred
October 27th

How do we know the difference between God's truth for us and Satan's lies?

Jon: "In John 10 Jesus likens himself to a shepherd and those who follow him to his sheep. He says in verse 27, 'My sheep hear my voice, and I know them, and they follow me.' Sheep won't follow false shepherds. They won't follow someone who isn't their shepherd. They follow *their* shepherd. How do they do this? They know their shepherd's voice. They know his smell. They know his figure. They've spent hours and days and years at his side. So if we want to be able to tell when Satan is trying to influence us, when false shepherds are trying to influence us, we need to spend hours and days and years with the Good Shepherd, Jesus Christ."

Anna: "The lies one accepts will evolve into one's truth when unaware of crucial lifesaving principles. The allure of half-truths has the ability to distort one's perceptions when misapplied. Evil attacks, especially one's mind. It plants seeds of skepticism within one's world, which manifests division in one's soul and disconnection from one's ultimate source of strength. Understanding God's truth guides one into having a discerning and wise application of one's past, current state, and imminent future. Standing firm, heeding conviction, not being defined by one's childhood abuse, and edifying one's spirit and soul by studying the Bible and having a personal relationship with Jesus, will help distinguish what actually is from the enemies' lies."

Question Three Hundred And One
October 28th

Do you think that child molesters can be rehabilitated and, if so, trusted around our children?

Jon: "It was Jesus who said in Matthew 19:26, 'With man this is impossible, but with God all things are possible.' If God so desires that a person be rehabilitated and that person works hard and in fact becomes rehabilitated, then that person is trustworthy. The problem is that no one can be sure that this person will not relapse into that which they were rehabilitated from. Caution is primary here. The other problem is that putting children before a former child abuser is like putting alcohol before a former alcoholic. Reason tells us that the likelihood of a former abuser becoming a present abuser increases dramatically when the abused subject — person or drink — is within close proximity."

Anna: "Some do desire to change, yet will relapse, and others are extremely dangerous, cannot be trusted, and do not want rehabilitation. This fact, though frustrating and baffling, is simply reality. Rehabilitation varies dependent upon one's psychopathology, predatory patterns, sexual behaviors, victim counts, belief systems, and level of remorse etcetera. Evil is running wild and attempting to take down anyone, especially the young, misled, and the blind-sided. Humankind is fighting a spiritual battle, an unseen war that wants to ensnare and destroy one's innocence and hope. Good and evil exist on all plains and the seeds of molestation have spiritual roots. A molester with perceived rehabilitation, or not, should not be around children alone."

Question Three Hundred And Two
October 29th

A number of us were illegally adopted, stripping us of our society and culture. Is there a way we can make up for the loss of our true identities?

Jon: "There may be no way to make up for any loss of identity in this lifetime. But should we call our earthly identity our *true* identity? Surely what we experience and gain here on earth is important and contributes to our identity, but our *true* identity is in Jesus Christ. Our true identity is the way God sees us. Since unlike us God is omniscient, he knows us better than we know ourselves. As believers, how does God see each one of us? He sees us as blessed, chosen, holy, blameless, predestined, family, redeemed, and forgiven (Eph. 1:3-10). This is our true identity 'sealed with the promised Holy Spirit' (Eph. 1:13)."

Anna: "Not knowing where one comes from is heartbreaking and adoption can be very lonely, self-displacing, and attempts to take away one's heritage and individuality. One's identity development and detachment issues require serious validation through grieving and self-exploration. The pain of abandonment can be difficult to explain and can negatively affect one's distress modalities and relationship patterns. When life's circumstances strip one of inborn privileges, one can feel unseen and forgotten. One's biological family cannot be replaced but God's love cannot be replicated. There is always hope. God's saving grace and life's redeeming quality is experiencing that one's true identity is perfectly and graciously in Christ."

Question Three Hundred And Three
October 30th

As children, our very basic human needs went unmet, like the need to be loved, protected, and approved. Now as adults, we are not comfortable being in situations of dependency. For example, perhaps some of us are married to protective men but we simply do not trust the gesture. Can you suggest how we might go about resolving codependent issues?

Jon: "Dependency is something Christians ought to master because we are dependent on the Lord for everything. Acts 17:28 says, 'In him we live and move and have our being.' It is not that we must be able to depend on anyone. Rather, we must we able to depend fully on God. This will give us practice in depending on another. So when the time comes to depend on another, we will be prepared to do so. Moreover, when and if that dependency disappoints, it will not devastate us because we have learned that it is only God who will never disappoint."

Anna: "When one's psychological, emotional, or physical boundaries have been consistently violated, one's construct of trust was abused. What appeared to be routine was manipulated for self-destruction's gain. There are safe people in the world and a good measure of relational security is discerning one's values, intentions, and behaviors. To resolve codependency, one must connect one's insecurities and desires, to one's behaviors, relinquish control, and depend on God to fulfill one's needs. One's unhealthy reliance stems from sin's wake and fear."

Question Three Hundred And Four
October 31st

Some of us have the propensity to feign the goodness in some people. For example, we would rather tell our friends that our abusive parents are great people rather than tell them the truth about them. Could it be that we simply do not want to see their faults or for others to see them?

Jon: "There are two reasons for embellishing the status of those we associate with: pride or appropriateness. The first is sinful while the latter is prudent. When pride drives our embellishments of others, we are secretly lifting the self. We surmise that the more impressive we make those with whom we associate ourselves, the more impressive we will appear. This course of action will surely lead to destruction (see Pro. 16:18). The second reason for embellishing—appropriateness—is used when it may not be suitable or proper to reveal the negative character of another in inappropriate situations."

Anna: "Abuse creates detrimental misconceptions, dysfunctional relationship patterns, and crooked self-impressions. Hiding, running from, or denying what happened is common because of the complications and painful emotions that arise from abusive experiences. Recognizing the good as opposed to flippancy, inappropriate gossip of harmful information, and plain family condemnation is a loving and gracious way to live. However, covering up the truth leads to bondage, which opposes a fulfilled existence. When ready, express one's truth in confidence to God, and a trusted friend or counselor, for support, reassurance, healing, and personal and spiritual growth."

Question Three Hundred And Five
November 1st

What do we do if we want to share our stories of how we were abused as children with others but are simply too embarrassed to do so?

Jon: "Shame is one of the earliest felt emotions in the Bible. God's response to shame and embarrassment is the same now as it was then. After Adam and Eve had sinned in the garden, they heard the Lord coming toward them and hid themselves. They were embarrassed. Now of course God's omniscience necessitates that he knew where Adam and Eve were hiding, so what he does next is quite intriguing. Genesis 3:9 says, 'But the LORD God called to the man and said to him, "Where are you?"' God calls to the ashamed and embarrassed, *Where are you?* He desires we come out into the open and share ourselves appropriately with him and with others."

Anna: "Transparency of one's authentic self does not just happen without effort, discernment, and time. Throughout development, as one matures, one's innate desires intensify. This beautiful want from within is connected to one's purpose whether one chooses to embrace it or not. What one has been through truly matters, so please embrace this: crush evil's plan by sharing one's story to encourage oneself and others. Humiliation and shame extinguish one's light. God desires for Christ followers to confess one's testimony as proof, so that others will be deeply moved by the power of his grace, forgiveness, salvation, and love."

Question Three Hundred And Six
November 2nd

A number of us are being told that we have no intention of resolving our issues. What does it mean to have intention, anyway?

Jon: "Intentionality is a setting of the mind toward something. Colossians 3:2 says, 'Set your minds on things that are above, not on things that are on earth.' When he wrote this, Paul knew that whatever the mind was set toward would influence the rest of a person's thoughts, feelings, and even actions. If you think about it, almost everything a person does is a result of thought. Put more specifically, many of our feelings and actions are the result of our thoughts. Therefore, *what* we choose to think most often about must be deliberately chosen. Accordingly, the more we intentionally direct our thoughts toward resolving our issues, the more likely those issues will be resolved."

Anna: "Intention is one's willful desire to accomplish something, whether attached to an external objective, an extension of oneself, or a burning passion from within. It means one has assigned thought and purpose to one's behaviors and being. One's intent can be simplistic or convoluted, deceptive or beautiful, and understanding the root of one's issues will help enable one's soul to start resolving one's dissonance from one's past abuse. Thoughtfully deciding brings structure, security, and hope because one is sure of one's decisions. As the Holy Spirit transforms one from the inside out, one's thoughts, intentions, and actions start to truly fall in line with God's will and one's unique purpose."

Question Three Hundred And Seven
November 3rd

Many of us have come to the realization that we have always played the role of scapegoat in our family dynamics, the person who is made to bear the blame for others. How do we get out of this pattern of playing scapegoat?

Jon: "Some people place blame on us regardless of whether or not we are actually blameworthy. It is not the truth that is important to them, but our suffering. As wrong as it is for people to act this way, circumstances such as these provide opportunity for rejoicing—a common Christian paradox. 1 Peter 4:13 says, 'But rejoice insofar as you share Christ's sufferings…' Jesus took the blame and consequences for our sin. He didn't deserve it either. We can rejoice when we are blamed and suffer for something we didn't do because in doing so we share with the Lord Jesus Christ."

Anna: "Chronic critics, blamers, and slanderers are all dealing with a fundamental misconception: that they are perfect and do not affect or hurt others. Within abuse's system, souls are exploited. Not living out the projections and accusations of others is accomplished through embodying one's true identity. Scapegoating is a conspiracy to continually shame, evil's tactic. Not identifying as the problem, not carrying other's burdens or accepting the lies in Jesus' name is how this pattern ends. One must take ownership of who one is in Christ, not how one is treated or how others paint them to be."

Question Three Hundred And Eight
November 4th

If any of our spouses are abusing our children, should we divorce them?

Jon: "For Jesus and Moses the only reason one is permitted to divorce his or her spouse is over sexual immorality. In other words, Scripture permits divorce only over sexual sin such as adultery. Unfortunately, many cases of child abuse fall into this category. So there is biblical warrant for a husband or wife to divorce his or her spouse who has committed such sin. It should be noted, however, that Jesus qualifies in Matthew 19:8 that it is because of 'hardness of heart' that we are permitted to divorce for this reason. We can safely say that no one is obligated to divorce his or her spouse for sexual immorality but is merely permitted to do so."

Anna: "It cannot be stressed enough that safety is most important and when a child is being hurt then one must protect that child. Abuse intends to destroy and a child's soul is penetrable. Caring for a fragile being is a serious responsibility. Abuse and divorce will both have psychological and emotional ramifications upon the child if not addressed: depression, anxiety, anger, mistrust, rejection, abandonment, and self-blame. Soul preservation is dire and with serious challenges come greater decisions, yet always an opportunity for divine advantage. Marriage is sacred, one's commitment is serious, however, one cannot change another, only God can; pray, seek counsel, protect one's children, and take action toward preserving what one has."

Question Three Hundred And Nine
November 5th

Regarding our sufferings in childhood, many of us continue to look for sympathy from others and find none. Given that, does Christ pity us?

Jon: "As Jesus went throughout various cities and villages he encountered many crowds. Matthew 9:36 says, 'When he saw the crowds, he had compassion for them, because they were harassed and helpless, like sheep without a shepherd.' It is Christ's nature to have compassion on us. It is also his nature to want to do something to help us. And the best possible thing he could do for us is offer to be our shepherd — to protect us from the wolves and to lead us into the pasture of everlasting life. But all his compassion cannot force us to follow him. Will we toil after the lesser sympathies of this world? Or will we rest in the infinite sympathy of the Good Shepherd?"

Anna: "Pity is often deemed as negative, as having an implied inferiority that muddles the point of what genuine compassion brings to one's mind, heart, and spirit. An abusive upbringing is apathetic, cruel, and lacks devotion toward the well-being of others. This emotional abandonment is disappointing and self-compressing because one is left to battle one's sensitivities alone and without a solid understanding of how to do so. The greatest commiseration was God sending Christ to die for humankind because he understands perfectly the condition of one's soul and the suffering one has endured. He pities lovingly, humbly, and flawlessly."

Question Three Hundred And Ten
November 6th

How do we handle the emotional needs of others if we can't handle our own?

Jon: "The focus may be too situated over our own abilities and not situated enough over God's abilities. For when the focus is properly situated over God's abilities *we* are no longer the handler of our or anyone else's needs. Rather, *he* becomes the handler. This is why Psalm 37:5 says, 'Commit your way to the LORD; trust in him, and he will act.' It doesn't say God *might* act. It says God *will* act. And the two mechanisms that endorse God's action are faith and obedience. So there is a correlation between how much faith and obedience we exercise and how much God will act in our lives. The key to handling our needs and others' needs is trusting God to do the handling."

Anna: "One's mind is a weapon, yet a formidable adversary when easily swayed. This can affect susceptible individuals and cause emotional deregulation. Managing emotions can be tricky when one is sensitive by nature and has not yet come to terms with their past hurts and faulty self-beliefs. The ability to differentiate from another's emotional spurring within a cognitive reappraisal of truth versus reacting solely upon one's perceptions is emotional intelligence. Genuinely understanding that you are not supposed to carry another's feelings is transformative. One will learn to handle others in a way that is emotionally safe through internalizing less and by giving other's difficult needs to God."

Question Three Hundred And Eleven
November 7th

If Jesus was walking among us today, what do you think he would have to say to people who abuse children in any way, shape, or form?

Jon: "Surely we could imagine that Jesus would have harsh words for such a person. And perhaps he would (see Mat. 18:6). But in the Gospels, the people for whom Jesus reserved his harshest language were not those society called *sinners* but those society called *religious*. It was the Pharisees and the Sadducees who Jesus called hypocrites and blind guides, whitewashed tombs and broods of vipers (see Mat. 23:13-37). Assuredly, however, to the unrepentant child abuser Jesus would say what he says to all the unrepentant: 'I told you that you would die in your sins…' (John 8:24). So long as anyone continues to sin unrepentantly they will not inherit eternal life."

Anna: "Those who have turned from what is good should listen. Children are treasures and one is lost to not comprehend their worth. Abuse exposes one's human nature and is proof of one's disconnection from salvation's forgiveness and grace. When one is harsh, hypocritical, or judgmental, it tears another's spirit apart because one truly needs love and faithfulness, not cruelty or condemnation. The depth of one's soul is known and no one can hide. One's awareness is uncovered and one's intentions are clear; all truths will be revealed. One's hope and promise for salvation is within reach, however, one must repent and believe."

Question Three Hundred And Twelve
November 8th

Many of us who were sexually molested as children do not like people looking at us. We believe that they are thinking ill thoughts about us. How can we lessen this affliction?

Jon: "Proverbs 29:25 says, 'The fear of man lays a snare, but whoever trusts in the LORD is safe.' When we consider what others think about us to the point where we become fearful, we are setting traps for ourselves to walk into. The assumption that others are thinking negatively about us is the trap setting. The fear or anxiety which comes afterward is the trap closing on us. Better to spend less time thinking negative thoughts about man than we think trusting thoughts about God. A remedy for this problem every time we assume others are thinking ill of us is to substitute that assumption for a conscious assertion of our trust in God."

Anna: "Sexual abuse inflicts scars engraved upon one's heart and psyche. One's innermost self will not heal without addressing the molestation and how it has injured one's soul. Abuse is humiliating, demeaning, confusing, and instills self-doubt within its victim's mentality. When uncomfortable with whom one is purely because of what happened to them, self-conceived beliefs transpire from one's negative perceptions. Violations cause pain, mistrust, and being someone's sex object creates displeasure and disconnect between one's desires and beliefs. Ask God to transform one's mind through his truth and give one discernment and clarity in correlation to trusting others."

Question Three Hundred And Thirteen
November 9th

Some of our partners are physically and emotionally abusive to us. We have nowhere to go. What do we do?

Jon: "We have options that range in different degrees of severity and differ from situation to situation. The first option may be direct conversation with our offender. If this is not enough, we may consult a trusted friend or family member. If these are not available or do not work, contacting higher authorities such as a counselor or the local church may be the next option. Finally, if these are not enough, we may consult law enforcement, 'for the authorities are ministers of God' (Rom. 13:6) and 'he is God's servant for your good' (Rom. 13:4)."

Anna: "It is time to be honest and acknowledge one's spiritual state. The abusive environment convinces one to become less and less of who they were created to be and reluctantly conform to the abuser's control and chaos. When continually victimized, a warped sense of reality develops that mirrors the abuser's delusions. Feeling as if one is at fault, questioning oneself, or becoming numb and just existing battle one's former self-confidence and identity. Believing that one deserves better taunts one's possibilities and future. Ask God for wisdom and strength and safely get help because feeling hopeless within abuse's snare is lonesome. Devise a plan, prepare, and seek support from family, a friend, an abuse hotline, a counselor, or the law, because no one deserves to be abused."

Question Three Hundred And Fourteen
November 10th

Must we re-experience the traumatic memories of our childhoods to restore our psyches?

Jon: "The apostle Paul was imprisoned, beaten nearly to death, whipped thirty-nine times, beaten with rods, stoned, ship-wrecked three times, adrift at sea, exposed to the elements of nature, and often left hungry and thirsty (see 2 Cor. 11:21-29). What does Paul do with these memories? He writes in Philippians 3:13, '… one thing I do: forgetting what lies behind and straining forward to what lies ahead…' By focusing on the positive future-promises of God instead of his past trauma, Paul was able to become arguably the most accomplished apostle of Jesus Christ."

Anna: "To validate one's experiences for healing is empowering, yet can stimulate past abuse and precursor intense fear or post-traumatic stress when memories are invasive. Within a secure space, to re-experience one's suffering for curative measures can allow one to surmount mental and emotional snares. However, most pressingly, this should be implemented when one is ready and willing within the scope of one's grieving process and therapeutic journey. Must everyone relive all details of their abuse to move forward? No. Yet when one has dismissed, denied, or suppressed the abuse and is completely disengaged from life, one's reality certainly needs addressing. God desires to heal humankind's wounds but in order to be psychologically restored, one must allow God's Word, his truth, and Spirit to transform one's conscious mind to press on toward one's promising future."

Question Three Hundred And Fifteen
November 11th

There is another story in the Bible where babies are said to be beaten into fragments. Isn't this yet another example of child abuse?

Jon: "This no doubt comes from Isaiah 13. The inaugural verse is, 'The oracle concerning Babylon which Isaiah the son of Amoz saw.' So the chapter is a prophecy concerning what will happen to the people of Babylon who have sinned (Isa. 13:9), who are evil, wicked, arrogant, and ruthless (Isa. 13:11). And the harsh consequences described in verses 15 and 16 about these evil persons—for example, falling by the sword or watching their infants die—only apply to those evil persons who are 'found.' In other words, the prophecy did not apply to those evil persons who did not choose to stay and fight the Medes. Moreover, Scripture does not say if any *did* die in this way."

Anna: "Dysfunctional behaviors are often disguised as an acceptable means of retaliation. The demise of the human experience entails abusive and murderous conduct, which impedes upon one's innate worth and purpose. Systematic corruption targets the confused, abused, rejected, and helpless. What one does affects one's soul, spirit, and will be made known. People make choices, they act upon desires, which uplifts or tears down. Self-advantage and spiritual confusion is at the core of evil, and is most often ignorantly, blatantly, and demonically induced. Human nature is flawed, yet blessed with a God-given responsibility to love one another. Evil sadly has generational consequences."

Question Three Hundred And Sixteen
November 12th

Do you think that prayer promotes forgiveness?

Jon: "Before answering this question, we must first ask whether or not God is forgiving. Numbers 14:18 says, 'The LORD is slow to anger and abounding in steadfast love, forgiving iniquity and transgression.' Daniel 9:9 says, 'To the Lord our God belong mercy and forgiveness...' Forgiveness is not merely something God acts according to; forgiveness *belongs* to God. He is by nature forgiving. He cannot *not* be forgiving. Now we can answer our initial question. Genuine prayer promotes communion with God. Communion with God increases the amount of time we are exposed to God. By nature we become like that which we often expose ourselves to. Therefore, if God is forgiving, then the more we pray to him, the more forgiving we will be."

Anna: "Prayer demonstrates one's reprieve through a humble acknowledgement and self-declaration of where one's mercies, abilities, and opportunities lie. One's boldness within prayer reflects one's belief system, and asking with certainty when approaching the sovereign throne shows unshakable faith. This displays a hope in something greater than oneself yet is carried out through one's confidence and will. For optimal faith building, one's consciousness must stand firmly upon forgiveness, one's soul-saving message. When one communicates with whom one cannot see yet can unmistakably feel, one is depending upon truth's promises. The Holy Spirit is salvation's access to God, and prayer through Jesus Christ is one's anchor to God's grace and power."

Question Three Hundred And Seventeen
November 13th

Is it right and proper to mourn our lost childhoods?

Jon: "Jesus said in Matthew 5:4, 'Blessed are those who mourn, for they shall be comforted.' Notice Jesus didn't say, 'Blessed are those who mourn *over this or that*.' He said, 'Blessed are those *who* mourn.' For the one who is in Christ, their mourning—so long as it is without sinful embellishing or exploitation—is never improper. Beyond this still, the Christian who mourns is not left to their mourning. In other words, their mourning is not the end. Comfort is the end. Again, note that Jesus does not say mourners *'may* be comforted' but they *'shall* be comforted.' So if we mourn our lost childhoods now, we do so understanding that Christ guarantees our comfort, whether in this life or the next."

Anna: "Mourning the abuse one braved is vital, adaptive, and helps increase one's personal stability. When the woes within are not addressed, one's emotional toll becomes too heavy. Acknowledging the past helps secure one's present state and one's domination over immorality. That confused child can be a newfound adult when one chooses to set oneself free from the past. What abuse attempted to destroy can certainly have purpose. The dysfunctional agenda has surfaced and one can truly live victoriously through one's hope-centered core beliefs. When faith arises in Jesus, what was completely lost is transformed through a spiritual rebirth; one's soul experiences freedom and one's glory is claimed."

Question Three Hundred And Eighteen
November 14th

Some of us are scared that if we get into some sort of treatment plan, whether spiritual and/or psychological in nature, Satan will take over our minds and we will lose them to him. Is this possible?

Jon: "We can well imagine Satan desiring we adopt an attitude such as this one. He doesn't want us to seek help. He doesn't want us to overcome our afflictions. He doesn't want us to improve spiritually and psychologically. Rather, he wants us to believe that if we try, we will fail. He wants us to live in fear. Well, not so for the Christian. For, as the Scripture says, Jesus Christ is already victorious over even death, 'that through death he might destroy the one who has the power of death, that is, the devil' (Heb. 2:14). Praise God! Satan has no power over the faithful in Christ, nor will he ever."

Anna: "The ability to contemplate, conceptualize, and make daily decisions through one's will is an amazing freedom. Unless one has made a pact with the devil or has given one's soul over to him without conscious withdrawal, one has rule over selfdom. Satan attempts to deceive humankind in their pain and sinful excursions when living in disbelief, spiritually unprotected, and lukewarm in one's faith. However, one must choose to believe his lies. Study and reflect upon God's Word to secure one's mind and heart to truth, and have faith in Jesus' righteous covering, for the believer is divinely sheltered."

Question Three Hundred And Nineteen
November 15th

A handful of us know people who get so angry that they can't speak. How can we support them?

Jon: "The best thing we can say to angry people is nothing. That is, it is best not to say anything at all to an angry person. Someone who has become so angry that they can't form words likely cannot be reasoned with. If there comes a time when we must speak, we do well to obey Proverbs 15:1, 'A soft answer turns away wrath, but a harsh word stirs up anger.' The key is understanding the difference between negative words and positive words. Negative words fuel the flames of anger, while positive words extinguish them. Surely, the ability to speak positively to an angry person is simultaneously one of the most difficult and profitable of interpersonal skills."

Anna: "Compassion, patience, and understanding are powerful instruments when supporting someone who has difficulty communicating when angry. Experiencing threatening and abusive interactions can lead to a deficiency in tolerating one's negative cognitions and internal escalations. When one shuts down when in distress, one's desire to maintain control defensively modifies. Conversion directs one's subjective experiences, one's emotional turmoil, toward one's physical body. Anger alludes to an important notion, that one has emotional depth and the symbolisms of one's vulnerabilities are being expressed. Asking what one needs and praying to God in Jesus' name when unsure of how to respond is selflessness in love and uplifting support."

Question Three Hundred And Twenty
November 16th

There is no end to those of us who truly believe that being abused as children has caused us to become atheists. We do, however, maintain a glimmer of curiosity: How do unbelievers know that the Bible is true?

Jon: "Unbelievers do not know that the Bible is true because an unbeliever is one who claims to know that the Bible is not true. That's what it means to be an *un-believer*. They do *not* believe. Therefore an unbeliever cannot know that the Bible is true. One must turn from their unbelief and toward belief in order to know that the Bible is true. For, 'these things God has revealed to us through the Spirit' (1 Cor. 2:10). How do we obtain the Spirit? The Holy Spirit is received *through* faith (Gal. 3:14). It is not truth that is the obstacle, but unbelief."

Anna: "Pain can delude one's perspective. When one's world-view has been shaped through abuse's message of unworthiness and lack of purpose, the biblical perspective seems foolish because it teaches the counter. Abuse deprives one's existence and it enables identity confusion when attempts to differentiate fail within the dysfunctional system. Remember, one's needs are intrinsically motivated because one has purpose. Visualize the galaxy, the twinkling stars, and the earth suspended within the atmosphere. How could one not be curious? The Bible is God's dynamic Word, his unfolding plan, his gift for humankind, obtainable for all to experience and receive."

Question Three Hundred And Twenty-One
November 17th

Our sense of how we should properly discipline our own children has been skewed by our abusive upbringings. How do you both think that we should discipline our children?

Jon: "Proverbs 22:6 says, 'Train up a child in the way he should go; even when he is old he will not depart from it.' Whatever we teach our children while they are young will remain with them when they are old. We have a responsibility to instill good moral values as early as possible. Since God is the locus of morality, it is vital we base the way we discipline our children according to godly instruction. This of course will come from God's Word. If Scripture says anything about disciplining children, it is that discipline is necessary (Pro. 23:13), an act of love (Pro. 13:24), and its absence sabotages the child's future (Pro. 19:18)."

Anna: "Families progress with boundaries, when healthy behaviors are modeled, affirmed, and corrected through accountability, and ultimately with forgiveness, and grace covering the household. Disciplinary action established with self-control, truth, authority, and love is quite impactful. When parental motives or reactions become entangled with selfish desires, one's priorities need to be addressed. Positive reinforcement is necessary, yet when a child's behaviors are consistently praised as opposed to the child, that child may interpret that who they are, flaws and all, is simply not good enough. Upright discipline falls in line with God's biblical teachings, wisdom, communication, mercy, and when one firmly follows the direction of the Holy Spirit."

Question Three Hundred And Twenty-Two
November 18th

A number of us are bigger and stronger than our partners and we take out our frustrations on them. For example, our bosses may shout at us at work, but instead of taking care of the problem there, we go home and shout at our partners. How do we stop?

Jon: "Anger is a gateway to greater offenses. The more we entertain it, the wider open the gate swings. If we cannot stop our anger by an act of will we ought to seek counseling, especially if we are physically larger than whomever we become angry with. We must install an additional source of accountability. This is arguably why James 5:16 says, 'Therefore, confess your sins to one another and pray for one another, that you may be healed.' Confessing something personal and embarrassing to another is difficult, but it is necessary for powerful and effective accountability."

Anna: "Displacement can be powerfully effective or extremely destructive. When attempting to regulate one's emotions, whether intentionally or inadvertently, feelings can be projected onto what is currently deemed the bad object, which perpetuates unfulfilling processes. Increasing one's ability to attune to what is circumstantially appropriate is difficult when regressive behavioral patterns were modeled. Displacing anger in moments of escalation is common. However, when one's impulses become habitual and cause relationship ruptures, emotional resolution skills need building. When conviction becomes repentance, and one's soul is surrendered to God's will and Spirit, one's ability to emotionally regulate will progress."

Question Three Hundred And Twenty-Three
November 19th

Why are many of our abusers wealthy while we, their victims, remain destitute?

Jon: "Job asked the question this way: 'Why do the wicked live, reach old age, and grow mighty in power?' (Job 21:7). Jeremiah, this way: 'Why does the way of the wicked prosper? Why do all who are treacherous thrive?' (Jer. 12:1). The Psalmist: 'O LORD, how long shall the wicked, how long shall the wicked exult?' (Ps. 94:3). We are so quick to equate *prospering* with *good*. But if this were the case, we could hardly consider the life of Christ good. And this is obviously wrong. The problem isn't with Christ, but with our understanding of what is *good*. Finding good in money, the wealthy may feel no need for a savior in Christ—making them the truly destitute."

Anna: "The world's ways are impure yet one's choices will bring reward or consequence, temporarily or permanently, and not conditionally upon one's beliefs and motivation. This is why abusers have the opportunity to gain worldly success even when their offenses have not been exposed. What one values is what constitutes for self-achievement. The people who appear to be winning in life do not necessarily have integrity, nor must they finish with honor. Free will motivates one's behaviors and creates one's destiny. However, what is upright spiritually mitigates the unfairness of life, and one's devotion to God will overcome, and victory will be reached through one's eternal faith in Jesus Christ."

Question Three Hundred And Twenty-Four
November 20th

Why do a number of us still ache for the very parents who abused us and hurt us so deeply?

Jon: "Even those who have abused us have been made in the image and likeness of God (see Gen. 5:1). Observing his likeness in them, we sympathize with their condition and ache as a reaction to the great marring their humanity has undertaken. Jesus says in Matthew 5:44, 'But I say to you, Love your enemies and pray for those who persecute you.' Our aching for our abusive parents is a sign that we are according to Jesus' command. It is a sign that we love them. This ought not strike us as *confusing* but as *confirming*, namely, that Jesus Christ has done a great work inside us to incline us to love those we may otherwise consider unlovable."

Anna: "Humankind was created to love and when one's childhood was filled with abuse, one intensely desires emotional support, relational security and attention. Rejection stabs deep into one's soul, so deep it feels as if one will not survive, as if one's very worth has been completely denied, undeservingly renounced. Emotional starvation creates a hunger to be seen, heard, and validated. There is nothing wrong with desiring their love; what is disheartening is that they did not know how to give it. God will comfort one's heartache and he loves more fully than one could ever imagine, yet one must grieve what was lost."

Question Three Hundred And Twenty-Five
November 21st

There is nothing funny about being abused as a child. But some of us who had been abused do try and keep a sense of humor about this life. Isn't it better to have a sense of humor rather than being so serious all the time?

Jon: "Ecclesiastes 3:4 says, 'a time to weep, and a time to laugh; a time to mourn, and a time to dance…' If we expect humor to be present throughout life, we will be sorely discouraged. On the other hand, if we expect life to be humorless we will be equally discouraged. So one cannot say that humor is *better* than humorlessness or vice versa except in the sense that one will be more appropriate at one time than the other. The teaching of Scripture is to balance humor and seriousness without allowing one's life to be overrun by either."

Anna: "Humor is a gift yet often used to deflect one's emotional pain. Humor attempts to mask one's uncomfortable experiences and to lightheartedly change the projection of one's mood. Humor uplifts and also exposes the obvious and unspoken. A sense of humor is priceless and so is discerning the seriousness of life's intent. Defense mechanisms are handy but when overused and misused they may become self-antagonistic or self-delusive. When one's earnestness forgets joy, the somberness of past abuse can take over and become burdensome. Righteous humor adds variety to one's life; so smile, and thank the Lord."

Question Three Hundred And Twenty-Six
November 22nd

Some of us speak before we think. It could be said that we have no "filters" for our mouths. How can we learn to pause before we let hurtful words fly?

Jon: "Scripture says, 'let every person be quick to hear, slow to speak' (Jas. 1:19). Do you see the genius in God's Word here? Notice the correlation between speaking and listening. Hasty listening is the remedy for hasty speech. In other words, we can slow our speech by hastening our listening. The more time we spend listening, the less time we have to speak. There should be an imbalance. The scale should be tipped: more listening, less speaking. But we are not diminishing our speech. Rather, we are cultivating and increasing our ability to listen."

Anna: "Patience and self-control can attribute to the success of a conversation by simply being selective, tactful, and gracious when speaking. Reacting hastily is different than replying or cleverly defending oneself. To linger on negativity and permeate through what is good, and filter chosen information can stir damaging ideas that lead to a reckless, impulsive, or cruel verbal delivery. Having self-command and listening takes effort. Paying attention to one's thoughts and emotions will increase self-awareness and understanding. Sadly, the tongue can be a powerful and crafty tool used to degrade others, because it speaks what one feels. Allowing God's Spirit to transform one's heart and motives will allow one to be more patient and composed."

Question Three Hundred And Twenty-Seven
November 23rd

We come from such destructive childhoods that just the thought of any sort of salvation for our souls is elusive to us. What is salvation, anyway, and what could it mean for our living souls?

Jon: "That our living souls have received salvation means that our souls will *keep* living. This does not mean that without salvation we will not continue to exist. Biblically speaking, *life* after death does not necessarily refer to existence but to existence *in heaven with God*. For those who are or will be in hell will exist there. But it is difficult to call this living. In any case, 1 Thessalonians 5:10 says that we receive salvation 'so that whether we are awake or asleep we might live with [God].' Our belief in Jesus Christ eternally binds us to God. And we are bound to him in this life and in the next."

Anna: "Not receiving deliverance from one's detrimental upbringing stirs perceptions and aggravations that one was not worth saving. This is untrue. Dysfunction distributes falsified messages of inadequacy and unworthiness. This leads to an unfulfilled existence when one is not firmly planted within an accurate belief system. Salvation is faith's assurance, which mentally and emotionally relieves one's anxieties and fears when meditating upon personal truths. One's soul lives eternally and salvation determines its permanent residence. An authentic and active belief in Jesus dictates one's disposition and anticipated privilege that one will forever reside in God's kingdom."

Question Three Hundred And Twenty-Eight
November 24th

Child abuse has caused a selected number of us to experience such conditions as headaches, back pain, and difficulty swallowing with no medical evidence showing that anything is wrong. Could the cause be spiritual and/or psychological?

Jon: "In 1 Corinthians 11, Paul addresses problems the Corinthians' church was having when they ate the Lord's Supper. They were quarreling, dividing, eating selfishly without sharing, and even becoming drunk. This had caused the church to partake of communion in a guilty and unworthy manner. Paul says in verse 30, 'That is why many of you are weak and ill, and some have died.' The point is not that our health issues are *necessarily* caused by poor spiritual practices, but that they *could* be. How do we remedy this? By examining ourselves as we ask God to reveal and restore any poor spiritual practices we may be engaged in."

Anna: "Different combinations of psychological and emotional misunderstandings and afflictions affect one's spiritual state on complex levels. Mental distress can manifest into physical symptoms due to a premature regulation and communicatory process. When persistent anxieties appear due to suppressed traumas, thoughts, and emotions, conversion processes expressed through one's internal body systems arise. Without confessing, expressing, and surrendering one's painful secrets, psychological and emotional bondage will not subside and will manifest. Applying God's truth over the abuse's lies will help to develop more stability within one's soul, spirit, and body."

Question Three Hundred And Twenty-Nine
November 25th

FGM/C, female genital mutilation/cutting, is a cultural practice centuries old. Millions of women have been cut so that we never enjoy sex and have to be cut again to deliver our children into this world. Does the Bible support the cutting and mutilating of female genitalia?

Jon: "Absolutely not. The Bible is categorically against any and all unjust harm. And it is especially against the harming of reproductive organs because they are necessary for carrying out God's command to humanity to be fruitful and multiply and fill the earth (Gen. 1:28). But this does not mean that surgery done in order to, say, allow a woman to deliver her baby is wrong, for it may be necessary in order to save the baby's or the mother's life. The principle here is that harm done to someone's body for harm's sake or for some other evil purpose is unbiblical."

Anna: "Different cultures practice unique traditions and female circumcision is one. Obvious disparities, oppression, and social abuse within different regions associated with sex and gender grievously transpire. The psychological and emotional effects of FGM/C can bring confusion upon a woman's identity. Dysfunction's grip is strong and the detrimental beliefs held as an individual and as a collective system will cause deep deceptions, disunity, and harm. The Bible does not support injustice, evil, and is proof of God's combat against it; a way has been made for one's depravity to be healed, dignified, and glorified through Jesus Christ."

Question Three Hundred And Thirty
November 26th

There is a story in the Bible where the priest's daughter dishonors her father by fornication and is told she will be burned to death because of it. How could a father do this to his daughter?

Jon: "Firstly, this is not a story in the Bible. It is part of the Levitical Law (see Lev. 21:9). Moreover, there is no evidence that this law ever needed to be carried out. This is not the right question, however. The right question is *how could a person sin against God?* God is wronged in sin, not the sinner. What punishment do persons who sin against a perfectly holy and just God deserve? Do we have better knowledge than an omniscient God has? Pride and hypocrisy make us assume we deserve no punishment for our wrongdoings and that sinners know better how to punish sin than a sinless God does."

Anna: "Unfortunately, some fathers abuse their daughters and this depravity is only worsening. Human behavior can be atrocious and it is no wonder why there is so much suffering. The pain we inflict upon one another is perplexing, astonishing, and sadly, corruption is moving more expeditiously. Lost souls simply act upon evil yet the consequences are deep. A father is just a man, and a man must choose his fate like everyone else. Sin is humankind's curse and the irreverence for God and one's soul is sadly one's demise, and only Jesus Christ truly rectifies this."

Question Three Hundred And Thirty-One
November 27th

Plenty of us learned that failure in childhood—failing to wash a dish, roll up a hose, clean a room properly—meant blame and condemnation. Isn't there some value in failure?

Jon: "How could Paul say in 2 Corinthians 12:10, 'For when I am weak, then I am strong'? Or how could he say, 'I am content with weaknesses, insults, hardships, persecutions, and calamities'? His point was that without recognizing his own failures he would be unable to recognize his need for God's grace. It was through his failures and his weaknesses that he was able to see that need. The greatest value in our failures then is that they reveal to us our need for a savior. That need brings us to Christ. Christ brings us into relationship with God the Father. And that relationship means no blame and no condemnation (Rom. 8:1)."

Anna: "Abusers have a highly negative and selfish perspective, and tend to set unreachable expectations. Even when a controlling person has a lapse within their rigid ideals, anger and mistrust have already been embedded and any satisfaction is short-lived. Failure connects directly to humanity's fallen nature and should be expected. Striving toward something that is of personal significance builds character, yet when one does not accomplish what was intended or expected, how one handles the misstep is important. Humility, resilience, confidence, perseverance, triumph, and dependence upon God can all be shaped and propelled from defeat."

Question Three Hundred And Thirty-Two
November 28th

Some of us who were sexually molested as children never feel clean. And when we say never, one could place us in a vat of bleach, scrub our skin with a stiff wire brush and it would not remove the putrid trash from the depths of our souls. Will we always—for the rest of our lives—feel this filthy?

Jon: "Peter was prejudiced against Gentiles and considered them unclean. So to prepare him for his service to the Gentiles, the Lord showed Peter a vision and told him to eat food he would have similarly considered unclean. Astonishingly, Peter's response to God was, 'By no means, Lord; for I have never eaten anything that is common or unclean' (Acts 10:14). A voice said to him, 'What God has made clean, do not call common' (Acts 10:15). We have been made clean by the blood of Jesus Christ (Heb. 9:14). Finite cannot make unclean that which infinite has made clean."

Anna: "'Always' is a definite implication that can manifest itself within one's perception. Sexual abuse leaves an imprint within one's psyche, heart, and spirit like no other. When one's purity is perceived as tainted, the beginning of one's emotional dissolution begins. What is filthy is what the molester did! This is exactly why immorality destroys; the lie it tells permeate one's senses, intrudes one's psyche, and resides within one's soul. One is made new and completely cleansed through one's faith in Jesus."

Question Three Hundred And Thirty-Three
November 29th

At times, for a lot of us, our image of ourselves differs from how others see us. For example, some say that we are too thin while we see ourselves as fat. Why is this?

Jon: "Inappropriate judgments will come from man. Never God. If we make judgments only according to our own opinion or the opinions of other men or women, we will likely end up believing inappropriate or damaging ideas. If we base our judgments on God's truth, however, we will believe appropriate and strengthening ideas. God said to Samuel in 1 Sam. 16:7, 'For the LORD sees not as man sees: man looks on the outward appearance, but the LORD looks on the heart.' A correct judgment of a person is based on what is inside their heart and mind. This is why it is important to line up our thoughts and desires with God's."

Anna: "When physical self-distortions propel ruminations or behaviors based upon falsified perceptions, one's risk for body dysmorphia increases. Self-deprecating belief systems that derive from highly critical, controlling, and abusive families manifest in unfortunate ways. Self-exaggerations can lead to serious eating disorders where one needs support and counsel. The environmental messages one received regarding acceptance or attractiveness along with abusive, demeaning circumstances will lead one to perceive oneself as wrong, unlovable, or internally and physically unpleasant. God prizes one's soul, he sees into one's heart, and he loves one dearly, more than one could ever imagine."

Question Three Hundred And Thirty-Four
November 30th

A certain number of us suffer from physical handicaps that keep us bound to a bed and/or a wheelchair. Do you know how horribly painful it is to not be able to move, to defend yourself, when someone is abusing your body?

Jon: "Many of us will never know this kind of pain. So it will be difficult for those who have suffered in this way to significantly connect with others on this matter. Betrayed and handed over to be crucified they whipped Jesus, beat him, stabbed him, pulled out his hair, and spit on him. On the cross he could not move his arms or legs. Nails had been hammered through them, anchoring them to the wood. Jesus did this not only so that those victims of abuse might inherit eternal life, but also so that in him they would have someone who was himself a victim of abuse. Jesus knows."

Anna: "Living within a trapped reality with the inability to protect oneself must be deeply disheartening. Held captive to one's mind and body while simultaneously being violated by another is downright disturbing and unjust. To have zero control, to not have the ability to fully advocate for oneself, to feel forgotten, could drive one to hate others, self, and sadly, even God. The uncertainty and despair could be too much for most to handle. Nothing written can take away one's tortuous experiences yet God is just and through faith one's royal crown and glory awaits."

Question Three Hundred And Thirty-Five
December 1st

It is through faith, for a great deal of us, that we receive solace from the various wounds of our childhood abuse, like from worry, sadness, and bad memories. What can we say to those people who are telling us that we are using our faith in God as a crutch?

Jon: "Everyone has a crutch. No one can always stand on their own. Maybe intellect is one man's crutch. Maybe money is another's crutch. Maybe food is another's. Maybe power, or success, or drugs, or alcohol are yet another's. The question is, *What ought to be our crutch?* Nothing in this world is dependable in all circumstances. Money comes and goes. So does success and drugs and even life itself. We must lean on that which is not of this world. We must lean on that which is eternal. We must lean on that which can be leaned on at all times. We must lean on God."

Anna: "A life without support is an existence without stability. To pretend one can live freely depending upon one's own will is foolish. Where one has been, what one has endured, what one has seen is more of a reason to grasp truth's pillar. Human beings were created to be in authentic connection to life's source, God, and when not, one is spiritually ungrounded. Unfaithfulness and complete independence are more of the enemy's ploys. God is a God of permanence, not an excuse; he is one's sole strength and sustainment."

Question Three Hundred And Thirty-Six
December 2nd

What can we do to help abolish child abuse?

Jon: "In Romans 10, Paul asks that if salvation comes to those who believe, how can anyone believe if they haven't heard? His point is that if faith comes by hearing, then there must be one who is sent to preach that message of salvation. The key is communication. Paul knew that he could not preach the gospel alone. All Christians must preach. In the same way, one person or one event alone cannot end child abuse. It takes a community. It takes time. If child abuse can be lessened through awareness, how will anyone be made aware if we are not delivering the message?"

Anna: "Accountability and crisis prevention starts within the immediate family system. Turning a blind eye, sweeping issues under the rug, or ignoring the catastrophic volcano in the room should no longer be tolerated, period. Infectious awareness, complete honesty, utter sacrifice, and the willingness to speak out no matter the cost would help with minimizing abuse. To hurt a child, on any spectrum, shines a vivid light upon the truth and how rampant immorality is within humankind's minds, hearts, and homes. The Bible foreshadows that evil is upon us, chaos is on the rise, and abolishing wickedness will only happen when this world passes away and yet, as a believer, one is called to take action and speak truth directly through the power of the Holy Spirit."

Question Three Hundred And Thirty-Seven
December 3rd

During our childhoods, a number of us were restrained and isolated from society; kept in closets, kept from socializing with our peers, and kept from developing a sense of who we are. Given this, we are painfully naïve as to how to properly conduct ourselves in social settings. Can the Bible help us to know how to properly function in society?

Jon: "The Bible is the pinnacle of moral direction. It is the best guide for the people of any society. Jesus said in Matthew 22:40, 'On these two commandments depend all the Law and the Prophets.' Those two commandments are to love God and to love one's neighbor. When we love God and love our neighbors we become the perfect citizen. In other words, when we follow those two commands we function flawlessly in our society. We must be aware that while the secular wish to erase the Bible from society, it is biblical principles they wish to be treated according to."

Anna: "Neglect's impact is heart-wrenching. A lack of stimulation and relational connectivity causes a child's cognitions to develop slowly, which enforces an insecure or reactive attachment. Disconnection and fear drives social anxiety, especially when self-efficacy and support are minimal. Social settings can be nerve-racking and when one's interactions and coping mechanisms impede upon social advancement, hope appears lost. The Bible instructs one on how to live functionally within God's will, so seek his knowledge through his Word."

Question Three Hundred And Thirty-Eight
December 4th

A majority of us have come to learn that blame is at the core of most emotional disturbances. This is something that we have learned as a fact and is not necessarily clear to us as to how it actually presents itself. That said, can you describe blame for us?

Jon: "We can blame in two directions: inward and outward. We can blame ourselves and we can blame others. Blame is negative in nature as it is an accusation of fault for some wrong. It is offensive. So when we question the moral character of another, we naturally invite retaliation and more negative feelings. Therefore we want to make sure that blame is rightly placed. This means we must spend time thoroughly considering whether or not we have blamed someone correctly and whether the blame is worth the retaliation and addition of new negative feelings. We will respect and be responsible with blame or we will regret and suffer the consequences."

Anna: "Owning responsibility for one's thoughts, emotions, and behaviors is mature and exudes wise consciousness. However, where blame lies does not mean one should shame. Shame can strip one's desire to productively exist. Just like no one can always be right, no one person is perpetually wrong. Blame often leads to self-disappointment, which can thwart one's confidence. Taking ownership for one's wrongs is key, but continual self-blame is detrimental toward one's identity. Accountability apart from forgiveness is not righteousness."

Question Three Hundred And Thirty-Nine
December 5th

Masses of us who were abused in childhood push love away. Why is this?

Jon: "Many of us have a misconception of love. We define it based on our experiences with other people. So when other people harm us we associate love with fear. But 1 John 4:18 says, 'There is no fear in love, but perfect love casts out fear. For fear has to do with punishment, and whoever fears has not been perfected in love.' We ought to associate love with God and base our definition of love on him rather than our experiences with man. Since God never harms us, there is no reason to fear his love. In fact, his love repels fear. For it is because of his love expressed in Jesus Christ that the punishment we deserve for our sins is removed forever."

Anna: "Pushing love away and relational sabotage stem from the same sources: an implanted seed of fear, unworthiness, good-for-nothing, burdensome, rejection, and abandonment. Self-protection and self-preservation present in contradictory ways when one attempts to avoid vulnerable and painful situations. Ambivalent and avoidant attachments create dysfunctional behavioral patterns, which manifest from one's traumas. These disrupted connections cause turmoil within one's cognitive processes, because feeling unloved goes against one's innate intuitions and purpose. The devastation of one's childhood interactions, the fear and anxiety it creates, is light years away from God's all-encompassing plan; do not push him away, for he truly loves perfectly."

Question Three Hundred And Forty
December 6th

There are countless things in this life that we do not know for certain. But for a lot of us, we know this positively: We adored our abusive parents when we were young. What's wrong with parents who reject a child's love?

Jon: "There are many reasons a parent might reject their child's love. Parents are human and therefore susceptible to mental, emotional, and spiritual defects. Their imperfections are starkly contrasted by God's perfection. Jesus said in Matthew 19:14, 'Let the little children come to me and do not hinder them, for to such belongs the kingdom of heaven.' God not only welcomes his children's love, he commands that no one prevent them from doing so. In God we have a Father who is always present and willing to receive our love—a Father who fights to ensure that we can always love him and receive his love."

Anna: "Sadly, loveless parents push away what is good. When one has been ignored and continually torn down by another's words or actions, one's ideals of a robust relational-self depreciate. One will emotionally detach to cope when their environment creates constant confusion and stress. Apathy is created from an intense disinterest to re-experience rejection and pain. Deep-rooted fears, the desire to control one's security, and dysfunctions fog one's innate desires. Those who reject innocence and love have been influenced by lies that intend to destroy one's God-given ability to fellowship with and care for others."

Question Three Hundred And Forty-One
December 7th

Plenty of us weren't abused by our parents but actually were sexually, physically, and emotionally abused by our siblings. Shouldn't we, nonetheless, hold our parents accountable for not stopping them?

Jon: "Ephesians 6:4 says, 'Fathers, do not provoke your children to anger, but bring them up in the discipline and instruction of the Lord.' To the best of their abilities and efforts, parents are to raise their children in a godly environment. This includes insuring that one child is not causing harm to another child. If a parent knowingly and willingly allows one child to harm another, they will be held accountable before an almighty God. This is why the rejection of God and his Word is so dangerous. If we are not receiving his perfect instruction, then we are receiving imperfect instruction. A rejection of godly parenting is a rejection of good parenting."

Anna: "If a parent was aware that one of their children inflicted abuse of any kind upon another, and did nothing, emotional, psychological, relational, and spiritual consequences ensue. Desiring acknowledgment and accountability for one's part is different than continual condemnation or fixed resentment. The past cannot be changed, yet the reality of what happened can be confronted. The personal repercussions of not doing what was honorable wreak havoc upon one's soul. Addressing one's truth without contempt, with humble and pure intent, is admirable and God-breathed. God will hold one accountable for what they were aware they should have done yet did nothing."

Question Three Hundred And Forty-Two
December 8th

Whether or not remaining quiet around people was caused by our inborn temperament and/or by not being allowed to use our voices when we were children, why do most people become so upset at those of us who prefer not to speak?

Jon: "James 1:19 says, 'Know this, my beloved brothers: let every person be quick to hear, slow to speak, slow to anger.' And Proverbs 29:20 says, 'Do you see a man who is hasty in his words? There is more hope for a fool than for him.' Speaking too often and with too many words is worse than foolishness. This is why James commands us to be slow with our speech. It is not that we must talk slowly, but that we must be slow to talk at all. When a person becomes angry at our slowness of speech, they reveal not only our wisdom but also their own foolishness."

Anna: "Silence can be interpreted as one not complying, or as a covert method of control. To one who reacts, or internalizes other's behaviors, nothingness can be perceived as threatening. Communication is fundamental, and when absent at crucial times, it can highlight one's insecurities and mistrust. Human beings are often attracted to qualities they do not possess, and then yearn for specific things that others are not equipped to give. Most people want to be needed and loved, and when one feels rejected, it is perceived that one is inadequate. When others are still, ask and listen for God."

Question Three Hundred And Forty-Three
December 9th

In terms of looking to God as a father figure, how do we know the Father in heaven when we never experienced one on earth? We cannot even imagine what that might feel like.

Jon: "The Bible says that when we receive God's Spirit, we are adopted as his children (Rom. 8:14). Because we are his children, we may call him 'Abba', 'Father' (Rom. 8:15). Earthly fathers may provide us some earthly inheritance, but because God is our heavenly Father, we become heirs of eternal glory (Rom. 8:14-17). We need not imagine. We can in this present moment experience our heavenly adoption: 'For through him we both have access in one Spirit to the Father' (Eph. 2:18)."

Anna: "When one's earthly father was emotionally, physically, and/or sexually abusive, the abused one may take on the role and very valid feelings of being damaged, bad, used, unworthy, and deserving of punishment and oppression. One's perception and interpretation of one's image of God is now represented by one's father figure, which was developed and established through unhealthy experiences. Even when one does not experience stability, nurturing, or protection from their natural father, God's Spirit supernaturally manifests within so one can come to understand how a true father figure authentically loves within relationship. God's healing powers and perfect love will transcend one's earthly experiences when one acknowledges Jesus and wills God to do so."

Question Three Hundred And Forty-Four
December 10th

Some tens of millions of children are abused each year. If we are to believe that God doesn't do away with child abuse because he gave humankind free will, perhaps we should ask Satan to stick his proverbial fork in it—child abuse—and let the air out of its existence. What do you think about asking for Satan's help in this regard?

Jon: "No. Satan is not our assistant, he is our adversary (1 Pet. 5:8). He is not a supporter, he is a sinner (1 John 3:8). He is no friend, he is a fraud (2 Cor. 11:14). He is a murderer and a liar (John 8:44; 1 Cor. 11:3; Rev. 12:9), a loser (Rom. 16:20), a serpent (Rev. 12:9), a coward (Jas. 4:7), a thief (John 10:10), a schemer (Eph. 6:11), and above all, evil (1 John 5:19). This is not the resume of one whom we ought to ask favors of. Nor is it the resume of one whom we ought to be involved with in any respect whatsoever."

Anna: "Assuredly as God exists, child abuse will end, but for now, boldly rise up and continue to face one's purpose. Even though one's circumstance was completely unfair, without the bad, could one truly appreciate what is good? Satan revels in humankind's pain. He has no shame. He should not be underestimated, he does not help, he tries to infect one's mind, emotions, and will. Anything that is good comes purely from God."

Question Three Hundred And Forty-Five
December 11th

What if we choose to take our secrets of being abused as children with us to our graves? Will we go to hell?

Jon: "Absolutely not. The only thing that causes one to enter hell is willfully rejecting faith in Jesus Christ (see John 8:24). When, where, how, why, and what we choose to share with others is strictly our business. It is our choice to share or not share. No one can or should force us to do so. We must be honest with ourselves, however, and accept that sharing our secrets with others—even God—may benefit our spiritual and psychological health. Sometimes hiding secrets is more damaging than revealing them is. But if we decide that we would benefit from sharing, it is important that we do so only with trusted acquaintances or proven credible professionals."

Anna: "No. However, covering one's truth or pretending that one's trauma is not important enough to acknowledge and grieve will have personal side effects. One's reality does not change when one denies the past and its abusive existence; it more often than not will make things more burdensome. Smothering one's childhood pain neutralizes one's voice and what is not processed will hinder one's psychological, emotional, and spiritual development. Personal freedom is uncovered in the humility of one's authentic testimony and that one cannot conquer this life alone. Hell is only reserved for those who consciously reject Jesus and the Holy Spirit."

Question Three Hundred And Forty-Six
December 12th

A lot of us walk around on eggshells, not saying anything about being abused as children, while our abusers, our parents and/or caregivers act as if nothing happened. While this sickens us, how important is it to keep family peace?

Jon: "There is no peace where man must suffer to keep peace. At least not for the one who suffers. For, to suffer is to not be at peace. Just as peace could only be restored between God and man after the sufferings of Christ were finished, so too can peace only be restored between man and man after the sufferings of man are finished. It may be that in order to bring peace to our family, we must first bring them our suffering. While there is nobility in suffering for others, if it brings more harm than good then suffering loses its nobility."

Anna: "Maintaining peace over exposing the truth to not disrupt one's family unit is not one's responsibility. True peace manifests from within and is not temporary. When one yearns for love, support, and acceptance, one will do almost anything to make it happen, even deny one's self. Self-martyrdom is interesting within abusive dynamics because the one who was initially targeted now feels they must protect what the abuse created. The most important mission one has is attached to one's belief in Jesus, and one should not let anything, especially one's family dysfunction, manipulate or dominate one's divine privilege and purpose."

Question Three Hundred And Forty-Seven
December 13th

Too many of us have only experienced nothing but disgrace throughout our childhoods. As a result, we are attracted to people who treat us disgracefully. We want to end this. What qualities should we look for in a mate and/or people in general?

Jon: "The primary attribute we ought to seek in a mate is godliness. When someone is godly, they obey God's commands. When someone obeys God's commands, they not only keep from doing wrong to others but they practice doing good to others. This is what we want in a mate: someone who to the best of their ability will refrain from harming us while providing us love. Those who will properly love us are those who first properly love God. If we desire a gracious mate, we ought to seek one who is in consistent commune with an infinitely gracious God."

Anna: "Dysfunction and abuse affect one's soul through a seed of disgrace, a falsified self-perception founded upon another's hurtful behaviors and negative circumstances. A beautiful place to begin is understanding the qualities one desires to possess within. Holiness, authenticity, faithfulness, trustworthiness, kindness, patience, and other similar characteristics and spiritual attributes can be embodied when one is planted firmly within one's identity and purposed driven mentality. Based upon faith rooted within biblical truths, and one's Christ-centered philosophy that one is forgiven by grace and no longer disgraced by sin, one will exude love and seek what one treasures."

Question Three Hundred And Forty-Eight
December 14th

Can we rely on psychics or mediums to help us solve the problems related to our childhood abuse?

Jon: "If those who claim to have psychic powers really do have psychic powers, then why don't they prevent child abuse before it happens? The most plausible answer is that those people do not have psychic powers. If they do, they should be held accountable for not preventing child abuse. In any case, whether or not people do have psychic powers, we should not rely on them. We should rely on God. If the psychic must claim that his or her powers do not include knowledge of future incidents of child abuse, then their powers are limited. Better to rely on unlimited God than limited man. Some things are too hard for man, but 'Is anything too hard for the LORD?' (Gen. 18:14)."

Anna: "What is deemed mystical can be somewhat enticing when considered within human limitations. However, the practice of divination is unholy. Psychics attempt to channel demonic spirits that swindle, deceive and mislead naïve, curious, ignorant, wavering, and desperate souls. Temporary knowledge or perceived foresight compared with spiritual wisdom, God's wisdom, cannot be compared. The believer in Jesus Christ should seek out and depend upon God's Word and will for answers pertaining to one's past hurts, present problems, and future hopes. Deceptive spirits will attempt to mislead and veer one off their divine path."

Question Three Hundred And Forty-Nine
December 15th

This may sound a bit grave, but some of us believe that we were meant to experience childhood abuse so that we would grow up and do something about it. To a certain degree, is this to be respected?

Jon: "Not only is this respectable, it's God's position. Remember what Joseph said to his brothers who conspired to kill him: 'As for you, you meant evil against me, but God meant it for good...' (Gen. 50:20). There is no evil that occurs that God cannot bring great good from. This does not mean that evil is permissible, but that God will have the final say in what comes about from evil. Evil is still evil. But we can play a part in God's bringing good from evil when we choose to do good as a consequence of that evil. Good will always win."

Anna: "To live within a courageous and hopeful framework is downright respectable, and is an inspiring perspective to witness when lived out. Faith in oneself and the core belief that one can truly make a difference is crucial for one's mental health and spiritual light. Taking action to protect innocent children is admirable and needed in these abusive times. Certain situations have been brought about to specifically demonstrate God's power, yet most often, one's circumstances are a product of evil's manipulation within human behaviors. One's childhood abuse was unjust, however, one can wholeheartedly use what was meant to destroy for good."

Question Three Hundred And Fifty
December 16th

Over time, will practicing being in the present moment, in the here and now, push our fearful childhood memories further and further away?

Jon: "It may be that maximum contentment regarding our difficult childhood memories will not come by merely pushing them away. This may not be enough. We may have to do more, namely, come to terms with our memories and therefore remove their power entirely. Psalm 23:4 says, 'Even though I walk through the valley of the shadow of death, I will fear no evil, for you are with me; your rod and your staff, they comfort me.' There is great comfort in knowing and affirming that when we confront these memories, we are not alone. For the One who has already conquered evil and who casts out fear with perfect love is with us."

Anna: "To be present will decrease one's current stresses, slow down one's thoughts, and in essence calm one's soul. However, one's anxieties and experiences need validation with differentiation. When one's fearful memories have been suppressed, time will often reap ambivalence toward one's mental, emotional, and relational instability. Attempting to push one's abusive memories away, to cut them off, to forcefully disengage, is re-abandoning and rejecting oneself. Gaining freedom through self-awareness and grieving allows one's negative thoughts and uncomfortable feelings to consciously be acknowledged and powerfully surrendered. What one has been through deserves consideration, not emotional envelopment, but genuine concern, like God's Spirit attends to the one who believes."

Question Three Hundred And Fifty-One
December 17th

So many of us found our voices and they will never ever be silenced again. What does Scripture and psychology have to say of the lost and found?

Jon: "John the Baptist had sent his disciples to inquire about Jesus' legitimacy (Mat. 11:1-19). Jesus tells John's disciples to report back to him that the blind now see, the lame now walk, lepers are now cleansed, the dead are raised, and the poor receive the Gospel. Now we too have experienced the power of Jesus Christ. We have been transformed. And that transformation is a testimony to Jesus' power, which we will proclaim to those whom God places in our path. Before any and all who seek for legitimate answers in life, we will point to Jesus Christ and tell of the wonders he has accomplished among us. The found will point the way for the lost."

Anna: "One's voice is connected to one's beliefs and passions, or lack thereof. What one says is a measure of one's heart and character. Surviving abuse and its silencing effects takes its toll, but with courage and perseverance one can rediscover who one truly is. The subduing of one's spirit through abuse's intimidations causes one to drift away from one's identity. Knowing who one is equates to being found within one's mind, will, and purpose. God's amazing Son, his saving grace, is where one is truly found; one's identity, one's voice and divine calling, is one's testimony of Christ."

Question Three Hundred And Fifty-Two
December 18th

Many of us realize now the importance of keeping a sense of humor, of surrounding ourselves with people and programs that make us laugh. Along these lines, do you think it would be a good idea for us to learn to laugh at ourselves as well?

Jon: "Proverbs 17:22 says, 'A joyful heart is good medicine, but a crushed spirit dries up the bones.' It is difficult to laugh when the heart is not joyful. And that's what we need to protect ourselves from. We do want to be able to laugh at ourselves from time to time, but only when appropriate. We do not want to laugh at ourselves when the matter is at the same time crushing to our spirit. This is self-deprecation and ought to be avoided. On the other hand, Scripture affirms that laughing—even at ourselves—in an appropriate way is like balm or ointment for our souls."

Anna: "Finding the humor within one's flaws and life's difficult circumstances can help one cope and get through trying times. The effectiveness of humor boils down to one's motives, one's frame of mind, and one's perceptions. The ability to bounce back or deflect fiery flames is a lifesaving skill, one that protects one's soul and spirit. Laughter is medicinal and its self-countering properties can truly rescue one from self-sabotage. Humorous amusements can ease one's anxieties and soothe one's troubles. Giggle, laugh, ignite one's childlike self, and let one's joyous spirit shine."

Question Three Hundred And Fifty-Three
December 19th

A great number of us are going to begin and end our days praying for all those who were and are currently stricken by childhood abuse. Will you join us?

Jon: "Heavenly Father, we praise you for your glory. And we thank you for allowing us access to your glory through your Son Jesus Christ. May we be filled and strengthened by your Holy Spirit to glorify you with our thoughts, our words, and our actions. May we be ever transformed, becoming more and more like Jesus as we proclaim his name to the world. And would you, in the mighty name of Jesus, protect all children who are now threatened by abuse. In the name of Jesus, would the evil plans and intentions of abusers be thwarted as your angels protect and minister to the abused. Above all, may not our but your will be done. Amen."

Anna: "Yes, wholeheartedly, it is truly an honor, and a privilege. Prayer is, without question, one of the foremost influential means a believer has. Having a goal, a genuine concern, being moved to help, and being proactive reveals the position of one's faith, mind, heart, and spirit. Owning the authority one has over any circumstance and future hope is inspiring and life-changing. Selflessly advocating for others in Jesus' name will move evil obstacles. One's access to God is righteously attained through one's belief in Jesus and the power of the Holy Spirit."

Question Three Hundred And Fifty-Four
December 20th

When all is said and done, when all is tried and failed, what do you have to say to those of us who remain stuck in the pain of our childhoods?

Jon: "Do not give up. Noah and his family were hopelessly adrift at sea before they finally landed ashore. The Israelites were caught between Pharaoh and the Red Sea just before God parted the sea, allowing them escape. Israel then wandered in the wilderness for forty years until it was finally brought to the Promised Land. Jesus suffered and died upon the cross just before he was raised from the dead. Galatians 6:9 says, 'And let us not grow weary of doing good, for in due season we will reap, if we do not give up.' This season will pass, and a new one will come. The future brings our deliverance."

Anna: "Childhood alone is difficult and when overcoming abuse, feeling trapped within one's past, mind, and fears can seem inescapable. When one believes they cannot, sadly, they will not. One must fight and one must continue to try. Perspective is tied to one's core belief system and one's perceptions can be manipulated when not secured in truthfulness. For example, being contingent upon shifting circumstances or another's unstable behaviors. Affixing to the past is one's present choice. One's faith in Jesus equals freedom, God-breathed intimacy, which requires the genuine expression of one's thoughts and emotions for personal and spiritual restoration."

Question Three Hundred And Fifty-Five
December 21st

How important is it for us to walk a spiritual path?

Jon: "We are spiritual creatures. If we ignore our spirituality, then we ignore one of the most significant parts of our lives. But it must be emphasized that this is not an endorsement of *mere* spirituality, but of *Christian* spirituality. And it must be further emphasized that Christian spirituality means glorifying God in all our words, thoughts, and actions through faith in Jesus Christ and in the power of the Holy Spirit. To put this into a metaphor, the right spiritual path may only be walked toward God, beside Christ, and following the Spirit. Any other path, albeit spiritual, will lead us astray. This truth is hard for many, but it's better to know the truth than a lie."

Anna: "Spiritual development is very important for one's psychological, emotional, and relational growth. Because one's spirituality is rooted within one's worldview, it will profoundly affect one's thought processes, decision-making, and behaviors. Spiritual conviction differs from worldly emotion and one's level of maturity is dependent upon one's spiritual awareness. The path one walks will carry out one's purpose and lead one into their destiny. Having a spiritual intellectualism is different than being heart-driven by God's Holy Spirit. Not all spirituality is good or Christ-centered. It is important to live one's life according to God's Word and will. Apart from Christ, apart from God's Holy Spirit, one will not truly become who one was created to be."

Question Three Hundred And Fifty-Six
December 22nd

Is there any benefit in finding out whether or not our abusers are survivors of childhood abuse?

Jon: "Knowing that our abusers were themselves abused can help us understand the causes that led up to our injury. And this can do two things. First, it can provide for us some solid historical facts surrounding our experience of abuse. From this, difficult memories that are vague and confusing may gain new stability and therefore manageability. Second, this knowledge can motivate those of us who were abused to not perpetuate the cycle. In other words, knowing that if we abuse someone they are likely to abuse another is powerfully convicting. If one abuses, so too may their victim. The weight of all that potential abuse inflicted on all those potential victims may be enough to keep one from the act."

Anna: "Knowing the truth is beneficial when one is ready to accept it. Abusers are often abused themselves and empathically conceptualizing this could help make sense of one's painful experiences. However, knowing an abuser's history will not change what happened but may shed light into one's psychopathology and spiritual state. Self-advantage will blossom when one's outlook, beliefs, hopes, and desires coincide, and break through psychological and spiritual barriers. Empathy is a beautiful quality and increases with righteous awareness and compassion. When a victim relates to an abuser through one's trauma, unhealthy relationship cognitions could ensue. However, when forgiveness is one's motive toward healing, then understanding one's abuser can be healthily within God's will."

Question Three Hundred And Fifty-Seven
December 23rd

What does Scripture and psychology have to say to those of us who possess the will to persist in this life, despite our unjust start?

Jon: "When our will is to persist in this life, our will is in line with God's. For, his will is to provide us a hopeful *future* (Jer. 29:11). He wants us to persist. But persist in what? Jesus says in John 15:4, 'Abide in me, and I in you. As the branch cannot bear fruit by itself, unless it abides in the vine, neither can you, unless you abide in me.' If we do not persist *in Jesus*, our persisting will be in vain. But when we continually practice faith in and obedience to Jesus Christ, our persisting in life will not be mere persistence. It will be a persistence which bears divine fruit."

Anna: "Psychological and emotional development rely on resilience and persistence. Humility and transformation are spurned through one's painful experiences. Abuse hurts, it disappoints, it infuriates, yet fuels something from within that cannot be tamed once released: the desperate pursuit of one's dignity and hope. Perseverance beautifully unfolds and is necessary to complete one's purpose. Immorality's nudge is incessant, but when one takes ownership of false beliefs, the dysfunction faced can be victoriously conquered. The injustices Jesus endured, the tenacity he embodied to withstand, is what changed the world; do not stop, and do not hesitate in Christ. March on, brave soul, march on."

Question Three Hundred And Fifty-Eight
December 24th

One of the greatest things we have learned is that we cannot truly heal on our own. We need to lean on people we can trust, including God. And we imagine that this is a lifelong journey. Yes?

Jon: "God's work in our lives will not only take time, but that time will pass in seasons. Jesus says in John 15:2, 'Every branch in me that does not bear fruit he takes away, and every branch that does bear fruit he prunes, that it may bear more fruit.' When we are *in* Jesus, and when we believe in and depend on him, we will experience fruit in our lives. However, it is important to note that fruit comes in seasons. The seasons of fruitlessness are just that: seasons. They will pass. And in the midst of them God still abides in us, pruning and preparing us for the next season."

Anna: "Life's journey can be oh-so meaningful when one truly has the support needed to get through the difficult times one faces. Realistically, people will disappoint you because everyone is flawed, and they are fighting a personal battle of their own. In these times, remember, one is never truly alone, and one's journey does not end. There is hope in knowing that times will change and as one grows in Christ, one's awareness, character, and wisdom beautifully blossoms. Healing is trusting that God is fully capable and that he will remain faithful throughout everything."

Question Three Hundred And Fifty-Nine
December 25th

Thinking about forgiveness—perhaps it would help us to forgive others if we say to ourselves: We, too, are not without sin?

Jon: "When we think about our fallenness before God, it would be wrong to think that one person is more fallen than another person. It can be rightly said, of course, that there are some persons who have sinned more than others. An adult will have committed more sin than an infant. But *amount* of sin isn't the issue. The issue is whether or not anyone has sinned at all, and we all have sinned (Rom. 3:23). Therefore everyone is fallen. Everyone is condemnable before God. No one is better off than anyone else. Everyone is in need of and desires forgiveness. So we will to forgive as we will to be forgiven."

Anna: "Accepting that everyone makes mistakes and hurts others, whether unintentionally or not, is key in life's humbling forgiveness process. True strength is apparent when one discerns the depth of what has truly happened, yet willingly chooses to be gracious and merciful. Being tolerant toward others, while not justifying one's hurtful or negative behaviors, but understanding that every person is valued more than one's conduct shows a brilliantly wise nature. So yes, no human is sinless and no one will escape judgment. Bitterness, resentments, and psychological walls build when one does not set down their criticisms and condemnations, nor looks at others through Jesus' eyes."

Question Three Hundred And Sixty
December 26th

We, and we alone, are responsible for maintaining our emotional stability. What does Scripture and psychology have to say about taking responsibility for oneself?

Jon: "Galatians 6:5 says, 'For each will have to bear his own load.' And this applies to many areas of life. No one can do for us the work necessary to advance our spiritual and psychological well-being. Neither can anyone do for us the work necessary to earn a living, nor to learn. Our most imperative responsibility, however, is that we place our faith in Jesus Christ. God will not force us into a saving relationship with himself. But when we take responsibility to believe in God, God takes responsibility to work in us. Therefore, while our work is our responsibility, it will not be done without the help of an all-powerful God."

Anna: "Emotional stability and maturity is a predictor for one's state of mind and level of autonomy. Personal responsibility is telling and reflects one's awareness level, self-esteem, goals, and value system. One's free will is truly an honor and, when taken seriously, fearless actions transpire. Self-obligation is maintaining and nurturing one's self-perspective, core beliefs, and behaviors in alignment with what is healthy, good, and true. One is accountable for what one thinks, does, or does not do. The Holy Spirit's peace will transcend one's emotional being, and will magnify one's soul when allowed to lead one's life. Act upon God's Word and not simply on feeling, which is one of the responsibilities one has been called to."

Question Three Hundred And Sixty-One
December 27th

Most of us now understand that we need to spend more time being grateful for this brief life that God has gifted us rather than remain self-absorbed. One of the ways we'd like to express our gratitude is by serving others. Will focusing on others help us to stop playing the victim?

Jon: "Jesus' mandate to his disciples in Luke 12:33 was to 'Sell your possessions, and give to the needy.' Why do this? Jesus said in verse 34, 'For where your treasure is, there will your heart be also.' It is good in and of itself to give to those in need. But that's not Jesus' point. His point is that when we give to others, it is not only others who receive something good. We receive something good, namely, a good heart. When we help others flourish, we flourish. Focusing on others will not only distract us from ourselves, but it will produce for us a new heart less interested in the self."

Anna: "Serving others can most definitely shift one's self-perspective and worldview. When painful experiences consume one's mind, self-pity and self-absorption can set in. When self-focus shifts toward selflessness, one's internal dissatisfactions can minimize. One's beliefs become distorted when loathing is internalized into a diminished sense of personal worth. A self-centered perspective pushes away God-given opportunity for emotional connection and fellowship. God's abiding presence is a constant reminder of why one has breath: to help others with purpose for his glory."

Question Three Hundred And Sixty-Two
December 28th

For those of us who are just starting to have faith and for those of us who have none—does keeping faith really work?

Jon: "Faith is an investment that returns more than is deposited. We give faith, and receive eternal life (John 3:13). This reality alone is so overwhelmingly advantageous that one ought not need another motivation to place their faith in Christ Jesus. But it is worth knowing that faith also heals (Acts 14:9-10) and it purifies (Acts 15:9). Faith comforts (Rom. 1:12) and it sanctifies (Acts 26:8). It saves (Eph. 2:8) and it justifies (Rom. 3:28). It answers prayer (Mat. 21:22) and it rewards (Heb. 11:6). What must we do to inherit these realities and more? Merely hold in our minds and in our hearts that Jesus is Lord and that God raised him from the dead."

Anna: "Faith works wonders when it is courageous. Trust, when fastened to healthy beliefs no matter what storms unfold, secures one's purpose. Living out one's faith daily, despite one's childhood circumstances, does not mean one will not have continued tribulations or resurfaced and new, painful experiences. One's obstacles should not affect one's core belief system; often, the bigger the test is an even greater opportunity to apply one's faith. Believing God's Word, standing firm that what he says is absolutely true, leaning upon his promises, and holding tightly to one's hope not only work, but will bring healing and comfort to one's spirit and soul."

Question Three Hundred And Sixty-Three
December 29th

Hope is no longer elusive to so many of us. We are hope-filled in the knowledge that we can heal from our childhood abuse. Is there something that we can do to never lose hope again?

Jon: "Romans 15:4 says, 'For whatever was written in former days was written for our instruction, that through endurance and through the encouragement of the Scriptures we might have hope.' This passage gives us two methods for increasing our hope. The first is by enduring. As we continually endure through hardship, we become resilient in character. And a resilient character more easily hopes than a non-resilient character. The second method for increasing our hope is reading God's Word. As we read Scripture we stoke the flames of hope. Hope burns hotter and brighter the more our eyes meet the sacred pages and the more our will determines to endure."

Anna: "Hope mitigates despair, just as thankfulness is connected to one's attitude and longing is attached to one's understanding, identity, and purpose. Hopefulness is the belief that one is called to live out one's truth through the transformation of one's soul, spirit, and personal testimony. Staying afloat while almost drowning, believing, and truly remembering what it took to hold on that one could be rescued and saved, is hope. When one's focus is set on God, through Jesus' death and resurrection, hope is no longer fleeting; it is definitively in God's Word and foreseen truths. Hope is nurtured through one's relationship with Jesus."

Question Three Hundred And Sixty-Four
December 30th

Because many of us now perceive ourselves as lovable human beings, we no longer fear questioning the pain of our childhoods. Indeed, love does spurn fear. Do you believe, then, that most anything is possible for us as long as we exist from a standpoint of love?

Jon: "1 Corinthians 13:7 says, 'Love bears all things, believes all things, hopes all things, endures all things.' Verse 8 says: 'love never ends.' And verse 13 says that among faith, hope, and love, love is the greatest. We don't prize love because it gives us what we want. And we don't prize love for its own sake. We prize love because God prizes love. We esteem it with highest value because God esteems it with highest value. So it isn't that love makes all things possible, but that loving God and others puts us in a position where God can accomplish anything through us."

Anna: "Humankind exists because of love. However, just because this is true, one must choose to believe it wholeheartedly. When this divine principle is fully understood, without a shadow of any doubt, the possibilities become endless. Even though one experienced the horrors of childhood abuse, and believed all hope was lifted from the innocence of one's youth, love was always there; it lovingly awaits, and will always remain. With God's unfading love, with his wisdom and might, one is capable of accomplishing absolutely anything through him if he so wills it."

Question Three Hundred And Sixty-Five
December 31st

As we go courageously forward in this life—sheathed in the full armor of God, his Word our sword—may we have your blessings?

Jon: "May the Lord bless the reader of this book. May the words that have brought glory to God be solidified in their heart and mind, and the words that have not brought him glory be forgotten. May their wounds be healed. May their pain be redeemed. May their despair be turned into hope, their hate to love, and their hopelessness to hope. May they be filled with the Holy Spirit to draw nearer to and direct others toward Jesus Christ. Numbers 6:24-26: 'The LORD bless you and keep you; the LORD make his face to shine upon you and be gracious to you; the LORD lift up his countenance upon you and give you peace.'"

Anna: "You are blessed through your faith in Jesus Christ. My hope for you is to fearlessly seek God and ask him to reveal his truths that bring forth a spiritual cleansing that will continue to nurture your perspective and desires. With your sword ready to be drawn and your full armor on, discern and protect yourself from the enemies' lies and propel into love's magnificent purpose. Courage truly flourishes when you believe the truth of God's promises, so believe. Faithfully seek his Word, so you will sustain your spirit and soul. Invite God's Spirit to lead while calling upon his strength to move. When asking God daily for his protective covering, healing, and peace, is when you will truly be unafraid."

Please visit the authors at

www.whatwereafraidtoask.com

The Long Road to Heaven
A Lent Course Based on the Film
Tim Heaton
This second Lent resource from the author of *The Naturalist and the Christ* explores Christian understandings of "salvation" in a five-part study based on the film *The Way*.
Paperback: 978-1-78279-274-1 ebook: 978-1-78279-273-4

Abide In My Love
More Divine Help for Today's Needs
John Woolley
The companion to *I Am With You*, *Abide In My Love* offers words of divine encouragement.
Paperback: 978-1-84694-276-1

From the Bottom of the Pond
The Forgotten Art of Experiencing God in the Depths of the Present Moment
Simon Small
From the Bottom of the Pond takes us into the depths of the present moment, to the only place where God can be found.
Paperback: 978-1-84694-066-8 ebook: 978-1-78099-207-5

God Is A Symbol Of Something True
Why You Don't Have to Choose Either a Literal Creator God or a Blind, Indifferent Universe
Jack Call
In this examination of modern spiritual dilemmas, Call offers the explanation that some of the most important elements of life are beyond our control: everything is fundamentally al-right.
Paperback: 978-1-84694-244-0

The Scarlet Cord
Conversations With God's Chosen Women
Lindsay Hardin Freeman, Karen N. Canton
Voiceless wax figures no longer, twelve biblical women,
outspoken, independent, faithful, selfless risk-takers, come to
life in *The Scarlet Cord*.
Paperback: 978-1-84694-375-1

Will You Join in Our Crusade?
The Invitation of the Gospels Unlocked by the Inspiration of
Les Miserables
Steve Mann
Les Miserables' narrative is entwined with Bible study in this
book of 42 daily readings from the Gospels, perfect for Lent
or anytime.
Paperback: 978-1-78279-384-7 ebook: 978-1-78279-383-0

A Quiet Mind
Uniting Body, Mind and Emotions in Christian Spirituality
Eva McIntyre
A practical guide to finding peace in the present moment that
will change your life, heal your wounds and bring you a
quiet mind.
Paperback: 978-1-84694-507-6 ebook: 978-1-78099-005-7

Readers of ebooks can buy or view any of these bestsellers by
clicking on the live link in the title. Most titles are published
in paperback and as an ebook. Paperbacks are available in
traditional bookshops. Both print and ebook formats are
available online.
Find more titles and sign up to our readers' newsletter at
http://www.johnhuntpublishing.com/christianity.
Follow us on Facebook at
https://www.facebook.com/ChristianAlternative.